PSYCHOANALYSIS ON THE MOVE

Joseph Sandler has been an important influence in psychoanalysis throughout the world during the latter part of the twentieth century, contributing to changing views on both psychoanalytic theory and technique. He has also been a bridging force in psychoanalysis, helping to close the gap between American ego psychologists, and British Kleinian and object relations theorists.

Psychoanalysis on the Move: The Work of Joseph Sandler provides a comprehensive and accessible overview of Sandler's contribution to the development of psychoanalysis. The contributors trace the development of the main themes and achievements of Sandler's work, in particular his focus on combining psychoanalytic theory and clinical practice.

Timely and important, *Psychoanalysis on the Move: The Work of Joseph Sandler* should make interesting reading for psychoanalysts, psychotherapists, and all those who wish to know more about one of the most creative figures in psychoanalysis of the past few decades.

Peter Fonagy is Training and Supervising Analyst in the British Psycho-Analytical Society. He holds the Freud Memorial Chair in Psychoanalysis at University College London and is Vice President and Chair of the Research Committee of the International Psychoanalytical Association. **Arnold M. Cooper** is Stephen P. Tobin and Arnold M. Cooper Professor Emeritus in Consultation-Liaison Psychiatry at Cornell University Medical College and is currently Editor of the *International Journal of Psycho-Analysis* and Deputy Editor of the *American Journal of Psychiatry*. **Robert S. Wallerstein** is Training and Supervising Analyst at the San Francisco Psychoanalytic Institute and Emeritus Professor and former Chairman of the Department of Psychiatry, University of California School of Medicine.

THE NEW LIBRARY OF PSYCHOANALYSIS

General Editor: Elizabeth Bott Spillius

The New Library of Psychoanalysis was launched in 1987 in association with the Institute of Psycho-Analysis, London. Its purpose is to facilitate a greater and more widespread appreciation of what psychoanalysis is really about and to provide a forum for increasing mutual understanding between psychoanalysts and those working in other disciplines such as history, linguistics, literature, medicine, philosophy, psychology and the social sciences. It is intended that the titles selected for publication in the series should deepen and develop psychoanalytic thinking and technique, contribute to psychoanalysis from outside or contribute to other disciplines from a psychoanalytic perspective.

The Institute, together with the British Psycho-Analytical Society, runs a low-fee psychoanalytic clinic, organises lectures and scientific events concerned with psychoanalysis, publishes the *International Journal of Psycho-Analysis* (which now incorporates the *International Review of Psycho-Analysis*) and runs the only training course in the UK in psychoanalysis leading to membership of the International Psychoanalytical Association – the body which preserves internationally agreed standards of training, of professional entry, and of professional ethics and practice for psychoanalysis as initiated and developed by Sigmund Freud. Distinguished members of the Institute have included Michael Balint, Wilfred Bion, Ronald Fairbairn, Anna Freud, Ernest Jones, Melanie Klein, John Rickman and Donald Winnicott.

Volumes 1–11 in the series have been prepared under the general editorship of David Tuckett, with Ronald Britton and Eglé Laufer as associate editors. Subsequent volumes are under the general editorship of Elizabeth Bott Spillius, with, from Volume 17, Donald Campbell, Michael Parsons, Rosine Jozef Perelberg and David Taylor as associate editors.

ALSO IN THIS SERIES

PSYCHOANALYSIS ON THE MOVE

The work of Joseph Sandler

Edited by Peter Fonagy, Arnold M. Cooper and Robert S. Wallerstein

London and New York

First published 1999
by Routledge
11 New Fetter Lane, London EC4P 4EE

Simultaneously published in the USA and Canada
by Routledge
29 West 35th Street, New York, NY 10001

Typeset in Bembo by Routledge
Printed and bound in Great Britain by
TJ International Ltd, Padstow, Cornwall

British Library Cataloguing in Publication Data
A catalogue record for this book is available from the British Library

Library of Congress Cataloguing in Publication Data
Psychoanalysis on the move: the work of Joseph Sandler / [edited by]
Peter Fonagy, Arnold M. Cooper, Robert S. Wallerstein.
Includes bibliographical references and index.
1. Psychoanalysis. 2. Sandler, Jospeh. I. Fonagy, Peter, 1952– .
II. Cooper, Arnold M. III. Wallerstein, Robert S. IV. Series.
BF173.P7757   1999
150.19'5'092–dc21   98-47364

ISBN 0–415–20548–4 (hbk)
ISBN 0–415–20549–2 (pbk)

CONTENTS

CONTENTS

CONTRIBUTORS

Jorge Canestri is Training and Supervising Analyst at the Italian Psycho-analytical Association and the Argentinean Psychoanalytic Association. He is a Full Member of the International Psychoanalytical Association and is trained in Linguistics and Epistemology. Consultant to several research programs in Italy and other countries on the analysis of discourse and on multilingualism, he has published numerous psychoanalytical papers in Italy and elsewhere. He is presently Director of the Institute of Psycho-analysis of the Italian Psychoanalytical Association, Member of several Committees of the International Psychoanalytical Association and Director of a home page on 'Psychoanalysis and logical mathematical thought'. He has written (with Jacqueline Amati-Mehler and Simona Argentieri) *The Babel of the Unconscious: Mother Tongue and Foreign Languages in the Psycho-analytic Dimension.*

Yolanda Gampel is Training Analyst at the Israel Psychoanalytical Society. Yoland Gampel is Past President of the Israel Psychoanalytical Society and is currently Senior Lecturer in the Department of Psychology and in the School of Psychotherapy, Tel Aviv University

Max Hernández is a Member and former President of the Peruvian Psychoanalytic Society and is a Member of the British Psycho-Analytical Society. He is currently Training and Supervising Analyst at the Peruvian Institute of Psychoanalysis. He has been Vice President of the International Psychoanalytical Association and has been a recipient of the Sigourney Award.

Michael Hölzer has been Deputy Chief at the Psychotherapeutic Hospital, Stuttgart since 1997. He was Postgraduate Research Fellow at Downstate Medical Center, New York between 1984 and 1986. He has trained in psychotherapy and psychoanalysis at the Department of Psychotherapy at Ulm University, the Ulm Institute of Psychoanalysis (IPA), and the German Psychoanalytic Association in Ulm.

Horst Kächele trained in psychotherapy at the Department of Psychotherapy, Ulm University and in psychoanalysis at the Ulm Institute of Psychoanalysis (IPA). He has been Associate Professor Ulm University, Chief of Section for Psychoanalytic Methodology at Ulm University; Chief of Center for Psychotherapy Research, Stuttgart; Chair of Psychotherapy at the Faculty of Medicine, Ulm University; and Chair of Psychotherapy and Psychosomatic Medicine at the Faculty of Medicine, Ulm University.

Otto F. Kernberg is Director of the Personality Disorders Institute and the Cornell Psychotherapy Program at The New York Hospital, Cornell Medical Center, and Professor of Psychiatry at the Cornell University Medical College. He is President of the International Psychoanalytical Association and is also Training and Supervising Analyst of the Columbia University Center for Psychoanalytic Training and Research. He is the author of seven books and co-author of five others. He is also Guest Editor of a volume on the *Narcissistic Personality Disorder of the Psychiatric Clinics of North America*. His most recent book, *Ideology, Conflict, and Leadership in Groups and Organizations*, was published in 1998.

Serge Lebovici is Emeritus Professor of Child Psychiatry at the University of Paris. He is Training and Supervising Analyst at the Paris Psychoanalytic Society. He is Honorary Vice President and Past President of the International Psychoanalytical Association and is Past President of the World Association of Infant Mental Health.

Moisés Lemlij is a Member and Past President of the Peruvian Psychoanalytic Society and Associate Member of the British Psycho-Analytical Society. He is Training and Supervising Analyst at the Peruvian Institute of Psychoanalysis. He has twice been Vice President of the International Psychoanalytical Association and is currently Associate Secretary to the IPA.

Erhard Mergenthaler has been Director of the Section Informatics in Psychotherapy at the Department of Psychotherapy and Psychosomatic Medicine, University of Ulm since 1988. Together with Horst Kächele, he started and realised the Ulm Textbank project. His major research interests are in psychotherapy processes and text analysis.

Robert Michels is the Walsh McDermott University Professor of Medicine and University Professor of Psychiatry at Cornell University. He is a Supervising and Training Analyst at the Columbia University Center for Training and Research.

Ethel Spector Person is Professor of Clinical Psychiatry at the College of Physicians and Surgeons, Columbia University, and Training and Supervising Analyst at the Columbia University Center for Psychoanalytical Training and Research. She is the author of *Dreams of Love and Fateful*

Encounters: The Power of Romantic Passion and *By Force of Fantasy: How We Live Our Lives*. In addition, she is Editor of the IPA's Monograph Series, the most recent volume of which is *On Freud's 'A Child is Being Beaten'*.

Owen Renick is Editor-in-Chief of *The Psychoanalytic Quarterly*. He is Chair of the Program Committee of the American Psychoanalytic Association and Supervising and Training Analyst at the San Francisco Psychoanalytic Institute.

Roy Schafer is Training and Supervising Analyst at the Columbia University Center for Psychoanalytic Training and Research. His recent books include *Retelling a Life, Tradition and Change in Psychoanalysis*, and *The Contemporary Kleinians of London*. He has a private practice in New York City.

Hanna Segal is Training and Supervising Analyst and Honorary Member of the British Psycho-Analytical Society, Fellow of the Royal College of Psychiatrists and past holder of the Freud Memorial Chair of Psychoanalysis at University College London. She is Past Vice President of the International Psychoanalytical Association and Past President of the British Psychoanalytic Society.

Theodore Shapiro is Professor of Psychiatry at Cornell University Medical College and is Training and Supervising Analyst at the New York Psychoanalytic Institute. He is also a former Editor of the *Journal of the American Psychoanalytic Association*.

Robert S. Wallerstein is Emeritus Professor and Former Chair of the Department of Psychiatry, University of California San Francisco School of Medicine, and is also Training and Supervising Analyst at the San Francisco Psychoanalytic Institute. In addition, he is Past President of the American Psychoanalytic Association Past President of the International Psychoanalytical Association.

Daniel Widlöcher is Professor Emeritus of Psychiatry at the University Pierre et Marie Curie, Paris. He is Honorary Chief of the Psychiatric Department, Hôpital de la Salpêtrière, Paris, and Full Member and Training Analyst of the French Psycho-Analytical Association. He is also Lecturer and Senior Lecturer in Psychology at Paris University and Professor of Psychiatry at the Salpêtrière Medical School, and has been Director of a research unit in the National Institute of Medical Research (INSERM) from 1985 to 1997.

1

JOSEPH SANDLER'S INTELLECTUAL CONTRIBUTIONS TO THEORETICAL AND CLINICAL PSYCHOANALYSIS

Peter Fonagy and Arnold M. Cooper

INTRODUCTION

Joseph Sandler[1] has been one of the most creative figures in the past several decades in bringing about what Ogden (1992) has termed a 'quiet revolution' in psychoanalytic theory. His contributions form a coherent progression of thought on psychoanalysis and the analytic process, and he has been a formative influence on psychoanalysis during the latter part of this century. His accomplishments reflect an almost unique capacity to combine empirical research skills with the highest order of understanding of psychoanalytic theory. In a long series of extraordinary papers, one can observe the evolution of his thinking, from his more traditional frame of reference arising from his analytic training to his complex integration of ego psychology and object relations theory, which has become increasingly dominant.

This intellectual odyssey has been characterized by a consistent methodological effort to keep theory tied to clinical activity. While all of us have paid lip service to the intimate relationship of theory and practice, it was Sandler who used the Hampstead Psychoanalytic Index as the framework for researching how psychoanalytic concepts apply to the clinical situation, in contrast to what we expect them to mean. As a result, he initiated a series of redefinitions and reconceptualizations of some of the basic building blocks of psychoanalysis. His training as an experimental psychologist, statistically sophisticated and familiar with psychological tests and rating scales, gave him a fresh perspective on traditional concepts, and he supported and altered them on the basis of empirical research. His immersion in child development at the Anna Freud Centre also influenced his intellectual development.

Sandler's earliest published works, preceding his analytic training, focused on psychological topics ranging from Rorschach studies to statistical analysis. After graduating from analytic training in 1952 at the age of twenty-five, he wrote his first analytic paper to fulfil a membership requirement of the British Psycho-Analytical Society. Published in 1959 and now recognized as a classic, 'The body as phallus: a patient's fear of erection' described the necessary conditions for psychological development and functioning that elicit anxiety when threatened. This was the first of an astonishing series of papers that has shaped the way psychoanalysts think, written, often with collaborators, over four decades.

The task of presenting the key components of Sandler's psychoanalytic contributions in the space allotted for it in this volume requires a capacity for moulding and synthesizing psychoanalytic concepts and ideas that probably only Sandler himself possesses. Robert S. Wallerstein's breathtaking perspective on the development of psychoanalysis over the past half-century provides an historical backdrop for Sandler's evolving thought over the same period. Wallerstein identifies three major themes in his overview:

1   the increasing importance attributed to the analytic relationship, which has become equal to interpretation and insight as an agent of psychic change;
2   the increasing influence of object relations and other fresh perspectives challenging classical psychoanalytical concepts; and
3   the trend towards greater sensitivity in psychoanalysis to postmodern concepts of evidence where clinical data are no longer seen as isolated and independent from the person of the interpreter.

Our aim in this initial chapter is to highlight what may be Sandler's most important and lasting contributions, to link these with the chapters in this volume, and to encourage the reader to pursue this rich vein of creative and scholarly work through our commentary and Sandler's extensive bibliography.

REPRESENTATION AND AFFECTS

The representational world

The most important new psychoanalytic concept introduced by Sandler is his frame of reference for the representational world. Described fully in a paper coauthored with Bernard Rosenblatt (Sandler and Rosenblatt 1962), the representational world had earlier formed the background to his 1960 paper on the superego (Sandler 1960b) as well as others (e.g. Sandler 1962a). Sandler's notion of a representational world concept is rooted, among others, in the work of Piaget (1936, 1937), Jacobson's (1953a, 1953b, 1954a, 1954b,

1954c) concept of self-representation, and Head's notion of body schema (1926). The representational world is one of a family of psychological models that came into their own with the cognitive revolution in psychology, spurred by the analogy between the human mind and digital computers, long after Sandler's adoption of the concept. Consequent to the use of the mental representational concept in cognitive science, psychodynamically oriented psychologists, as well as psychoanalysts, have adopted Sandler's notion as the dominant framework for the conceptualization of the internal representation of object relationships (e.g. Blatt and Behrends 1987; Bowlby 1973, 1980; Horowitz 1991; Kernberg 1976; Stern 1985; Stolorow and Atwood 1979; Westen 1991).

Sandler's internal working model antedates but resembles Bowlby's influential formulation. Both view relationship representations as consisting 'in essence, of a set of expectations relating to the mother's appearance and activities' (Sandler 1960b: 147). In Sandler's (1962a) conceptualization, representations of self and other have a 'shape'; they also have a critical affective component that assists in the organization and integration of sensations and perceptions arising out of interpersonal experience. Once a self-representation is formed, object representations can be established. Sandler's metaphor links the representational model to structural theory: the ego is the theatre and representations are characters on the stage. We are aware of the characters enacting the drama, but remain blissfully ignorant of the essential props the theatre requires for staging the play.

Sandler found it necessary to introduce this idea in order to be able to update and clarify many basic concepts in psychoanalysis (see below). For example, the process of *introjection* of early childhood corresponds to a change in status of parent representations that does not involve a change in self-representation. *Incorporation*, on the other hand, implies a change in self-representation to resemble the perceived image of the object. *Identification* is a momentary fusion of self- and object representations that preserves their boundaries and separateness.[2] An instinctual wish may be seen as a temporary modification in the representation of the self or the object; conflict can result in the exclusion of these representations from consciousness. Defences rearrange the contents of the representational world (e.g. projection modifies the shape of the object representation to make it resemble the unconscious self-representation). Similarly, primary narcissism is the libidinal cathexis of the self-representation; object love is the transfer of this cathexis to the object representation. Secondary narcissism is the withdrawal of libidinal cathexis from the object representation now directed to the self-representation.

In these early papers, Sandler saw no inconsistency between the notion of the representational world and classical Freudian metapsychology: 'It is an auxiliary way of looking at things, of pulling parts of the psychoanalytical model together' (Sandler 1962a: 98). In the introduction to *From Safety to Superego*, Sandler (1987a) referred to it as 'a useful supplementary frame of reference' (58). Notwithstanding his modesty, it is evident to all serious scholars that his meticulous, systematic development of the representational world framework, as introduced by Jacobson (1954c) in her paper on 'Self and the object world', was the bedrock of the 'quiet revolution' of psychoanalytic thought over the past quarter of a century.

The concept of feeling states

In two papers, on *narcissism* (Joffe and Sandler 1967) and on *sublimation* (Sandler and Joffe 1966), Sandler proposed a profound revision of psychoanalytic theory, placing feeling states rather than psychic energy at the centre of the psychoanalytic theory of motivation. His paper on the safety concept (1960a; see below) anticipated this innovation, but his earlier papers on narcissism and sublimation forcefully challenged many of the original assumptions of libido theory. Joffe and Sandler (1967) questioned the appropriateness of libido theory as an explanation for narcissism. In brief, they observed that libido theory and clinical observation appear to be at odds, in that secure individuals show love and concern for their objects while insecure ones show higher levels of self-interest and self-preoccupation.

As an alternative, Joffe and Sandler (1967) offered the representational world frame of reference with its focus on the representation of feeling states and values:

> The clinical understanding of narcissism and its disorders should be explicitly oriented towards a conceptualisation in terms of a metapsychology of affects, attitudes, values and the ideational contents associated with these, from the standpoint of both present function and genetic development.
>
> (Joffe and Sandler 1967: 64)

Disorders of narcissism arise out of the mental pain associated with the discrepancy between the mental representation of the actual self of the moment and the representation of the ideal shape of the self.

Problems of self-esteem are higher-order derivatives of the basic affect of pain. The pain is constantly present but may be made more bearable by psychic techniques, such as by seeking narcissistic supplies, overcompensating in fantasy, and identifying with idealized and omnipotent figures. If these adaptive manoeuvres fail, a depressive reaction may develop. Feelings influence the values attached to mental representations; the value may be positive, negative, or both, but it is the feeling shape of the representations that is critical for narcissistic disorders.

In a similar vein, Sandler and Joffe (1966) took issue with the energy transformation theory of sublimation originally proposed by Hartmann *et al.* (1949). They showed that sublimation is not isomorphic with any skill or activity, but instead is motivated by feelings of pleasure evoked by the removal of the activity from the domain of crude, instinctual pleasures. The activity used for sublimation is endowed with feelings derived from gratifying object relationships where the activity is represented as part of the self, and the product or the tool is derived from the representation of the object. Sublimation evokes a relationship beyond the level of simple need satisfaction. In a later paper, Sandler (1976a) further clarified this concept by pointing out that sublimations are symbolic actualizations that are *unconsciously understood* by the individual.

These affect and representation models were initially integrated in an important paper on *adaptation* (Joffe and Sandler 1968). In it, the aim of all ego functioning was identified as the reduction of 'conscious or unconscious representational discrepancy and through this ... basic feeling state of well-being' (451). Many applications of the concept of a motivational system based on feeling states were explored, and the concept of adaptation was reconsidered as 'the relinquishing of ideals which are no longer appropriate to present reality' (451).

In a chapter on the role of affect in psychoanalytic theory, Sandler (1972) put its motivational significance unequivocally: 'while drives, needs, emotional forces, and other influences arising from within the body are highly important in determining behaviour, from the point of view of psychological functioning they exert their effect through changes in feeling' (296). Sandler saw the entire ideational content of the experiential field as embedded within a matrix of feeling states that give direction to all adaptation.

Sandler's emphasis on feeling states created a bridge between classical drive theories and object relations theories. A key point was his assumption that feeling states are subjective experiences representing a state of self in relation to another person. Many creative contributors to the study of object relationships, particularly early mother–infant interactions, have gone on to make extensive use of Sandler's model (e.g. Emde 1988; Stern 1985) as an alternative to poorly fitting drive theory accounts.

In a 1978 lecture on 'Unconscious wishes and human relationships', Sandler made explicit his conviction that the wish is the basic unit of psychoanalytic discourse, whereas instincts and drives are basic psychological tendencies. In further papers (e.g. Sandler and Sandler 1978) the break with classical drive theory became explicit. The historical progression of his ideas was masterfully traced in a paper delivered in 1985 in New York (Sandler 1989).

The superego, the ego ideal and the ideal self

In a critical and well-known paper, Sandler (1960b) introduced a radical revision of the concept of the superego. In introducing the 'pre-autonomous superego schema', altering classical Freudian formulations of the superego and

Kleinian notions (e.g. Klein 1927, 1933, 1958), he explained how preoedipal children can develop moral object-related behaviour. More importantly, he showed that the superego contains approving and permissive, as well as prohibiting, features, by providing the child with a background feeling of being loved. Structuralization of the superego remains associated with the Oedipus complex, and implies the capacity to invoke these affective states without the supervision of the parental object.

As part of the processing of case material in the Hampstead Index, Sandler, with Alex Holder and Dale Meers (Sandler *et al.* 1963), uncovered major ambiguities in the concept of the ego ideal (e.g. a conscience, an ideal self-representation, ideal parental introjects). Applying the model of the representational world, they suggested that the ego ideal was a version of the self that had the desired shape of the self. This representation arose as a compromise between desired instinctual gratification and the child's need to gain the love and approval of parents or introjects. The discrepancy between the self and the ideal self-representation was seen as inversely proportional to self-esteem. Shame, for example, could arise from a failure 'to live up to ideal standards' (*ibid.*: 157), whereas guilt arose out of a perceived difference between the ideal self and the self as dictated by introjects.

Pain and depression

In two papers, Sandler and Joffe (1965b; Joffe and Sandler 1965) reconsidered depression from a representational world perspective. They argued that the term previously had been used imprecisely, without making the essential distinction between states of unhappiness and misery (pain) and depression as an affective response. They advanced the view that psychic pain may be understood as the discrepancy between an actual state of self, and an ideal or wished-for state based on memories or fantasies. This discrepancy was seen as the common ingredient in all forms of unpleasure, including anxiety. Aggression thus was a normal response to such discrepancy.

Developmentally, there is a movement towards the appreciation of reality that entails relinquishing previously enjoyed states of satisfaction. With developments then, the ideal state moves away from magical and omnipotent experiences towards an appreciation of reality – optimally with minimum pain. Giving up ideal states may be analogous to the process of mourning rather than depression. However, ideal states of well-being involve mental object representations. Loss of the object may be usefully translated, then, to mean loss of a state of self for which the object was a vehicle. Depressive responses may follow when the individual fails to respond to psychic pain with an adequate discharge of aggression. The adaptive response is individuation, a process of working through that involves abandoning the pursuit of lost ideal states and adopting new ones that are syntonic with reality, as well as with internal states. This process occurs throughout life, but is developmentally typical of particular stages determined by biology and culture.

The depressive response – capitulation in the face of pain – is the opposite of individuation; it is maladaptive in that it may dull psychic pain because of the associated inhibition but 'it is not aimed at recovery' (Joffe and Sandler 1965: 423). Depression is thus a final common pathway to a wide range of influences that can include constitutional factors as well as environmental and intrapsychic ones.

The background of safety

In a 1959 presentation, Sandler (1960a) significantly expanded the motivational constructs available to psychoanalysts. He introduced the background of safety, a revolutionary concept that placed the operating principle of ego in a positive framework of trying to maximize safety or security rather than to avoid anxiety. Although Sandler recognized the inverse complementarity of anxiety and safety, he was able to show that the pursuit of safety is an overarching construct, compatible with instinct theory, that has the capacity to organize defences, perceptions and fantasies. In addition, Sandler reaffirmed the status of instinctual drives as 'prime motivators of behaviour' (365). Nevertheless, this concept provided a motivational framework far better articulated with the interpersonal object relations tradition than a simple drive theory model.

The clinical application of the concept was illustrated in Sandler's (1959) report on Mrs B, which showed how the feeling of safety overrides displeasure in terms of pain and suffering. Thus 'stress' can become 'reassurance'. Patterns of perception can represent safety, so success can be perceived as a threat and failure can become linked to feelings of familiarity and safety.

This apparently simple concept has proved essential not only to Sandler's elaboration of object relations theory, but also to other areas. For example, in a later paper, Joffe and Sandler (1968) applied it to *autonomy*, which was seen as a reflection of the range of strategies available to maintain one's basic feeling of safety in the face of threats of disruption from the drives, the superego or the external world.

The concept of safety also has an affinity with Hermann's (1923) clinging instinct and Bowlby's (1973) secure base notion. For these authors, safety was a biological force,[3] whereas for Sandler it was distinct and lacked the excitement normally associated with drive gratification. In fact, Sandler (1989) opposed the two, demonstrating that the urge to gain feelings of well-being and safety must be stronger than instinctual gratification in order to keep a check on the latter when its expression implies danger. Safety is the most radical example of the new motivational framework proposed by Sandler based on feeling states in place of drives.

A theory of trauma

In an important but less-well-known contribution, Sandler (1967) undertook a revision of the concept of trauma, prompted in part by the difficulty of defining it in absolute terms either as an intrapsychic experience of being overwhelmed or as a particular category of external events. In a theoretical advance that remains important today, he specified that the pathological sequelae of trauma do not depend on the child's initial experience of helplessness in the face of the event, but rather on the child's post-traumatic condition. He suggested that what may lead to traumatization (i.e. the clinical sequelae) is the continuing strain on the ego, determined principally by the degree of inner conflict that remains after the trauma, crippling personality growth and leading to the development of borderline, delinquent, or psychotic pathology.

Owen Renik, in Chapter 3 of this volume, builds on Sandler's reformulation of drive theory and the primacy of the wish for well-being and safety. His brilliant explication of phenomenological aspects of trauma-related disorders shows that traumatic dreams depicting the trauma (for example, examination dreams) frequently have a reassuring outcome and may be understood as wish fulfilment dreams where the underlying wish is for safety and well-being. Similarly, the sometimes incapacitating symptom of persistent flashbacks after traumatic experience may also promote a background feeling of safety, because they contain a reassuring memory of having survived. The memory is distorted, however, by typical survivor guilt that masks the happy ending. Renik highlights the complementarity of the fulfilment of the wish for safety and the mastery of trauma.

A similar theme is pursued by Yolanda Gampel in Chapter 4, but with a greater emphasis on technique. Victims of trauma and violence struggle to achieve a background of safety as a dialectical complement to their state of anxiety. Gampel postulates a fascinating opposition between Freud's notion of the uncanny and Sandler's notion of safety. The uncanny is without signification and cannot be translated into words, just as social experiences of extreme violence literally numb the observer's power of thought. The loss of the background of safety in trauma throws the victim into a 'background of uncanny' where deficits of symbolization are inevitable and there is no boundary between fantasy and reality. Transmission of these experiences across generations occurs because the trans-subjective space between infant and caregiver acquires the background of uncanniness. Gampel's formulation of flashbacks after trauma, in contrast to Renik's, is based on the difficulties encountered by survivors in assimilating the experience against a background of loss of signification.

Thus both these authors draw on Sandler's concept, yet offer somewhat different formulations. It is tempting to conclude that Renik's formulation may be more appropriate to milder forms of interpersonal trauma, while Gampel's is restricted to extreme forms of social violence.

The basic psychoanalytic model

The culmination of Sandler and Joffe's work was a paper (Sandler and Joffe 1969) on the basic psychoanalytic model. In addition to spelling out many of the theoretical innovations generated as part of their work on the Hampstead Index, they introduced a number of critical distinctions to psychoanalytic psychology. Perhaps the most important was the reminder to distinguish carefully the experiential from the non-experiential realms of psychoanalytic theorization. Whereas the former referred to Sandler and Joffe's representational model, the latter entailed mechanisms, structures and apparatuses. The non-experiential is inherently non-conscious, although it is not repressed or dynamically inhibited. The distinction between a fantasy (conscious or unconscious) and the organized function underpinning it (fantasying) remains an evocative example.

The model makes clear that experience is not the agent of action; change is brought about by structures in the non-experiential realm, which cause corresponding changes in the experiential. Thus self-representation cannot be an agent, but it is an entity that will determine how mechanisms of the mind behave. This paper located Sandler's model in a relatively clear position *vis-à-vis* Greenberg and Mitchell's (1983) dichotomy between drive and relational models. Sandler's model placed relational formulations within the framework of a structural psychology, albeit considerably modified from Freud, Hartmann, Kris, Loewenstein and Rapaport. While modifying structural theory, Sandler refused to abandon the ambition of psychoanalysis as a general psychology of structures and basic mental processes.

In later papers, Sandler made extensive use of this important distinction. For example, in a paper on 'The structure of internal objects and internal object relationships', Sandler (1990) made clear his view of internal objects as 'structures' within the non-experiential realm, albeit constructed out of subjective experience, conscious or unconscious. Once created, such non-experiential structures can modify subjective experience, including the child's experience of the actual objects.

REPRESENTATIONS OF OBJECT RELATIONS, PAST AND PRESENT

Actualization and role responsiveness

A key concept in the second phase of Joseph Sandler's writing was the use of actualization in a literary sense 'to make actual' or 'to realise an action'. He (Sandler 1976a) traced the roots of actualization to chapter 7 of Freud's (1900) *Interpretation of Dreams*, which discussed wish fulfilment in fantasy as a repetition of the perception linked with need satisfaction. Sandler suggested that dreaming provides satisfaction because the dreamer observes his own dream, thus achieving *an identity of perception.*

Naturally, consciousness has to be protected by appropriate disguise and symbolic representation. Nevertheless, it is possible to achieve an unconscious identity of perception. Consciousness provides the link with intentional action (movement) and thus explains the pressure of the unconscious contacts towards awareness and actualization. We act in ways to achieve a correspondence between a wished-for reality and a real or actual one. To fulfil this function, an unconscious scanning process has to be postulated that observes the reactions of others, the contents of consciousness, etc., and derives from these the underlying unconscious wished-for fantasy.

The idea of actualization was put to excellent use in a paper on role responsiveness that appeared about the same time (Sandler 1976b). In this highly influential work, Sandler showed how patients wishing to actualize an unconscious fantasy create role relationships. They cast themselves and the analyst in a specific relationship that actualizes a variety of unconscious needs and defences. The patients attempt to act on the external world and bring about changes so as to make it conform to an unconscious fantasy. Sandler (1976b) suggested that analysts should allow themselves a 'free-floating responsiveness' (44), whereby they accept – at least in part – and reflect on the role assigned to them and put it to good use in understanding their patients. He cited the example of the woman whose unconscious fantasy was of soiling or wetting herself and having an adult around to clean her up. Over many sessions, she cried and asked for tissues. The analyst in this case was forced into the role of a parental introject. Of critical importance here is that a part of the patient's mind is devoted to scanning and understanding the total analyst–patient situation because it is the entire role relationship that represents an identity of perception with the unconscious fantasy. Countertransference then must be understood as part of this process, which extends beyond the boundaries of the clinical situation and reflects the regular functioning of the unconscious mind.

Roy Schafer, in a beautiful essay on the concept of enactment (see Chapter 5), draws on Sandler's notion of role responsiveness in attempting to understand why and how analysts comply with the patient's unspoken need for manipulation. Although he accepts Sandler's formulation that the actualization of unconscious fantasy gives analysts a useful tool for identifying enactments in their patients, he also draws attention to dangers inherent in attempting to be over-definitive about the meaning of enactment. He questions attempts at uncovering, discovering or recovering definitive truths about the meaning of behaviour in analysis. Instead, he stresses that the analyst is restricted to constructing a version of the patient's representational world, and that what is discovered will depend on the analyst's principles of construction. In this regard, he is certainly in line with Sandler's suggestions about the discovery of the contents of the past unconscious (see below).

Schafer fully accepts the relativism implied by his position. If enactments are constructions, they will be affected by the story line (the theoretical orientation) of the analyst. However, he counsels against abandoning one's orientation to shift freely among the interpretive lines of different schools. He considers eclecticism suspect intellectually, emotionally and epistemologically.

Internal object relations

In a seminal paper with Anne-Marie Sandler (Sandler and Sandler 1978) Sandler drew together and demonstrated the immense heuristic value of his expanded notion of motivation. The frame of reference provided by representation and the concept of identity of perception offered an entirely new and ingenious theory of internal object representations. He showed how wishful fantasies are represented as interactions between self and object, the basic aim being to bring about a primary affective 'good' state while distancing a bad one. Thus the object plays as important a role as the self in the mental representation that embodies the wish. Object relationships are thus fulfilments, not only of instinctual wishes, but also of the needs for safety, reassurance and affirmation. Such needs accompany the actualization of a wished-for childhood relationship, albeit heavily disguised at times.

Overt relationships are derivatives of underlying wishful fantasy role relationships. As these representations are reinforced during the course of development, personality is formed and the individual becomes increasingly inflexible in the roles demanded of self and others. Character traits can thus be understood as well-established role responsiveness structures that serve to actualize a wished-for representation of a relationship, which in turn is a derivative of one existing in unconscious fantasy (Sandler 1981). The fulfilment of the wish derives from a correspondence between the perception of reality and what is wished for, that is, actualization (Sandler 1990).

The psychological structures that constitute the representation of these wished-for relationships are not conceived of simply as perceptions of the interaction between the child and the actual parent. Instead, the perception of these relationships is subject to defensive transformations resulting from the ego's need to gratify yet defend against unconscious wishes. The defensive modification occurs in response to the underlying intra-psychic mental representation. Because the structures that embody both the self and the internal representation are determined in part by the child's fantasy life, the object, as represented in the child's mind, will be a distortion derived sometimes almost entirely from fantasy constructions. The image of the object may be distorted so that it represents split-off aspects of the unconscious self-image that would normally arouse unpleasant affect (e.g. feelings of guilt or shame). Thus the manifest relationship that emerges in the psychoanalytic setting (or in everyday encounters) is most frequently a heavily disguised version of the unconscious fantasy – originally represented in relationship terms – rather than a simple repetition of internalized patterns of interpersonal relations. Nevertheless, the resulting internalized pattern may serve to create the unconscious illusion that the love object is present.

The remarkable usefulness of this framework is well illustrated by its power to provide a satisfactory account of some of the most puzzling aspects of human behaviour. Many 'dialogues', as Sandler (1990) termed them, between self and object are extremely painful yet paradoxically retained by patients. Nevertheless, as Sandler (1990) pointed out, these dialogues provide a feeling of safety because they allow the patient to continue experiencing the presence of the object. They are necessary, even if persecuting or guilt-provoking, because in fantasy the internal object can continue through this presence to function as the embodiment of unacceptable aspects of self-representation, thus enhancing the individual's experience of overall safety in terms of the mental economy of affect. In addition, their continuity may enhance safety through the mere familiarity of their presence.

A comprehensive account of the developmental aspects of Sandler's model of internal object relationships is presented in a recent paper published in the *Infant Mental Health Journal* (Sandler 1994). In it, Sandler summarized many of the ideas he has brought to the field of infant development, including the notions of the representational world and its development through internalization of the interaction between the self and the object, of affect as the basic motivator of infant behaviour, and of the 'shapes' of mental representations as helping infants to maintain internal equilibrium of their emotional states. Sandler (1993) has also described the infant's developmental task as being to build up an internal world on the basis of subjective experience. He ascribed critical importance to the role of fleeting primary identification (fleeting confusion between self and other), which complements the process of boundary setting between the object and the self.

Serge Lebovici, in Chapter 6, expands on Sandler's notions about the development of self-representation in infancy. The model he proposes is consistent with Sandler's, insofar that representations are not seen as agents but rather as motivators of action and thought to be distinguished from the concept of the ego. In this highly sophisticated exploration of self-development, Lebovici focuses on how the subjective self comes into being (via what he calls 'subjectification'). He extends Sandler's model in describing subjectification as a bi-directional dyadic process whereby infants incorporate adults' thoughts about them into a core part of the self.

In Chapter 7, the leading Kleinian psychoanalyst Hanna Segal offers her views on the object. Her simple but beautiful essay highlights the extensive overlap between current mainstream Kleinian thought and Sandler's model of the internal world of objects. Although Segal's theoretical roots differ greatly from those of Sandler, each of these eminent thinkers has evolved a model of internal representation of the external object that assumes both constitutionally given, non-experiential structures and environmentally determined, experiential structures. Segal links the development of internal object relations to Chomsky and generative grammar, a theory of structure inherent to the organism that predefines or constrains the development of symbolic representation. (The link between the natures of object relations and of language at the nonexperiential level is also taken up by Theodore Shapiro in Chapter 8.)

Segal and Sandler are in broad agreement on how the fantasy life of infants may determine the nature of their perception and, therefore, their representation of the object; and how, once they internalize this representation, it, in turn, colours their inner experience. The bi-directional movement implied by Segal is also implicit in Sandler's formulation. Nevertheless, there may still be incompatibilities between the two in regard to the nature of the movement between self and other, between inner and outer. We believe that Sandler's explication of projective identification is particularly helpful in spelling out more concretely the oscillation of projective identification and introjection that occurs during development, as well as how its presence surfaces in the clinical psychoanalytical encounter.

Theodore Shapiro's contribution takes Hanna Segal's model a step further. Shapiro explains the syntax of object relations as consisting of an agent, an action and an agent–action relationship (e.g. turning active into passive or representing a relationship of seduction). He suggests that this syntax may be specific to patients in analysis, and whereas the representations between the protagonists may alter with time, the 'syntactic relationship' will remain the same. He goes beyond syntax, however, to show how object relations may be conceived of at the level of semantics, for example, to understand how memory and unconscious fantasy are encoded. Finally, Shapiro notes that a third linguistic level, that of pragmatics (where meaning is derived from the experience of communication), may be helpful to understanding the evolution of meaning in the therapeutic setting. Sandler's concept of role responsiveness, for example, could be conceived of as an aspect of pragmatics.

Projective identification

Sandler's formulation of projective identification, as outlined in his chapter in an exceptionally interesting edited volume (see Sandler 1987b), was a particularly useful attempt to link a dominant Kleinian notion to the sophisticated representational point of view now generally adopted by most theorists. Clinical observations in which the psychoanalyst appears to be experiencing a feeling more appropriately attributable to the patient were seen by Sandler as a wishful fantasy of the patient that included the analyst. The fantasy involved modification of the representation of the object in the patient's mind so that it contains unwanted aspects of the self-representation. To actualize the fantasy, the patient attempts to modify (or control) the behaviour of the analyst, so that it will conform with the distorted representation. Retaining self–object boundaries is essential in order for the mechanism to fulfil its defensive function of dissociating unwanted aspects of the self while maintaining the illusion of controlling them through control of the object.

This concept may also be illustrated within the context of the transgenerational transmission of representations evident in infancy (Fraiberg *et al.* 1975; Sandler 1994). The mother's interaction with her child is based on her representations of past attachment relationships. In such encounters, the mother may modify the representation of her child, making it identical to an unwanted aspect of herself. She may then manipulate the infant to behave consistently with her distorted representation. Naturally, this process works both ways; infants may, from time to time, be obliged to distort their representation of their caregivers in order to deal with unmanageable affect and bring about behavioural reactions in the adults that confirm the accuracy of their mental representation. The model is basically a dynamic one, in that what the child experiences as unmanageable is by no means absolute but, rather, strongly dependent on what is perceived to be experienced by the caregiver as unmanageable and unacceptable in the child. Gradually, through this process, the child's self-representation may increasingly resemble that of the caregiver. The dialectic process that occurs intrapsychically between self- and other representations (within the framework of the representation of the interactions between them) will work towards an isomorphic set of representations in the two individuals.

The three box model

In a series of scholarly papers published in the 1970s, Sandler and his co-workers (chiefly Alex Holder and Chris Dare) made the most coherent attempt in the history of the discipline to crystallize the frames of reference of classical psychoanalysis (Sandler 1974; Sandler, Dare and Holder 1972a, 1972b, 1972c, 1974, 1978, 1982; Sandler, Holder and Dare 1972, 1973a, 1973b, 1973c, 1975, 1976). This programme of work culminated in a hallmark paper by Sandler and Sandler (1984) which highlighted the inconsistencies that have arisen as a direct consequence of the concurrent use of these incompatible frameworks.

Sandler and Sandler (1984) proposed a far more coherent frame of reference to distinguish two aspects of unconscious functioning. The first system or 'box' consists of 'those infantile reactions, infantile wishes or wishful fantasies that developed early in life and are the outcome of all the transformations that defensive activities and modifying processes have brought about during that period' (418). This system is the child within the adult, primitive in terms of mental structure but by no means restricted to sexual and aggressive impulses. Sandler and Sandler (1987) see the system as consisting of unconscious fantasies with wish-fulfilling, problem-solving, reassuring and defensive aspects. Indeed, it embodies the ego of the young child as well as the superego formation of the early years. From the point of view of cognitive sophistication, representations within this structure are less well elaborated and are dominated by childhood theories. Never directly accessible to consciousness, it is essentially unchangeable. What is changeable, though, is how the adult psyche accommodates to derivatives of the past unconscious.

The second system or 'box' is also unconscious; representations within it may be more or less subject to censorship. It is equivalent to Freud's unconscious ego, but also contains unconscious representations normally assigned to the superego. It differs from the first system in that it is oriented to the present rather than the past. Conflict-solving compromises are created within it, facilitating intra-psychic adaptation; the most important of these is the creation and modification of current unconscious fantasies and thoughts. Whereas external stimuli applied to the first system may trigger past unconscious fantasy, the second system involves the constant modification of representations of self- and object interactions that are less peremptory and disruptive than the mental products of the first system. It is cognitively more involved and more closely linked with representations of the present-day reality. It also shares the property of unconscious systems in tolerating contradictions.

The nature of the second censorship, at the border of the second and third systems, differs qualitatively from that on the border of the first and second. Whereas the latter may be conceived of as analogous to Freud's repression barrier, the former is principally oriented towards avoiding shame, embarrassment and humiliation. The third system is conscious and only irrational to the degree that it may be licensed by social convention.

The clinical significance of the distinction is self-evident. The first box is a continuation of the past in the present. It lacks cognizance of the need for adaptation because it is based on infantile aspects of the child's self. The second box is the present unconscious, consisting of here-and-now adaptations to the conflicts and anxieties triggered in the first box. It follows from this model that material in this part of the mind is more likely to be accessible to interpretation, so it must be considered appropriate for intervention – all the more so because the analyst's authority positions them to overcome the second censorship by providing an atmosphere of tolerance that weakens the inhibition based on shame, embarrassment and humiliation. Interpretations, even in a transferential context, that attempt to immediately access putative, peremptory fantasies or to directly address the child within, without first addressing their derivatives in the second system, inevitably muddle the two forms of the unconscious and reduce the impact of the intervention.

Hernández and Lemlij, in their carefully sculpted contribution presented in Chapter 9, draw on Sandler's distinction between Oedipal and preoedipal internalizations of objects (i.e. the past and present unconscious). Using the theory of internal object relations, they helpfully elaborate why the past unconscious functions in qualitatively different ways from the present unconscious. They point out that preoedipal internalizations remain largely preverbal. Similarly, preoedipal internal objects are more likely to function in an anthropomorphic manner (as if concrete internal persons) and less likely to be structure-like, behaving as internal processes. The concepts Hernández and Lemlij propose are helpful in understanding manifestations of severe character pathology, such as borderline states, where early object representations predominate. Sandler's notion of the experience of the internal presence associated with internalized object representations may apply more to preoedipal internalizations than to ones that follow the establishment of the repression barrier. These authors also imply that the psychoanalytic recognition of internal objects as entities, theoretically and clinically useful as this discovery undoubtedly has been, may have come about as part of the 'widening scope' of clinical work, because their manifestation is more readily discernible in primitive personality structures where preoedipal internalizations predominate.

Unconscious fantasy

It was in an early paper on the metapsychology of fantasy (Sandler and Nagera 1963) that Sandler first referred to the distinction between fantasies that are descriptively unconscious and fantasies that arise as a consequence of the act of repression and so may be called dynamically unconscious. Fantasies originating in the system unconscious provide the ideational content of unsatisfied wishes but do not constitute a wish fulfilment; rather, they are a representation of the gratifying experience. In contrast, preconscious fantasies are attempts at wish fulfilments or are derivatives of wish-fulfilment fantasies. Preconscious fantasies may, of course, reflect the failure of wish fulfilment in that they incorporate defensively modified derivatives. What is dynamically unconscious acts as the source of what is preconscious or descriptively unconscious, the latter striving towards consciousness in order to achieve identity of perception.

This paper, which was based on the work of the Index group, also clarified the distinction between conscious fantasy (or daydreams, which through the loosening of reality testing created a wish-fulfilling situation in the imagination known to be not real); a preconscious, descriptively unconscious fantasy (non-conscious daydreams); and unconscious fantasy (repressed preconscious fantasies that, once repressed, function like memories of gratification, deserving the term 'fantasy' only in that they were the source of conscious or preconscious fantasies). The process of unconscious fantasizing was seen as an ego function located in the non-conscious ego and involving both childlike and more mature forms of thought, that is, a constant 'back and forth' movement within the system preconscious. In a chapter on sexual fantasies

(1975) and in the important paper (1983) on the links between psychoanalytic theory and practice, Sandler reinforced the importance of recognizing that not all unconscious wish-fulfilment fantasies could be traced back to sexual or aggressive instincts; rather, some may be fulfilling wishes for safety, protecting against threats to self-esteem presented by feelings of guilt and shame or even from the external world.

With the development of the three box model, the notion of unconscious fantasy could be elaborated further (Sandler and Sandler 1986). Unconscious fantasies in the second box (the present unconscious) function adaptationally by involving constant modifications of self- and object representations, thus restoring again and again the individual's equilibrium, much like a gyroscope stabilizes a physical object through centrifugal and centripetal forces. The peremptory urges and fantasies of the past unconscious disturb mental equilibrium but are worked on (elaborated) in the second system to restore homeostasis. Wishes and impulses that arise in the deeper layers of the present unconscious threaten the individual's current equilibrium. These fantasies are dynamically kept from consciousness by the internalized social judgement of the second censorship. In reaction to narcissistic hurt, for example, grandiose omnipotent fantasies help restore equilibrium but become inconsistent with the child's more mature thoughts and so are kept out of consciousness; if allowed in, they are extensively modified (made plausible through rationalization). Unconscious fantasies modified by defensive activity are gratified by making reality consistent with them via externalization (actualization) and by making such actions plausible through rationalization. Psychotic phenomena have a similar re-equilibrating function but sacrifice the criterion of social plausibility.

In Chapter 10, Daniel Widlöcher offers a highly innovative model of unconscious fantasy, rooted in part in Sandler's formulations. He makes the radical proposal that unconscious representations are invariably of hallucinatory actions (i.e. 'action presentations'). From this model, he is able to derive many of the properties of the traditional notion of the unconscious, such as displacement and absence of contradiction. He argues that actions occur independent of each other; each is an entity in its own right. One action may replace another, but contradiction is inconceivable because they cannot be represented simultaneously. Understanding within psychoanalytic treatment takes time, not simply because such understanding addresses itself to the past but also because it is not a narrative but, rather, an action that is represented; it is not a memory but, instead, a currently experienced event. Echoing the Sandlers' conclusion concerning the past unconscious, he suggests that genuine direct therapeutic access to such experience will always be problematic because memory of action is not governed by the same rules as memory of knowledge.

In an immensely interesting and creative contribution (Chapter 11), Ethel Spector Person applies Sandler's unconscious fantasy model and three box model to help us understand the impact of social and cultural changes on conscious and unconscious fantasy. She begins by distinguishing between three different types of fantasy – only one of which, the generative fantasy, may be susceptible to change as part of cultural evolution. Using the example of gender-specific fantasies, she extends Sandler's notion of the present unconscious to suggest the existence of a cultural unconscious, where stories and narratives specific to a culture may shape the choice of life paths, modes of gratification, and the priority placed on certain values. Then, relying on the notion of the second censorship as being based on the injunctions of the child's social context, she suggests that the impact of cultural change on generative fantasies occurs via social constraints placed on what is acceptable and what is anticipated to engender a shaming, embarrassing or humiliating reaction.

CLINICAL CONCEPTS

Transference

In a valuable monograph with Chris Dare and Alex Holder based on a series of papers in the *British Journal of Psychiatry* in the 1970s, Sandler carefully scrutinized many of the fundamental clinical concepts of psychoanalysis (Sandler *et al.* 1973). Recently, their productive collaboration with Ursula Dreher has resulted in a new edition of this widely used text. Many of the concepts treated deserve presentation here but because of limitations of space, we shall concentrate on only a couple of the topics they reviewed.

In a 1969 paper with a number of colleagues at the Anna Freud Centre, Sandler put forward an important revision of the concept of transference (Sandler *et al.* 1969). The paper contrasted transferences in the analytic situation with transferences in everyday life, illustrating how problems with the concept may arise out of attempts to bring a metapsychological frame of reference to a clinical concept. The clinical and technical use of the term covers a broad spectrum of experiences, all of which concern object relationships in general. Sandler and his colleagues identified a number of phenomena representing aspects or dimensions of transference that should be distinguished for both technical and conceptual reasons (e.g. displacement of wishes, conflicts or reactions to others, externalization of parts of the representational system, character transferences, the so-called 'real' relationship, and the therapeutic alliance). They reformulated the question of what is and is not transference by asking: 'What dimensions of relationship enter into the special and artificial analytic situation, and how are these involved in the process of treatment?' (643). Thus the repetition of past relationships with defences against them is only one dimension of a complex phenomenon.

The elaboration of the model of internal object relations led Sandler (1990) to reformulate the concept of transference. He saw patients as gratifying, through some form of actualization in the analytic situation, their unconscious wishful fantasies via a disguised identity of perception (Sandler 1976a, 1990). The recognition of these internal object relationships in the transference does not constitute a perception by the analyst, but rather a *construction*, a framework imposed on the material brought by the patient.

Sandler (1990) further elaborated on the significance of this distinction. Constructions concerning the inner world of the patient pertain to a current state of affairs, not to memories, even if that state of affairs is marked by childlike features and clearly involves an object of childhood concern (an omnipotent parental figure or a dangerous and persecutory one). Recon-struction, although frequently confused with construction, attempts to provide a temporal perspective by rediscovering the state of affairs of the historical past. Those involved in the recent controversy concerning recovered memories of childhood sexual abuse (Sandler and Fonagy 1997) could greatly profit from a thoughtful reading of Sandler's writing on this issue.

The distinction between the present and past unconscious also proved helpful in the understanding of transference (Sandler and Sandler 1984). Unconscious transference fantasies are part of the present unconscious aimed to restore psychic equilibrium by manipulating self- and object representa-tions. They are kept from consciousness and expressed in displacement because they violate the principles of the second censorship, protecting consciousness from shame and humiliation. Sandler and Sandler (1987) point out that the patient's constant striving towards the actualization of the wishful fantasies in the present unconscious makes the analysis of transference the most convincing route to elucidation of the present unconscious. The hierarchical layering of unconscious fantasies in the second 'box' implies that interpretation of the transference should be as close as possible to the current central conflict and to the patient's immediate resistance. The present should always be interpreted before the past; if the latter is brought into the foreground, it should be done only to throw light on what is occurring currently.

Within this framework, the analyst and patient are seen as jointly creating an extended model of the patient's self and world. As a result, the patient acquires a perspective on that part of the self that is childlike – and thus frequently repudiated but made acceptable in the clinical context by the analyst's tolerant attitude.

Countertransference and the vicissitudes of guilt

In a superb summary paper integrating their writing on internal object relations and the past and present unconscious, Sandler and Sandler (1987) presented a brief but highly sophisticated understanding of the role of guilt in psychoanalytic work. They distinguished between guilt accessible to interpretation, seen as part of the present unconscious, and hypothetical primitive guilt embedded in the archaic fantasies of the past unconscious which cannot be perceived, only conceived and reconstructed.

They note a great number of manoeuvres to protect against the dis-equilibriating influence of guilt. These share the common quality of modifying the representation of the self–object interaction (the unconscious fantasy), with the aim of restoring homeostasis. Such manoeuvres may include actual feelings of guilt that are experienced about something else rather than the original source. In masochistic reactions, guilt is atoned for by directing aggression and sadism against the self. Role responsiveness may play a part by provoking the criticism of others when the unconscious fantasy of the self as being reproached or held in contempt by the introject 'leaks out' without the patient's awareness. The analyst may have countertransference awareness of critical feelings towards the patient. Sometimes the modified fantasy may mitigate guilt by further modifying the fantasy so that it depicts unjust criticism; the patient may actualize this fantasy by provoking unjust accusations, leading to an experience of entitlement and self-vindication. All these enactments may be understood by the analyst but not perceived by the patient without interpretation.

Otto Kernberg's exceptionally lucid discussion of countertransference (Chapter 12) builds on and advances Sandler's ideas on countertransference by distinguishing between acute and chronic countertransference reactions. Whereas the former are brief and isolated enactments of the role into which the analyst is placed, the latter are slowly developing, diffuse, invasive and pervasive distortions of the analyst's emotional disposition or capacity to work. While acute countertransference reactions are available for immediate internal exploration by the analyst, and may be readily available for analytic work, chronic reactions require more consistent working through by the psychoanalyst both inside and outside of sessions. Kernberg suggests a number of countertransference management techniques, including mentally normalizing the patient's reactions by comparing them to what the average analyst and patient would do in this situation and by adopting a stance that combines cognitive clarity, emotional concern and courage. Above all, a balance is needed between mutual patience in the long term and analytic impatience. The analyst must have tolerance for the development of the patient's mental capacities.

Regression

All Sandler's contributions are imbued with strong developmental orienta-tions. Nowhere is this clearer than in the papers dealing with regression. The first of these (Sandler and Joffe 1965a) dealt with obsessional phenomena in children and evoked the concept of 'the function of regression of aspects of the ego' (145). The model suggested that particular modes of ego functioning may be associated with varying degrees of pleasure, thus creating the potential to return to that mode of functioning in a way analogous to drive regression. Obsessional children manifest 'a particular style of the perceptual and cognitive functions of the ego' that indicate its fixation in the second and third year of life (436). In Sandler's papers on depression and individuation (Joffe and Sandler 1965; Sandler and Joffe 1965a, 1965b), regression is described as a response to frustration and suffering that arises from the need to give up early magical and omnipotent ideal states in favour of an appreciation of reality; it functions as an attempt to stave off helplessness and its possible sequel, the depressive response. Modes of ego functioning may be sources of feelings of safety and mastery and can thus exert as much backward pull as do libidinal fixations.

Sandler, in a 1967 paper with Joffe, was the first fully to recognize the major theoretical implications of Freud's (1933) notion of persistence when he emphasized that psychological

> structures are in the normal course of events never lost, but rather that new and auxiliary structures of increasing complexity are created, the newer structures becoming superimposed on the old in the course of development. The more complex emergent organisation must not only provide an effective means for discharge and control, but must also include systems of inhibition directed against the utilisation of the older structures.
>
> (Sandler and Joffe 1967: 264)

In Sandler's view, then, regression is a disinhibition within the older structure rather than an actual reversal or backward movement to that structure. The notion of persistence has continued to occupy a central position in Sandler's thinking. For example, in his Amsterdam presidential address at the 1993 IPA Congress, Sandler pointed to primary identification that invariably characterizes interpersonal perceptions (Sandler 1993). If we observe someone taking a false step off the kerb, we automatically right ourselves, giving evidence of the continued presence of primitive modes of thought that may be incorporated in the far more elaborate process of empathy.

In 1994 Sandler and Sandler extended the notion of persistence by applying the distinction between past and present unconscious to the phenomenon of regression. As observed clinically, regression (i.e. manifest regression) is not a going back in time but, rather, a relaxation of an anti-regressive function of the ego. In many ways, this anti-regressive function, which prevents the individual from functioning at a lower developmental level (using structures that have persisted through development), is central to the phenomenon of resistance in clinical psychoanalysis. The aim of psychoanalysis may be seen as one of permitting the patient to relax anti-regressive functioning in the service of the analysis. Allowing oneself to tolerate in consciousness previously intolerable unconscious wishes, positions one to find better solutions or compromises to conflicts between wishful fantasies and defensive self-protective motives. Thus benign regression or the controlled relaxation of the anti-regression function is a central agent of therapeutic change.

Contribution to epistemology

Almost all Sandler's contributions could be regarded as epistemological contributions. Perhaps beginning with the work on the Hampstead Index (Sandler 1962b), his overarching aim appears to have been to divest psychoanalysis of conceptual confusions, circularity, and reification. The pattern of his writing has been to explore the history of a term or concept in psychoanalysis, then to elaborate on the multiple and frequently mutually incompatible meanings attached to the term. Having analysed the historical changes in terminology, he explains how misconceptions emerged or discussions at different levels of abstraction were conflated. Then, with a minimum number of assumptions, he proposes a highly economical model that encompasses the multiple uses of the varying meanings of the construct under scrutiny. A good example of this approach is his paper with Christopher Dare on the psychoanalytic concept of morality (Sandler and Dare 1970).

Perhaps it was Sandler's experience in the Hampstead Clinic, as well as his intellectual evolution in the theoretical turmoil of the British Psycho-Analytical Society, that led him to the important insight that much of psychoanalytic theoretical development is preceded by the unconsciously constructed partial theories that evolve in the minds of practising experienced analysts, as they struggle to develop mental models of the minds of their patients. In his oft-cited paper (Sandler 1983) on the relations between concept and practice in psychoanalysis, he pointed to the necessity for such proto-theories, as well as the simultaneous presence of incompatible preconscious theoretical constructions in the minds of many analysts. Evidence for such heterogeneity in the mental models of analysts may be readily found in the multiplicity of uses of psychoanalytic concepts, whose meaning cannot be derived without also considering their clinical context. The correspondence between 'official theory' and such tentative intuitions determines the likelihood of their emergence in consciousness. Sandler's contribution is a tribute to the tolerance of ambiguity required of theoreticians like him who make essential contributions by explicating these ideas which, however generally held, remain inaccessible to most of us.

Robert Michels, in his remarkably cogent contribution (Chapter 13), elevates Sandler's notion of preconscious or unofficial theories to the level of an organizing construct for understanding psychoanalytic practice. He identifies several non-specific functions of psychoanalytic theory for the practising clinician. Theoretical ideas may serve as an inspiration for interpretative work, thus assisting therapy as an ongoing process. Theoretical understandings may maintain the analyst's basic clinical stance, whose attitude of listening may rely on the theoretical expectation that there is meaning in incoherence. The analyst's tolerance and uncritical non-judgemental acceptance, also highlighted by the Sandlers, may be rooted in a belief in the dynamic nature of the unconscious. The analyst's theoretical belief in conflict and determination may prompt an openness to additional meanings. Michels thus embraces Sandler's emphasis on private theory as underpinning practice. He advances this proposition by suggesting that non-specific as well as specific aspects of theoretical ideas may influence the clinician's basic stance, may generate rules and guidelines, and may provide comfort and security in a situation of uncertainty (as well as suggesting meanings and interpretations).

Jorge Canestri, in a wonderfully erudite and scholarly piece (Chapter 14), integrates two aspects of Sandler's thinking: his notion of the present unconscious; and the preconscious theories of psychoanalysis. Canestri proposes that preconscious theories of analysis are in the second box of the Sandlers' model. In other words, they would be better conceived of as fantasies rather than as theories. He outlines a programme of research to explore the psychoanalyst's preconscious ideas, both in supervision and in specially formed learning groups. He makes the reasonable claim that psychoanalysts are in a privileged position with regard to their theoretical constructs. Since these scientific fantasies have their roots in the unconscious, where the unconscious must by definition be known, it makes sense to study derivatives of these ideas in the thinking of analysts. He offers a tantalizing developmental progression of psychoanalytic theories, using Piaget and Garcia's epistemological history of geometry as a model, and suggesting that the criteria for evaluating theories should move from coherence to congruence of theories in an inter-figural configuration.

Sandler is one of an unfortunately relatively small number of psychoanalysts who are fully committed to the importance of research that complements clinical work. Fundamentally, he is an empiricist. He sees psychoanalytic theory as a frame of reference to be applied to observations, 'be it in diagnosis, therapy, education, or research' (Sandler 1960b: 128; see also Sandler 1962a). He recognizes the role of settings other than the consulting room as a way to test psychoanalytic assumptions: 'psychoanalysts are constantly making psychological assumptions, and whatever light can be thrown on these assumptions, whether in the consulting room or the laboratory, must be of immense value' (Sandler 1960b: 150).

It is therefore fitting that this tribute to Joseph Sandler should end with a fascinating empirical report by Horst Kächele, Erhard Mergenthaler and Michael Hölzer (Chapter 15). In their study of the verbal utterances of psychoanalysts, Kächele and his co-workers demonstrate an increase in the use of emotional words in long-term therapy, relative to short-term therapy. It is particularly interesting that the elevation is for a specific class of emotion words, those pertaining to objects rather than the self. The results suggest, in a manner highly consistent with Sandler's theoretical framework, that the analyst becomes increasingly familiar with the internal object world of the patient and is able to label emotional states pertinent to them.

SUMMARY

Sandler's extraordinary creative mind has led us towards a psychology of feelings, internal representations, and adaptation, closely tied to the behaviours of the analytic couple in the analytic situation. Besides contributing to our changing views of psychoanalytic theory, he has also influenced psychoanalytic technique. His concept of role-responsiveness is consistent with his view that the internal world involves internal representations of self and object, the actions between them, and the affects carried by those actions. The 'three box model' of psychic structure, emphasizing the importance of distinguishing present unconscious from past unconscious, has led to the fruitful re-examination of further metapsychological and clinical concepts, including transference and countertransference. The spirit of collaboration that sparked some of these papers speaks in part of the generous intellectual disposition that Sandler brings to his work.

Sandler has never slowed down. In 1970, with Holder and Dare, he began to publish the series of papers that eventually appeared as the volume *The Patient and the Analyst* (Sandler *et al.* 1973), a book that has been read by budding therapists and analysts alike throughout the world and is now in its second edition. He recently published his tenth book, covering the history of psychoanalytic ideas from the point of view of the aims of psychoanalytic treatment; it will undoubtedly be assured a place as a standard text in most training programmes (Sandler and Dreher 1996). Sandler is a dedicated teacher as well as scholar, and he has contributed to psychoanalytic education in almost every part of the world where there is psychoanalytic education. He is one of the few eminent psychoanalysts who has combined a clinical career with an academic position. As Sigmund Freud Professor in Israel and Freud Memorial Professor at University College London, he has been instrumental in forming a dedicated cadre of analytic researchers whose contributions are beginning to influence analytic ideas.

He has been a bridging force in psychoanalysis, attempting to find the inherent links between apparently opposing ideas, and helping to close the gap between American ego psychologists and British Kleinian and object relations theorists. Endlessly curious, he is ever on the search for mental functions that have been overlooked; most recently, for example, he has been working on 'anti-regression' – in an effort to understand how and why we retain higher-order mature functioning in the face of the temptation to allow regressive tendencies.

NOTES

1 Tragically, Joseph Sandler died during the course of the preparation of this volume. The editors and contributors are all gravely disappointed that he had no opportunity to see this volume in print, but are pleased to be able to honour his memory in this way.
2 Jaqueline Amati Mehler, in a superb recent chapter, which sadly could not be included in the present volume but has been published independently, demonstrates the value of Sandler's distinction for current psychoanalytic thought.
3 In a recent conference presentation, Sandler (1995) integrated his accounts with those of attachment theory and research.

REFERENCES

Blatt, S. J. and Behrends, R. S. (1987) 'Internalization, separation-individuation, and the nature of therapeutic action', *International Journal of Psycho-Analysis*, 68, 279–97.

Bowlby, J. (1973) *Separation: Anxiety and Anger*, vol. 2 of *Attachment and Loss*, New York: Basic Books.

——(1980) *Loss: Sadness and Depression*, vol. 3 of *Attachment and Loss*, New York: Basic Books.

Emde, R. N. (1988) 'Development terminable and interminable. II. Recent psychoanalytic theory and therapeutic considerations', *International Journal of Psycho-Analysis*, 69, 283–6.

Fraiberg, S. H., Adelson, E. and Shapiro, V. (1975) 'Ghosts in the nursery: a psychoanalytic approach to the problem of impaired infant–mother relationships', *Journal of the American Academy of Child Psychiatry* 14, 387–422.

Freud, S. (1900) 'The interpretation of dreams', in J. Strachey (ed.) *The Standard Edition of the Complete Psychological Works of Sigmund Freud* (vols 4–5, 1–715), London: Hogarth Press.

——(1933) 'New introductory lectures on psychoanalysis', in J. Strachey (ed.) *The Standard Edition of the Complete Psychological Works of Sigmund Freud* (vol. 22, 1–182), London: Hogarth Press.

Greenberg, J. R. and Mitchell, S. A. (1983) *Psychoanalysis and Object Relations Theory*, New York: Basic Books.

Hartmann, H., Kris, E. and Loewenstein, R. M. (1949) 'Notes on the theory of aggression', *Psychoanalytic Study of the Child*, 3–4, 9–36.

Head, H. (1926) *Aphasia and Kindred Disorders of Speech*, New York: Macmillan.

Hermann, I. (1923) 'Zur Psychologie der Chimpanzen', *Internazional Zeitschrift für Psychoanalyse*, 9, 80–7.

Horowitz, M. J. (1991) 'Person schemas', in M. J. Horowitz (ed.) *Person Schemas and Maladaptive Interpersonal Patterns* (12–31), Chicago IL: University of Chicago Press.

Jacobson, E. (1953a) 'Contribution to the metapsychology of cyclothymic depression', in P. Greenacre (ed.) *Affective Disorders: Psychoanalytic Contributions to Their Study* (49–83), New York: International Universities Press.

——(1953b) 'The affects and their pleasure–unpleasure qualities in relation to the psychic discharge processes', in R. Loewenstein (ed.) *Drives, Affects, Behavior* (vol. 1), New York: International Universities Press.

——(1954a) 'Contribution to the metapsychology of psychotic identifications', *Journal of the American Psychoanalytic Association*, 2, 239–62.

——(1954b) 'On psychotic identifications', *International Journal of Psycho-Analysis*, 35, 102–8.

——(1954c) 'The self and the object world: vicissitudes of their infantile cathexes and their influence on ideational affective development', *Psychoanalytic Study of the Child*, 9, 75–127.

Joffe, W. G. and Sandler, J. (1965) 'Notes on pain, depression, and individuation', *Psychoanalytic Study of the Child*, 20, 394–424.

——(1967) 'Some conceptual problems involved in the consideration of disorders of narcissism', *Journal of Child Psychotherapy*, 2, 56–66.

——(1968) 'Comments on the psychoanalytic psychology of adaptation, with special reference to the role of affects and the representational world', *International Journal of Psycho-Analysis*, 49, 445–54.

Kernberg, O. F. (1976) *Object Relations Theory and Clinical Psychoanalysis*, New York: Jason Aronson.

Klein, M. (1927) 'Symposium on child-analysis', in M. Klein (1948) *Contributions to Psycho-Analysis, 1921–1945* (152–84), London: Hogarth Press.

——(1933) 'The early development of conscience in the child', in M. Klein (1948), *Contributions to Psycho-Analysis, 1921–1945*, London: Hogarth Press.

——(1948) *Contributions to Psycho-Analysis, 1921–1945*, London: Hogarth Press.

——(1958) 'On the development of mental functioning', *International Journal of Psycho-Analysis*, 39, 84–90.

Ogden, T. (1992) 'The dialectically constituted/decentred subject of psychoanalysis, II: the contributions of Klein and Winnicott', *International Journal of Psycho-Analysis*, 73, 613–26.

Piaget, J. (1936) *The Origins of Intelligence in Children*, New York: International Universities Press, 1952.

——(1937) *The Construction of Reality in the Child*, New York: Basic Books, 1954.

Sandler, J. (1959) 'On the repetition of early childhood relationships in late psychosomatic disorder', in Society for Psychosomatic Research, *The Nature of Stress Disorder* (187–95), London: Hutchinson.

——(1960a) 'The background of safety', *International Journal of Psycho-Analysis*, 41, 191–8.

——(1960b) 'On the concept of superego', *Psychoanalytic Study of the Child*, 15, 128–62.

——(1962a) 'Psychology and psychoanalysis', *British Journal of Medical Psychology*, 35, 91–100.

——(1962b) 'The Hampstead Index as an instrument of psychoanalytic research', *International Journal of Psycho-Analysis*, 43, 287–91.

——(1967) 'Trauma, strain, and development', in S. S. Furst (ed.) *Psychic Trauma* (154–74), New York/London: Basic Books.

——(1972) 'The role of affects in psychoanalytic theory', in J. Sandler, *From Safety to Superego: Selected Papers of Joseph Sandler* (285–300), New York: Guilford Press; London: Karnac Books.

——(1974) 'Psychological conflict and the structural model: some clinical and theoretical implications', *International Journal of Psycho-Analysis*, 55, 53–62.

——(1975) 'Sexual fantasies and sexual theories in childhood', in Hampstead Child-Therapy Course and Clinic (ed.) *Studies in Child Psychoanalysis: Pure and Applied*, New York: International Universities Press.

——(1976a) 'Dreams, unconscious phantasies, and "identity of perception" ', *International Review of Psycho-Analysis*, 3, 33–42.

——(1976b) 'Countertransference and role responsiveness', *International Review of Psycho-Analysis*, 3, 43–7.

——(1981) 'Character traits and object relationships', *Psychoanalytic Quarterly*, 50, 694–708.

——(1983) 'Reflections on some relations between psychoanalytic concepts and psychoanalytic practice', *International Journal of Psycho-Analysis*, 64, 35–45.

——(1987a) *From Safety to Superego*, London: Karnac Books.

——(1987b) 'The concept of projective identification', in J. Sandler (ed.) *Projection, Identification, Projective Identification* (13–26), Madison CT: International Universities Press.

——(1989) 'Toward a reconsideration of the psychoanalytic theory of motivation', in A. M. Cooper, O. F. Kernberg and E. S. Person (eds) *Psychoanalysis: Toward the Second Century* (91–110), New Haven CT: Yale University Press.

——(1990) 'On the structure of internal objects and internal object relationships', *Psychoanalytic Inquiry*, 10 (2), 163–81.

——(1993) 'On communication from patient to analyst: not everything is projective identification', 38th International Psychoanalytical Congress Presidential Address: From listening to interpretation (1993, Amsterdam, Netherlands), *International Journal of Psycho-Analysis*, 74 (6), 1097–107.

——(1994) 'Fantasy, defense, and the representational world', Fifth World Congress of the World Association for Infant Psychiatry and Allied Disciplines (1992, Chicago IL), *Infant Mental Health Journal*, 15 (1), special issue, 26–35.

——(1995) 'On attachment to internal objects', paper presented at conference on The Clinical Implications of Attachment: The Work of Mary Main, London, UCL.

Sandler, J. and Dare, C. (1970) 'The psychoanalytic concept of morality', *Journal of Psychosomatic Research*, 14, 211–22.

Sandler, J., Dare, C. and Holder, A. (1972a) 'Frames of reference in psychoanalytic psychology. I. Introduction', *British Journal of Medical Psychology*, 45, 127–32.

——(1972b) 'Frames of reference in psychoanalytic psychology. II. The historical context and phases in the development of psychoanalysis', *British Journal of Medical Psychology*, 45, 133–42.

——(1972c) 'Frames of reference in psychoanalytic psychology. III. A note on the basic assumptions', *British Journal of Medical Psychology*, 45, 143–8.

——(1973) *The Patient and the Analyst: The Basis of the Psychoanalytic Process*, New York: International Universities Press.

——(1974) 'Frames of reference in psychoanalytic psychology. VIII. The topographical frame of reference: transference as an illustration of the functioning of the mental apparatus', *British Journal of Medical Psychology*, 47, 43–51.

——(1978) 'Frames of reference in psychoanalytic psychology. XI. Limitations of the topographical model', *British Journal of Medical Psychology*, 51, 61–5.

——(1982) 'Frames of reference in psychoanalytic psychology. XII. The characteristics of the structural frame of reference', *British Journal of Medical Psychology*, 55, 203–7.

Sandler, J. and Dreher, A. U. (1996) *What Do Psychoanalysts Want? The Problem of Aims in Psychoanalysis* (The New Library of Psychoanalysis, no. 24), London and New York: Routledge.

Sandler, J. and Fonagy, P. (eds) (1997) *Recovered Memories of Abuse: True or False?*, London: Karnac Books.

Sandler, J., Holder, A. and Dare, C. (1972) 'Frames of reference in psychoanalytic psychology. VI. The affect-trauma frame of reference', *British Journal of Medical Psychology*, 45, 265–72.

——(1973a) 'Frames of reference in psychoanalytic psychology. V. The topographical frame of reference: the organization of the mental apparatus', *British Journal of Medical Psychology*, 46, 29–36.

——(1973b) 'Frames of references in psychoanalytic psychology. VI. The topographical frame of reference: the unconscious', *British Journal of Medical Psychology*, 46, 37–43.

——(1973c) 'Frames of reference in psychoanalytic psychology. VII. The topographical frame of reference: the preconscious and the conscious', *British Journal of Medical Psychology*, 46, 143–53.

——(1975) 'Frames of reference in psychoanalytic psychology. IX. Dream processes in the topographical frame of reference', *British Journal of Medical Psychology*, 48, 161–74.

——(1976) 'Frames of reference in psychoanalytic psychology. X. Narcissism and object-love in the second phase of psychoanalysis', *British Journal of Medical Psychology*, 49, 267–74.

Sandler, J., Holder, A., Kawenoka, M., Kennedy, H. and Neurath, L. (1969) 'Notes on some theoretical and clinical aspects of transference', *International Journal of Psycho-Analysis*, 50, 633–45.

Sandler, J., Holder, A. and Meers, D. (1963) 'The ego ideal and the ideal self', *Psychoanalytic Study of the Child*, 18, 139–58.

Sandler, J. and Joffe, W. G. (1965a) 'Notes on obsessional manifestations in children', *Psychoanalytic Study of the Child*, 20, 425–38.

——(1965b) 'Notes on childhood depression', *International Journal of Psycho-Analysis*, 46, 88–96.

——(1966) 'On skill and sublimation', *Journal of the American Psychoanalytic Association*, 14, 335–55.

——(1967) 'The tendency to persistence in psychological function and development, with special reference to fixation and regression', *Bulletin of the Menninger Clinic*, 31, 257–71.

——(1969) 'Towards a basic psychoanalytic model', *International Journal of Psycho-Analysis*, 50, 79–90.

Sandler, J. and Nagera, H. (1963) 'Aspects of the metapsychology of fantasy', *Psychoanalytic Study of the Child*, 18, 159–94.

Sandler, J. and Rosenblatt, B. (1962) 'The concept of the representational world', *Psychoanalytic Study of the Child*, 17, 128–45.

Sandler, J. and Sandler, A.-M. (1978) 'On the development of object relations and affects', *International Journal of Psycho-Analysis*, 59, 285–96.

——(1984) 'The past unconscious, the present unconscious, and interpretation of the transference', *Psychoanalytic Inquiry*, 4, 367–99.

——(1986) 'The gyroscopic function of unconscious fantasy', in D. B. Feinsilver (ed.) *Towards a Comprehensive Model for Schizophrenic Disorders* (109–23), Hillsdale NJ: Analytic Press.

——(1987) 'The past unconscious, the present unconscious, and the vicissitudes of guilt', *International Journal of Psycho-Analysis*, 68, 331–41.

——(1994) 'Theoretical and technical comments on regression and anti-regression', *International Journal of Psycho-Analysis*, 75, 431–9.

Stern, D. N. (1985) *The Interpersonal World of the Infant: A View from Psychoanalysis and Developmental Psychology*, New York: Basic Books.

Stolorow, R. D. and Atwood, G. E. (1979) *Faces in a Cloud: Subjectivity in Personality Theory*, New York: Jason Aronson.

Westen, D. (1991) 'Social cognition and object relations', *Psychological Bulletin*, 109, 429–55.

2

A HALF-CENTURY PERSPECTIVE ON PSYCHOANALYSIS AND PSYCHOTHERAPY

The historical context of Joseph Sandler's contributions

Robert S. Wallerstein

It is indeed a pleasure to participate in a festschrift honouring the psychoanalytic contributions and achievements of Joseph Sandler, a close and long-time friend and colleague. He is indeed someone who, without being centrally revisionist or deviationist, has played a major conceptual role in the gradual transformation of the once-dominant ego-psychology paradigm, rooted in the vicissitudes of the instinctual drives and their management by an ever more complex and multifaceted ego, into a psychology of the management of feeling states and the interplay of internalized object relationships. Yet he has never lost the vital anchoring in issues of drive gratification and frustration, as the ego balances its conditions of danger and safety and adaptive regulation.

Among the arenas of our intersecting interests has been the evolving relationship of psychoanalysis with the derived psychoanalytic psychotherapies. This relationship has been shaped over time by the concomitant transformations in our theoretical and clinical understandings of the nature of psychoanalysis as both theory and praxis. This topic is therefore the focus of this presentation: the historical unfolding of the evolving relationship of psychoanalytic psychotherapy *vis-à-vis* psychoanalysis. My own interest in this subject began when I was a psychoanalytic candidate in the 1950s. I was fashioning, together with a group of colleagues, what turned out to be the thirty-year-long Psychotherapy Research Project of the Menninger Foundation. This intensive, longitudinal study of the processes and outcomes of the treatments of a group of forty-two patients, half in psychoanalysis and half in the derived and related psychoanalytic psychotherapies, followed them over the course of their treatments and their subsequent careers, and was not brought to a close until the publication of my book, *Forty-two Lives in Treatment*, in 1986.

This preoccupation has continued unremittingly since, both with a successor psychotherapy research project currently active in San Francisco, and with my work on a book on the half-century history of this development, out of psychoanalysis, of a differentiated array of psychoanalytically conceived psychotherapies geared to extend psychoanalytic knowledge to the wider array of the psychopathological spectrum not considered amenable to analysis proper. That book, *The Talking Cures: The Psychoanalyses and the Psychotherapies*, was published in 1995.

It is an overview of that story that I present here, that is, the story of the historical development of psychoanalytic psychotherapy out of psychoanalysis and of the ever-evolving, constantly imbricated, relationship between them, from the very beginnings in the mid-1940s, a half-century ago, through today, amidst current stocktakings within a culture and an intellectual world, in literature and aesthetics and philosophy, so heavily coloured by postmodernism, with its own consequential infiltrations into our psychoanalytic way of looking at things. Before I begin, however, an apologia. The events and ideas I will describe are almost all of them familiar. What I hope to add in my recounting is an organizing overview that makes them into a coherent unfolding, and presents my own perspectives on how – and perhaps to some extent why – an era of seemingly progressive, increasing conceptual clarity on these matters several decades ago has given way to a perhaps greater wisdom in which the issues seem far more complex and undeniably less clear or certain.

As with so much in our psychoanalytic understandings, such an accounting makes most sense when presented via its temporal unfolding, and so I begin with Freud and the birth of psychoanalysis. Psychoanalysis, developed as a purified product out of the congeries of therapeutic approaches in vogue in Freud's time, or experimentally introduced by him, soon became *the* scientific psychology and *the* scientific therapy. Yet Freud, although he devoted a monumental lifetime to the (almost single-handed) creation of *psychoanalysis* as a theory of mental life and a therapy of the disorders of mental life, never himself moved in the direction of any other therapy than 'strict and untendentious' (Freud 1919: 168) psychoanalysis. As early as 1905, Freud had already set down his criteria for amenability to this rationally understood and powerful new tool. The criteria stated there are those that have always marked our conception of the 'good analytic patient': the classically neurotic, those with transference neuroses, educated, motivated, of reliable character, in the prime of adulthood, and not in a situation of emergency. By implication – and in contrast – psychoanalysts had little or nothing to offer patients not suited to the classical analytic method, beyond the same suggestive and hypnotic techniques employed by their non-analytically informed confrères.

It is this view, that proper psychoanalysis was the only truly curative and scientific psychotherapy, that pervaded the period extending over the span of

Freud's lifetime; it marked the prehistory of psychotherapy within psycho-analysis. Freud made his own distinction between psychoanalysis as a curative therapy and all other psychotherapeutic efforts as a species of outmoded suggestion outgrown by analysis most sharply in his 1918 Budapest address, when he declared that the large-scale application of the therapy 'will compel us to alloy the pure gold of analysis freely with the copper of direct suggestion', but that in this mixture the most important ingredients would always be 'those borrowed from strict and untendentious psycho-analysis' (1919: 168).

These views were strongly supported by such major adherents as Ernest Jones and Edward Glover (1931). Glover further developed the view that all psychotherapy, other than analysis, correctly and exactly applied, was indeed *nothing but* suggestion; it rests on elements not fully analysed back to their genetic-dynamic roots and hence must ultimately be based on the strong transference (i.e. suggestive) authority of the therapist. In 1954, a quarter-century later, Glover expanded this viewpoint:

> A further case exists: should the analyst's interpretation be consis-tently inaccurate then quite clearly he is practising a form of sugges-tion, whatever else he himself may call it. It follows then that when analysts differ radically as to the aetiology or structure of a case – as they nowadays do with increasing frequency – one side or the other must be practising suggestion.
>
> (Glover 1954: 394)

But Glover also tried to soften this blow: 'Bad analysis may conceivably be good suggestion' (1931: 407).

In all this we can see the kind of narrowed reasoning – that there must be only a single 'correct' interpretive line in every analytic situation, and that any deviation based on inexactness, ignorance, or countertransference must therefore be suggestion – that led Glover, building on Freud, to this sharp dichotomization of therapy into only psychoanalysis or simply suggestion. Thus both he and Freud did an unwitting disservice to the future develop-ment of dynamic psychotherapy, in obscuring the theoretical and technical complexities involved in psychoanalytically oriented psychotherapy under the excessively encompassing rubric of suggestion, employed to cover (and thereby blur) a diversity of distinct principles and practices.

In this first era of the development of psychoanalytic psychotherapy within psychoanalysis (its prehistory), psychoanalysis was delineated as a clearly articulated therapy with defined, consensually agreed-upon principles and practices. All else – for all categories of patients not amenable to it – was swept into the ill-defined category of suggestion. Before I turn to the second era in the development of our conceptions of psychotherapy, grounded in psychoanalysis as theory, and yet clearly distinct from it in goals, in technical implementation and in range of applicability, I should digress for a moment about the role of Ferenczi, Freud's closest friend and collaborator. Ferenczi, whose psychoanalytic visibility and influence seemed to have been eclipsed in the first decades after his death in 1933, has recently enjoyed a remarkable revival as the acknowledged originator of a number of major emphases in psychoanalytic thinking that, in counterpoint to Freud, have likewise been a seminal influence on many developing trends in psychoanalytic and psychotherapeutic thinking. He initiated, for example, the effort to intensify and perhaps even shorten the analytic experience, the emphasis on affectivity in the analytic dialogue as a reaction against sterile intellectualizing, the focus on the interactive nature of the analytic relationship, the concern with countertransference as a source of deeper knowledge of analytic interaction, and the unremitting effort to seek ways to approach the sicker patients, those who later came to be known as the wider-scope patients. In all these matters Ferenczi took a stand that differed from Freud's, and much of the dialectical to-and-fro in succeeding decades during the development of analytic psychotherapy *vis-à-vis* psychoanalysis can be seen as an oscillation of the pendulum between the views of these two.

To turn now to the second era in the history of psychoanalytic psycho-therapy as a derivative of and an adaptation of psychoanalysis: for a variety of reasons particular to the historical development of *psychiatry* in the United States, dynamic psychotherapy reflected a distinctively American confluence of influences. These included the self-conscious, and at first successful, effort of analysis to ally itself with medicine and thereby capture academic psychiatry; the prior wide acceptance of the doctrine of Adolf Meyer, with its emphasis on detailed case histories to show causal relationships between events and symptoms; the growth of the mental hygiene movement with its melioristic call for professionally guided interventions; and the impact of American 'progressive education' and other pragmatically optimistic ideas. It was most directly the necessary and logical outcome of the successful campaign by American analysts to take over the psychiatric teaching centres, and then to find ways to modify their psychoanalytic techniques, so as to cope effectively with the great range of patients in those psychiatric hospitals and clinics who were not amenable to classical analysis. That is, in taking over American psychiatry, psychoanalysis had assumed responsibility for a far wider range of the mentally troubled than had Freud, Jones, Glover, Ferenczi and all their European confrères who were denied access to medical schools and psychiatric patient populations, and were therefore free to develop a more purified psychoanalysis with their neurotic patients in their private consulting rooms.

Particularly notable was Robert Knight, who, over the first post-World War II decade, led the way in framing the fundamental conceptions that have marked the nature of analytic psychotherapy as *psychoanalytic* therapy but distinct from psychoanalysis proper. Knight's central concerns as a leader in

American psychoanalysis were with its relationship to psychiatry. He (1949) first formulated authoritatively the proposed fundamental distinction within a psychoanalytically informed framework, between supportive and expressive psychotherapeutic approaches, that is, efforts aimed primarily at supporting the patient in suppressing symptoms and in handling the erupting psychological material, or efforts aimed conversely at expressing and understanding psychic content. His explicit bias was in favour of the more expressive approach as more definitive and therefore more desirable; supportive-suppressive measures were used only when exploratory techniques were contra-indicated (e.g. the patient's ego being too fragile, too inflexible, or too defended).

In further papers, Knight separated psychoanalysis as a purer, more thorough-going, and more ambitious variant of expressive psychotherapy. He also distinguished the different goals and indications for the three emerging therapeutic approaches (supportive therapy, expressive therapy and analysis proper). In addition, he was the first to outline an entire array of supportive techniques and to spell out overall the distinctions in goals, indications and techniques across this entire spectrum of psychoanalytic therapies.

Contemporary with Knight's writings were two contrapuntal efforts, one from the right, the other from the left. On the left were Franz Alexander (1946) and his colleagues, attempting to rescue psychoanalytical treatments (especially with obsessional, masochistic, and/or depressive characters) that were threatening to turn into 'insoluble transference neuroses' via an array of active interventions and manipulations, the best known of which was dubbed the 'corrective emotional experience' (Alexander and French 1946: 353). This was a deliberate effort to assume an emotional posture within the transference-countertransference interplay, the opposite of the dominant transference disposition, so that the patient could see more readily and forcefully the contradiction between the transference expectation arising out of past experience and the actuality of the analyst's impact, leading to a more incisive mutative event that would both intensify and shorten the analytic process. This approach is indeed reminiscent of some of Ferenczi's experiments with 'active therapy', to which Alexander acknowledged his indebtedness. Corollary to this development of the conception of the 'corrective emotional experience' is the notion that all this is just an improved version of psychoanalysis, which counters Knight's view that necessary or desirable modifications of technique in certain difficult treatment situations would nonetheless qualify as a form of variant psychotherapy, rather than as proper psychoanalysis.

On the ideological right of Knight was Kurt Eissler (1953). His chief concern and target was Alexander's deviationism, with its modifications of the standard analytic procedure and its amalgamation of all these innovations as equally 'psychoanalytic therapy'. Eissler was not especially concerned with Knight's efforts to demarcate psychoanalytic psychotherapy from analysis proper and, in fact, ignored the ongoing debate over delineating analytic psychotherapy from psychoanalysis. He focused instead on psychoanalysis itself as the purified legacy bequeathed by Freud, and fiercely tried to safeguard it against those like Alexander who would modify it, ostensibly in the clinical interests of patients, and still presume to call it analytic therapy.

Eissler did this by affirming that psychoanalysis required the utmost adherence to the 'basic model technique' of *interpretation alone*, which then led to proper insight, working through and change. As such, it was applicable to all those patients with what Freud called a 'hypothetically normal ego', paradigmatically, to classical cases of hysterical neurosis. With all others who require some departure from this austere model, Eissler allowed the limited use of noninterpretive interventions. But these departures, designated 'parameters', were subject to three firm strictures:

1   that they be introduced only when the basic model proved insufficient;
2   that they never exceed the unavoidable minimum; and
3   that they always be possible to eliminate by interpretation so that the final phase of treatment could proceed with a parameter of zero.

Anything else (e.g. all of Alexander's experimentations) would no longer qualify as psychoanalysis. Indeed, Eissler's article was widely hailed as codifying the proper dimensions of analysis and as being the proper establishment response to the Alexandrian heresy, linked, of course, to the then-unfashionable Ferenczi.

By this point, the psychoanalytic stage was set for the watershed year of 1954. Knight had been establishing the frame for an array of psychoanalytically guided therapies, extending the applicability of psychoanalytic concepts, albeit not the specific psychoanalytic technique, to the ever-widening array of psychiatric patients within the purview of the new generation of dynamic psychiatrists. At the same time, Alexander, building on Ferenczi, was trying to extend a modified form of psychoanalysis to at least some patients beyond reach of the classical method. Meanwhile, Eissler was affirming and defending the boundaries of proper psychoanalysis against all diluting forces. In this context, the American Psychoanalytic Association established a sequence of three major panels in the early 1950s, their ideas all summarized in a dozen articles published in 1954 in a single issue of the Association's journal. Collectively, these articles staked out the then-dominant conceptions about the nature of analytic psychotherapy that mark the second era in the relationship of psychotherapy to psychoanalysis, that of forging a consensus around an established diversity of goals and techniques (the spectrum of psychoanalytically based therapies ranging from the most supportive to the most expressive − psychoanalysis itself) within a unity of theory (that of psychoanalysis), an era of converging consensus that lasted another twenty years after its full delineation in these manifestos.

The central confrontation at these panels was between two major and diametrically opposed viewpoints on the most appropriate way to conceptualize the relationship between dynamic psychotherapy and psychoanalysis. Basically, the issue lay between the viewpoint advanced by Alexander and his colleagues (representing a distinct minority) and that of the great majority represented by Gill, Stone, Rangell and Bibring. Alexander's group saw the historical trend as blurring, if not obliterating, the technical distinction between dynamic psychotherapy and psychoanalysis, while Gill's group conceived the scientific problem as the more adequate clarification and preservation of the conceptual and operational distinctions between the two.

Having elaborated the complex details of these debates elsewhere (Wallerstein 1989), I will give only their highlights here. Alexander's call was for the total integration of psychoanalysis into academic psychiatry and medicine. Following Knight, he declared the only realistic distinction to be that between primarily supportive and primarily uncovering methods. His recommendation, then, was to collapse *all* expressive treatment modes, expressive psychotherapy in all its variants, and psychoanalysis proper, into the one category of psychoanalytic therapy. Like Knight, he adumbrated his own very similar list of techniques inherent to the supportive approaches. On the other side of the dichotomy are all the expressive approaches, analysis included, that Alexander identified as varying only in quantitative (not critical) dimensions, and with all distinctions of frequency, duration, use of the couch, etc., being declared trivial, not vital. Swept into this debate was the concept of the 'corrective emotional experience', and the juggling with frequency and spacing to counteract the risks of the 'insoluble transference neurosis', etc.

By contrast, those (the majority) who strove to maintain and 'sharpen' the distinctions among the range of psychoanalytically based therapies, including psychoanalysis, on the supportive-expressive continuum, aimed in their differential treatment planning to select the therapeutic modality that was best fitted to the individual patient's psychological structure. As opposed to those who were blurring these distinctions, collapsing them ultimately to the position that good psychotherapy is all analytic or is all analysis and then pushing the limits of this 'analysis' to its utmost extension (i.e. fitting the patient to the treatment), their concern was to choose the most appropriate treatment method from this diversified spectrum for each patient (i.e. fitting the treatment, rather, to the patient).

The clearest articulation of this position was that of Merton Gill. He began with a succinct definition of psychoanalysis, which enjoyed wide currency over the span of several decades, as 'that technique which, employed by a neutral analyst, results in the development of a regressive transference neurosis and the ultimate resolution of this neurosis by techniques of interpretation alone' (Gill 1954: 775). Gill's definition incidentally circumscribed psychoanalysis far more precisely than had Freud's earlier definition that *any* therapy that *recognized* only the two facts of transference and resistance and took them as the starting point of its work could call itself psychoanalysis (Freud 1914: 16). Gill had also made a major demarcation in an earlier paper between the supportive and the expressive psychotherapies in accord with the decision to try to strengthen the defences in those cases where this is all that is necessary, or in those cases where it is all that is safely possible, or to 'break through' the defences as a preliminary step towards reintegrating the ego. Like Knight and Alexander, Gill elaborated his own conceptualization of supportive techniques.

From this point, the rest was elaborated. A primarily supportive therapy becomes the preferred mode for patients too ill for analysis, whose egos are not sufficiently strong to withstand its regressive pressures and whose failed psychic equilibrium is to be restored via 'strengthening the defences' through the techniques set forth by Knight, Alexander, Gill and also Stone. A primarily expressive therapy becomes the preferred mode for patients with less pervasive illnesses who can tolerate the effort at 'analyzing the defenses' to the extent necessary, but who do not require the thoroughgoing reconstructive effort of a fully fledged psychoanalysis (in effect, those too well for analysis). Psychoanalysis then emerges as the treatment of choice for that quite small middle band of patients in whom 'the ego is sufficiently damaged that extensive repair is necessary [i.e. sick enough to require it], but sufficiently strong to withstand pressure [i.e. well enough to tolerate it]' (Gill 1951: 63–4). This way of conceptualizing the different therapeutic modes puts expressive psychotherapy into an 'intermediate' position between supportive therapy and psychoanalysis. Gill (1954) called it an 'intermediate type of psychotherapy' (789) done by the analytically trained or oriented, with goals between rapid symptom resolution (i.e. supportive therapy) and substantial character change (i.e. psychoanalysis), where techniques as well as results are intermediate, but clearly with interpretation – to the extent feasible and necessary – as the principal technical vehicle.

Two other distinct contributions to these 1954 panels should be mentioned. One was the paper by Edward Bibring delineating five basic therapeutic principles intended, through differential selection and combination, to characterize all psychoanalytic therapies. This fivefold classification, widely accepted at the time and still in active use in some quarters today, comprises suggestion, abreaction, manipulation (in the nonpejorative sense of neutralizing or redirecting existent pathological emotional systems), clarification and interpretation. In terms of differential selection and combination, Bibring (1954) called interpretation 'the supreme agent in the hierarchy of therapeutic principles characteristic of analysis, in that all other principles are subordinate to it; that is, they are employed with the constant aim of making interpretation possible and effective' (763). By contrast, the psychoanalytic psychotherapies (expressive or supportive) are characterized by a different deployment of these five fundamental therapeutic principles, different in spread, frequency and saliency.

The other noteworthy contribution is Leo Stone's (1954) famed 'widening scope' paper, together with Anna Freud's (1954) discussion. Stone's main thrust was a tolerant, albeit reserved survey of the trends towards widening the indications for the classical psychoanalytic technique. It ended with the statement:

> The transference neuroses and character disorders of equivalent degree of psychopathology remain the optimum general indications for the classical method. While the difficulties increase and the expectations of success diminish in a general way as the nosological periphery is approached, there is no absolute barrier.
>
> (Stone 1954: 593)

In keeping with the spirit of debate that characterized these panels, Anna Freud gave a highly laudatory discussion of Stone's paper but took sharp exception to any concession to the concept of 'widening scope'. She opted instead for a 'narrowing scope', a restricting of classical analysis to those categories of patients originally declared appropriate for it by Sigmund Freud – and in line with the dispositions of Knight, Gill, Rangell, Bibring, etc., who were shaping the majority consensus on these issues, of conceptually distinct therapeutic modalities and techniques, deployed with nosologically distinct categories of patients.

Thus there was in 1954 a crystallization of the era of converging consensus on the nature of analysis proper, as related to, but distinct from, each of the psychoanalytically derived psychotherapeutic modalities. What each consisted of, what constituted their similarities and differences, what the indications for each were, what techniques specifically composed each, and what goals each might reach were becoming progressively clarified, with every expectation for increasing specification as experience and knowledge grew. And this development was all in full harmony with the then-prevailing scientific world-view, marked by the steady progression of rational knowledge, deployment of the scientific method, and the hallmarks of positivism, empiricism and objectivity. Basically, the world could be studied scientifically and ultimately known, and here was further evidence to that effect even in the subjective realm of mental illness.

But the story does not end there, for the consensus reached in 1954 no longer exists. The consensus actually held for some period, especially in the United States where it originated and where it fitted so congenially into the natural-science-framed, dominant ego-psychological metapsychology. In 1969, fifteen years later, I chaired the first major panel ever held by the International Psychoanalytical Association on the subject of 'The relationship of psychoanalysis to psychotherapy'. This event marked the growing concern within the world-wide family of psychoanalytic endeavour with what has seemed for so long primarily a peculiarly American creation, the body of theory and practice of psychoanalytically-based ... psychotherapy, in all of its complex relationship with its psychoanalytic parentage.

(Wallerstein 1969: 117)

What emerged clearly from that international panel was that the issues (and the controversies) that had characterized the earlier panel reports seemed essentially unaltered, either by increased experience and expanded knowledge or by considerations from the wider vantage of analysts in the diverse world-wide centres of analytic activity, with all their differing ecologies and developments.

But then, a decade later, the Southern Regional Psychoanalytic Societies sponsored a symposium in Atlanta in 1979 at which three of the central protagonists in the 1954 discussions (Gill 1984; Rangell 1981; Stone 1982) were invited to update their views on psychoanalysis and psychotherapy a quarter-century on. It was clear that the 1954 consensus had broken down, and that we had entered a third era, that of 'fragmented consensus' (Wallerstein 1989). The details of the now radical divergence of views among the three who had been so united a quarter-century earlier have been spelled out at length elsewhere (Wallerstein 1989). Here I will only state them in the briefest encapsulation. Actually, Leo Stone's subtly nuanced views had survived the least altered. In fact, his remarkable consistency of viewpoint on the basic elements of psychoanalytic psychotherapy and of psychoanalysis over a three-decade span of writings contrasted sharply with the significantly altered views of the other two protagonists.

The individual whose views had shifted most radically over this intervening timespan was Merton Gill. After Knight, Gill was clearest in the early fifties in his distinct delineations of the three major psychoanalytic treatment modalities (the supportive, the 'intermediate' expressive and psychoanalysis itself), each with distinct indications, goals and techniques. His radical shift in views was a direct consequence of his evolving preoccupation with the overriding primacy of the interpretation of the transference as *the* criterion of what is psychoanalytic, and of his parallel elaboration of the 'two-person' versus the 'one-person' view of the two participants' contributions to the transference. These views were all developed in elaborate detail in Gill's 1982 monograph. This present focus on interpretation of the transference to whatever extent possible, as the hallmark of psychoanalytic therapy, became in essence a proposal to reassimilate what Gill had earlier taken such pains to demarcate separately as intermediate expressive psychotherapy, or in other words to blur, even to obliterate, the differences he once believed were so vital to maintain. In effect, it was a revival of the position of Alexander that Gill had once led the (largely successful) effort to reject. And since all else but this unremitting focus on transference interpretation was declared to rest fundamentally on 'witting and unwitting suggestion' (Gill 1984: 177), Gill seemed also to be returning to the era of Freud and Glover, of suggestion as the 'all else' in therapy, other than 'strict and untendentious psycho-analysis' (Freud 1919: 168).

There is yet, however, the third position – Rangell's – to be distilled out of the 1979 symposium. Intermediate between that of Stone and Gill, it was one of infiltration of psychoanalysis by psycho*therapeutic* techniques, while seeking to maintain conceptual clarity around their differences. This position can best be summarized in the following quotation from Rangell:

> But just as analysts apply analytic principles freely and copiously to their practice of dynamic psychotherapy, reciprocally and empirically, with ever-increasing complexity and length of psychoanalysis, the opposite also holds. There is no analysis without its share of each of the technical manoeuvres noted by Bibring (1954) ... (1981: 670). ... There is no analysis without some of these mechanisms, which are not inadvertent but built-in and by design. ... There is no analytic case treated by interpretation alone, in spite of Gill's definition of 1954. If this were a prerequisite, no treatment would qualify as analytic. This is an empirical conclusion based not on theoretical preconception but on my composite experience.
>
> (Rangell 1981: 671)

Parenthetically, I would add that the experience of the Psychotherapy Research Project of the Menninger Foundation as presented in my 1986 book, *Forty-two Lives in Treatment*, my clinical accounting of the treatment careers and subsequent life careers of our patient group over a thirty-year span, is entirely in accord with these altered views of Rangell based on his lifetime of solo practice. In our project this was cast in terms of our quite universal finding of an inevitable infiltration of what we called supportive modes and supportive interventions, even into the purest forms of psychoanalytic treatments, and equally of course, vice-versa, of infiltrations from psychoanalysis into psychotherapy.

What, then, were the various influences that accounted for the vastly altered climate of 1979, with its now fragmented consensus on the nature of psychoanalysis and of the dynamic psychotherapies and their relationship? There were indeed several, and, although they were distinct and can be outlined separately, they were also confluent and inextricably interrelated. They had to do with the growing focus on relationship factors – variously conceived and explicated – as co-equal determinants of the change process in psychoanalytic therapies, alongside the previous more unitary focus on the interpretive process alone, leading via repetitive working through, to insight and consequent change. That is, they represented a turn from the primacy of the objective, natural-science model of veridical interpretation of defence and underlying impulse, embedded in the so-called 'one-body psychology' of the ego/structural paradigm, within which had been formulated the original distinctions between psychoanalysis and the analytic psychotherapies, and their curative processes. Instead, there was a growing concomitant appreciation of the tenets of 'two-body psychology', within which relational and interactional perspectives have assumed an enlarging, ultimately co-equal importance in effecting treatment change, growth and 'cure'. This growing focus on relationship factors as vital components of the analytic change process represents, of course, the revival of attention to the analytic perspectives introduced originally by Ferenczi, and expounded later in a particular form by Alexander. These perspectives, which were massively repudiated at the time, have returned to a central position in psychoanalytic thought, accompanied by a remarkable resurgence of attention to Ferenczi's own seminal position (via his letters, his clinical diary, his legacy, etc.) as almost the co-originator, with Freud, of the roots of all our present-day thinking about psychoanalysis as a therapeutic enterprise.

In addition, the influences accounting for the changed perspectives by 1979 also had to do with the simultaneously increasing awareness and acceptance, throughout the psychoanalytic world, of our world-wide theoretical diversity or pluralism. With each of these newly evolving foci of conceptualization and explanation, the once seemingly clear-cut distinctions between psychoanalysis proper and the array of psychoanalytically derived psychotherapies have become more complex, more ambiguous and more arguable.

These emerging new perspectives on the theory of the psychoanalytic therapeutic process go back as far as 1934, with Sterba's paper on the therapeutic dissociation of the analysand's ego into an experiencing, and alongside it, an observing ego in alliance with the analyst's therapeutic efforts. Sterba provided the original conceptual basis for the subsequent unfolding (mostly in America) of the focus on the therapeutic alliance by Zetzel (1956) and on the working alliance by Greenson (1965), two theoretically distinguishable but closely related concepts, often used interchangeably. Zetzel and Greenson were in full accord on the need for an alliance concept, a cooperative relationship between analyst and analysand, in constant dialectical interplay with the transference, and also as a necessary frame within which the transference could safely unfold. Where they differed was in Zetzel's focus on the archaic roots of the capacity for such an alliance in the successful navigation of the earliest dyadic mother–child developmental phase, whereas Greenson focused on the highest secondary process, rational rapport of the analysand working purposefully with the analyst. These alliance conceptions have by now recovered a firm position (again, mostly in America).

During this same period, another substantial expression of the same relational considerations, focused more directly on the nature of the dyadic interpersonal relationship *within* the transference-countertransference interplay, was also achieving prominence through the writings of Hans Loewald (1960) and Leo Stone (1961). Unlike the alliance concepts, their contributions made a less dramatic initial impact and were not fully seen at the time as the far-ranging reconceptualization of the therapeutic action of psychoanalytic therapy that they represented, nor for the bridge they provided to the conceptions of interpersonal psychiatry pioneered by Harry Stack Sullivan and evident in the interpersonal theoretical perspective of his followers (especially in the William Alanson White Institute), now heading towards a closer meeting ground with the American psychoanalytic mainstream.

Stone's vision, less fundamentally revisionist than Loewald's, was an explicitly physicianly (i.e. caretaking) intent, as well as an educational mode that kept analysis from ever being purely investigative and exploratory. His monograph, together with Lipton's (1977) subsequent paper, demonstrated that what Eissler had defined as classical technique was not a continuation of Freud's original technique, but rather a gross redefinition to broaden it far beyond the limits of what Freud had intended or practised, which was in fact far closer to what Stone later enunciated. This effort finally helped pull the whole analytic world away from the rigidity and austerity of Eissler's formulation, which had seemed for so long the accepted establishment view of the proper dimensions of psychoanalysis.

For Loewald's part, in contrast to Stone's emphasis on the 'humanness' in the analyst–patient relationship, the analyst's role was as a 'new object' in the patient's life, with whom therapeutically productive 'integrative experiences' could be (should be) achieved. Analysis was seen as a resumption of blocked ego development, contingent on the relationship with the analyst as new object, and within the context of a necessary developmental gradient between analyst and patient like that between parent and child. By now Loewald's understandings have been quite uniformly incorporated into the overall psychoanalytic theoretical corpus. He has been hailed (Cooper 1988; Fogel 1989) as the revolutionary agent most instrumental in transforming the generally accepted theory of technique, based on the primacy of interpretation leading to insight, into the currently accepted co-equal status of the affectively loaded, interactive psychoanalytic relationship in effecting change.

Concomitant with the focus on the affective analyst–patient relationship as a central component in understanding the overall change process has been the emergence of a developmentally grounded, hierarchical model of psychoanalytic therapy, the technical approach to the patient and the relationship mode that is most salient at each point, differentially geared to the patient's stage-specific developmental phase. A central figure in elaborating this way of categorizing the varying psychoanalytic approaches, and their stage-specific rationales, has been John Gedo (Gedo and Goldberg 1973) and a sequence of successor books by Gedo.

Basically, Gedo and Goldberg outlined an epigenetic series of five sequential developmental models, each with characteristic dangers, defences and anxieties:

1   the reflex arc model of primary narcissism, designated the traumatic state,
2   the first self-object stage, designated that of psychotic disorganization,
3   the second self-object stage, designated that of the narcissistic personality disorders,
4   the tripartite structural model, that of neurotic character, and finally
5   the mature transformation of the evolved psychic apparatus, that of so-called expectable adult functioning.

To each of these, they accorded the central treatment strategies designated as

1   pacification,
2   unification,
3   optimal disillusionment,
4   interpretation, and
5   introspection,

each of these in turn defined, specified and illustrated.

Alongside all of these trends, this same timespan was witness to the major expansion of the 'widening-scope' concept in the systematic publications of Heinz Kohut (1971, 1977, 1984) on the narcissistic personality disorders, and of Otto Kernberg (1975, 1976, 1980) on borderline personality organizations. Kohut embedded his ideas within the framework of the new metapsychology he called self-psychology, built centrally around his conception of developmental deficit rather than intrapsychic conflict as the primary pathogenic locus, offering them first as a supplement to, and later as an alternative to, the prevailing traditional ego-psychology paradigm. Kernberg did not create a new theoretical paradigm, but rather offered an effort to amalgamate traditional American ego psychology with the British object-relational perspective, through erecting Freud's tripartite structural mental world out of the building blocks of internalized object relations (i.e. units of self- and object-representations and the affective valences that bind them).

The specific formulations of psychopathology and therapeutic strategy of both Kohut and Kernberg, as well as their similarities and differences, are too well known to need elaboration: what they have in common is the thrust to truly widen the scope of therapeutic psychoanalysis, by extending it (via Kohut's formulations) to bring the narcissistic disorders within the scope of analysability, and (via Kernberg's endeavours) to treat borderline disorders via a 'modified psychoanalysis'. In both instances, they have cut into the original clear-cut distinctions among the therapeutic provinces of supportive therapy, expressive therapy and full psychoanalysis.

On the other side of the Atlantic, from within the British Psycho-Analytical Society, Joseph Sandler undertook his own effort to assimilate British object-relational perspectives to traditional Freudian ego-structural concepts. He started as early as 1962, in his paper with Bernard Rosenblatt on the 'representational world', and continued over the next three decades with a series of papers, some alone, some with Walter Joffe in the earlier years, and some with Anne-Marie Sandler in the later years. His goal was very similar to Kernberg's, but with distinctively different conceptualizations, and not specifically linked to the understanding and treatment of the borderline personality. Sandler's formulations, like those of Kohut and Kernberg – and as is true of so much of the thinking in the British Society within each of its theoretical frameworks – also tended to cut across the original distinctions of 1954 between the specific therapeutic domains of psychoanalysis and its derivative psychotherapies.

Nor is this the end of this ever-more-complex story. The United States, once the site of the monolithic hegemony of ego-psychological metapsychology, has been home not only to such variant theoretical perspectives as Kohut's self-psychology, a full-blown alternative theoretical system, but also Margaret Mahler's (1975) developmental perspective arising out of her studies of the separation-individuation stages of early childhood, and Roy Schafer's (1976) 'action language', an effort to recast mental life into a psychology emphasizing the self as agent in creating personal destiny. Alongside all these, our country has seen the growth of enclaves of Kleinian and even of Lacanian psychoanalytic work, as well as the increasing professional exposure to leading representatives of the British Independent, or object-relations group, and of the modern British Kleinians. (Here again, Sandler has played a very specific bridging role. His 1987 book, *Projection, Identification, Projective Identification*, demonstrated, for example, the very useful extensions of the specifically Kleinian conceptualization of projective identification into the understandings of psychopathology and psychotherapeutics shaped within his own ego-psychological/object-relational theoretical framework.) It is exactly this plethora of competing theoretical systems now crowding the psychoanalytic marketplace, in our own country and all over the world, that has brought to the fore the issues raised in my two plenary addresses to the International Psychoanalytical Association Congresses (Wallerstein 1988, 1990). In the face of our increasing psychoanalytic diversity, our pluralism of competing theoretical perspectives, of linguistic and thought conventions, and of philosophy of science concepts of the fundamental nature of our discipline, what still holds us together as common adherents of a shared science and profession? Do we have at least a common clinical ground?

One obvious implication of this issue for our concern with the evolving relationship between psychoanalysis and the derivative psychoanalytic psychotherapies has been spelled out by Schafer (1985). His main point was simply that what could be taken for granted in Freud's day (an agreed-upon understanding of what constituted psychoanalysis, what constituted 'wild analysis' and what constituted psychotherapy that was not analysis) has all but disappeared today. Today, what is considered proper psychoanalysis within one theoretical perspective can simply be reclassified as only psychotherapy by the adherents of a competing perspective. Schafer in fact proposed retiring the phrase 'wild analysis' as no longer even heuristically useful, in favour of the concept of 'comparative analysis'.

To summarize this overview of the two major trends that have marked this massive shift from the clarities and relative certainties of the early 1950s about analysis and the analytic psychotherapies, to our contemporary sea of divergent and often discordant voices on these issues: the one has been the elaboration within psychoanalysis proper of the role of the analytic relationship as a co-equal and interacting determinant along with veridical interpretation leading to insight, in effecting therapeutic change, incorporating into psychoanalysis elements that had earlier been designated as components of psychotherapy that helped to mark it off from proper analysis (i.e. the trends rooted in the original contributions of Ferenczi); and the other trend, obviously related, but also separable, has been the growing awareness of and acceptance in America – the heartland of the psychoanalytic psychotherapy enterprise – of the theoretical diversity that has come to characterize psychoanalysis since Freud's day (i.e. the trends originating with Melanie Klein's altered – or deviant – metapsychological perspectives, already in Freud's lifetime). Given both of these powerful currents, the fragmenting of the seemingly crystallized consensus of the 1950s on the issue of the natures of psychoanalysis and of the analytic psychotherapies and of their relationship, this fragmenting can be seen in this context as an all-but-inevitable consequence.

There is still a final set of considerations on how our present-day theoretical and clinical discourse on these issues has been affected. Another current major influence can be construed as denying even the possibility of a renewed conceptual consensus with any basis for a scientific truth-claim that could warrant collective conviction. In some influential philosophical and psychoanalytic quarters, there has been a major theoretical turn to an espoused hermeneutic position for analysis, advanced persuasively by psychoanalytically concerned philosophers such as Habermas (1968) and Ricoeur (1970), and in advocated clinical application by Schafer (1992) and Spence (1982). Closely linked conceptually to this hermeneutic movement, anchored in a coherence rather than a correspondence theory of truth (see Hanly 1992) with the therapeutic aim of the best narrative fit replacing the quest for historic truth, is the entire substantial current movement within psychoanalytic thinking that has developed as an extension of the 'two-body' psychology and interactional concepts of the therapeutic process expressed, for example, in the intersubjectivity theory of Stolorow and his collaborators

(Stolorow and Atwood 1992) or in the social constructivism of Hoffman (1991). In these concepts of the therapeutic dialogue as an interplay in the transference-countertransference of two participating subjectivities, there is in theory simply no room for an objective observer as a potentially valid arbiter of reality.

What these varieties of hermeneutic, phenomenological or linguistically based conceptualizations and the relational, interactional, interpersonal, intersubjective and social constructivist conceptualizations have loosely in common is a varying degree of congruence with what has come to be known as the postmodernist stance towards theory, culture and knowledge. Kimberlyn Leary (1994) has offered a vivid account of the imbrication of postmodernist thinking with so many of the relational and subjectivistic trends in contemporary psychoanalysis. Leary lays out the ultimate logic of the postmodern or deconstructionist claim that, rather than the written text containing specific meanings put there by the author to be communicated to the reader, the text is ultimately but an arrangement of words that different readers with different subjectivities, and at different points in geographic space and historic time, respond to differently, so that its 'reality' and what it 'means' are constructed anew with each reader. Leary then demonstrates the very direct analogues to this philosophic literary posture in the writings, for example, of Schafer (1985, 1992) on analysis as a succession of narrative acts (a telling of life stories), and of Hoffman (1991), whose 'social-constructivist' perspective shifts the task of analysis from a concern with interpreting reality to a focus on the interaction by which therapist and patient create and shape, out of their mutual impact on each other, their uniquely constructed reality.

This 'postmodern sensibility in psychoanalysis', as Leary calls it, has indeed been a useful corrective to a number of problematic, and now outmoded, aspects of analytic thinking, like the tendencies towards a misplaced scientism that inhere in the natural-science ego-psychological paradigm; or the seduction into an authoritarian stance by the analyst committed to the erstwhile modern ideal of the presumed objective observer who can always correctly assume the role of 'arbiter of the patient's reality' (in a phrase from Gill) and declare accurately what is transference distortion and what is realistic perception; or the notion that there are no theoretical limits, other than in biology, to the uncovering of the past of a knowable mental life and development.

But where the postmodern perspective creates a problem for my argument concerning psychoanalysis and the analytic therapies, is in its tacit discouragement, as misguided and ultimately fruitless, of any quest that aspires towards ever-increasing clarity and knowable precision of consensually agreed conceptual distinctions, since in their essence our understandings are always historicized and contextualized – they are always no more than social constructions, geared to what is considered satisfactory or unsatisfactory understanding within each particular socio-historical zeitgeist. Yet we need not be caught up in the extremes of a relativist and socially constructed model of the postmodern world any more than in the earlier fully objective, natural-science model. It is true that psychoanalytic treatments involve two interacting subjectivities and sensibilities, and depending on the experiences of the encounter over time, can result in a range of finally agreed-upon storylines. But it is also true that, although analyst and patient together socially construct an understanding of the patient's life experience, that life experience exists independently of the analyst, and that therefore some storylines fit better than others, correspond better to the felt life experience, and the analyst and the patient can arrive reasonably open-mindedly at such judgements. There is still a real world – a reality – 'out there', or else humankind could not have developed a science and a technology that work and provide the material world within which we live.

Where, then, does all this leave our conceptualizations today in 1996 of the nature of psychoanalysis, and of psychoanalytic psychotherapy, and of their relationship? Certainly, it is a far more complicated and more uncertain, but also richer, more complexly nuanced conceptual landscape than that of the 1950s. Conceptual boundaries among the range of psychoanalytically based therapeutic approaches are far less clear today. They are also set at different places by adherents of different theoretical perspectives, and by practitioners with differing experiential bases and differing patient populations. And in that earlier period of consensus framed within an objective natural-science model, more than we ever clearly understood, those boundaries are also significantly moulded by our only partially conscious, partially articulated health value-systems, by our personal and private theories about health and illness and therapy, and of course by the assumptions underlying our scientific and philosophical allegiances.

Yet given all that, the other side of my enduring conviction is that, though with considerably more difficulty, one can still find one's way, and that there are broad distinctions between psychoanalysis and psychoanalytic psychotherapy. My own choice is, of course, guided by my own lifetime commitment to the kind of scientific psychotherapy research that can be done, and is done, given all the epistemological and ontological constraints imposed by the world-views that mark each particular zeitgeist. The findings and conclusions of our thirty-year-long Psychotherapy Research Project at the Menninger Foundation (Wallerstein 1986) were indeed congruent with the perspectives articulated by Rangell (1981) in the 1979 Atlanta Symposium: that there is a much greater mutual infiltration of psychoanalytic and of psychotherapeutic (i.e. supportive) interventions than had been earlier conceptualized, so that indeed boundaries are today less clear, more shiftable and more reflective of varying intellectual allegiances. Nonetheless, differing modes of approach do still exist and are differentially employed within the limits of our individual best judgements, and will no doubt be continually refined with accruing clinical experience and conceptual advance. And in this, I and a new group of co-workers have been engaged in San Francisco with a successor project dubbed Psychotherapy Research Project II, to bring more precise methods of inquiry to bear on a hopefully more definitive study of the processes and outcomes of the entire spectrum of psychoanalytic therapies, however that spectrum is divided up. But that is another story. I trust that I have at least left the reader with some better bearings by which to find their own best way, clinically, theoretically or perhaps research-wise, in this domain.

REFERENCES

Alexander, F. and French, T. M. (1946) *Psychoanalytic Therapy: Principles and Applications*, New York: Ronald Press.

Bibring, E. (1954) 'Psychoanalysis and the dynamic psychotherapies', *Journal of the American Psychoanalytic Association*, 2, 745–70.

Cooper, A. M. (1988) 'Our changing views of the therapeutic action of psychoanalysis: comparing Strachey and Loewald', *Psychoanalytic Quarterly*, 57, 15–27.

Eissler, K. R. (1953) 'The effect of the structure of the ego on psychoanalytic technique', *Journal of the American Psychoanalytic Association*, 1, 104–43.

Fogel, G. I. (1989) 'The authentic function of psychoanalytic theory: an overview of the contributions of Hans Loewald', *Psychoanalytic Quarterly*, 58, 419–51.

Freud, A. (1954) 'The widening scope of indications for psychoanalysis: discussion', *Journal of the American Psychoanalytic Association*, 2, 607–720.

Freud, S. (1905) 'On psychotherapy', *Standard Edition*, vol. 7 (1953), London: Hogarth Press, 255–68.

——(1914) 'On the history of the psycho-analytic movement', *Standard Edition*, vol. 14 (1963), London: Hogarth Press, 1–66.

——(1919) 'Lines of advance in psycho-analytic therapy', *Standard Edition*, vol. 17 (1955), London: Hogarth Press, 157–68.

Gedo, J. E. and Goldberg, A. (1973) *Models of the Mind: A Psychoanalytic Theory*, Chicago IL: University of Chicago Press.

Gill, M. M. (1951) 'Ego psychology and psychotherapy', *Psychoanalytic Quarterly*, 20, 62–71.

——(1954) 'Psychoanalysis and exploratory psychotherapy', *Journal of the American Psychoanalytic Association*, 2, 771–97.

——(1982) 'Analysis of transference, vol. I: theory and technique', *Psychological Issues, Monograph no. 53*, New York: International Universities Press.

——(1984) 'Psychoanalysis and psychotherapy: a revision', *International Review of Psycho-Analysis*, 11, 161–79.

Glover, E. (1931) 'The therapeutic effect of inexact interpretation: a contribution to the theory of suggestion', *International Journal of Psycho-Analysis*, 12, 397–411.

——(1954) 'The indications for psycho-analysis', *Journal of Mental Science*, 100, 393–401.

Greenson, R. R. (1965) 'The working alliance and the transference neurosis', *Psychoanalytic Quarterly*, 34, 155–81.

Habermas, J. (1968) *Knowledge and Human Interests*, trans. J. J. Shapiro (1971), Boston: Beacon Press.

Hanly, C. (1992) *The Problem of Truth in Applied Psychoanalysis*, New York: Guilford Press.

Hoffman, I. Z. (1991) 'Discussion: toward a social-constructivist view of the psychoanalytic situation', *Psychoanalytic Dialogue*, 1, 74–105.

Kernberg, O. F. (1975) *Borderline Conditions and Pathological Narcissism*, New York: Jason Aronson.

——(1976) *Object Relations Theory and Clinical Psychoanalysis*, New York: Jason Aronson.

——(1980) *Internal World and External Reality: Object Relations Theory Applied*, New York: Jason Aronson.

Knight, R. P. (1949) 'A critique of the present status of the psychotherapies', in Stuart C. Miller (ed.) (1972) *Clinician and Therapist: Selected Papers of Robert P. Knight*, New York: Basic Books, 177–92. Reprinted from *Bulletin of the New York Academy of Medicine*, 25, 100–14.

Kohut, H. (1971) *The Analysis of the Self: A Systematic Approach to the Psychoanalytic Treatment of Narcissistic Personality Disorders*, New York: International Universities Press.

——(1977) *The Restoration of the Self*, New York: International Universities Press.

——(1984) (edited by Arnold Goldberg with the collaboration of Paul E. Stepansky) *How Does Analysis Cure?*, Chicago IL: University of Chicago Press.

Leary, K. (1994) 'Psychoanalytic "problems" and "postmodern solutions"', *Psychoanalytic Quarterly*, 63, 433–65.

Lipton, S. D. (1977) 'The advantages of Freud's technique as shown in his analysis of the Rat-Man', *International Journal of Psycho-Analysis*, 58, 255–73.

Loewald, H. (1960) 'On the therapeutic action of psycho-analysis', *International Journal of Psycho-Analysis*, 44, 16–33.

Mahler, M. S., Pine, F. and Bergman, A. (1975) *The Psychological Birth of the Human Infant: Symbiosis and Individuation*, New York: Basic Books.

Panels (1954) 'The widening scope of indications for psychoanalysis; the traditional psychoanalytic technique and its variations; psychoanalysis and dynamic psychotherapy: similarities and differences', *Journal of the American Psychoanalytic Association*, 2, 565–797.

Rangell, L. (1981) 'Psychoanalysis and dynamic psychotherapy: similarities and differences twenty-five years later', *Psychoanalytic Quarterly*, 50, 665–93.

Ricoeur, P. (1970) *Freud and Philosophy: An Essay on Interpretation*, trans. Denis Savage, New Haven CT: Yale University Press.

Sandler, J. (ed.) (1987) *Projection, Identification, Projective Identification*, Madison CT: International Universities Press.

Sandler, J. and Rosenblatt, B. (1962) 'The concept of the representational world', *Psychoanalytic Study of the Child*, 17, 128–45.

Schafer, R. (1976) *A New Language for Psychoanalysis*, New Haven CT: Yale University Press.

——(1985) 'Wild analysis', *Journal of the American Psychoanalytic Association*, 33, 275–99.

——(1992) *Retelling a Life: Narration and Dialogue in Psychoanalysis*, New York: Basic Books.

Spence, D. P. (1982) *Narrative Truth and Historical Truth: Meaning and Interpretation in Psychoanalysis*, New York: Norton.

Sterba, R. (1934) 'The fate of the ego in analytic therapy', *International Journal of Psycho-Analysis*, 15, 117–26.

Stolorow, R. D. and Atwood, G. E. (1992) *Contexts of Being: Intersubjective Foundations of Psychological Life*, Hillsdale NJ: Analytic Press.

Stone, L. (1954) 'The widening scope of indications of psychoanalysis', *Journal of the American Psychoanalytic Association*, 2, 567–94.

——(1961) *The Psychoanalytic Situation: An Examination of its Development and Essential Nature*, New York: International Universities Press.

——(1982) 'The influence of the practice and theory of psychotherapy on education in psychoanalysis', in E. D. Joseph and R. S. Wallerstein (eds) *Psychotherapy: Impact on Psychoanalytic Training*, New York: International Universities Press, 75–118.

Wallerstein, R. S. (1969) 'Introduction to panel on psychoanalysis and psychotherapy: the relationship of psychoanalysis to psychotherapy – current issues', *International Journal of Psycho-Analysis*, 50, 117–26.

——(1986) *Forty-two Lives in Treatment: A Study of Psychoanalysis and Psychotherapy*, New York: Guilford Press.

——(1988) 'One psychoanalysis or many?', *International Journal of Psycho-Analysis*, 69, 5–21.

——(1989) 'Psychoanalysis and psychotherapy: an historical perspective', *International Journal of Psycho-Analysis*, 70, 563–91.

——(1990) 'Psychoanalysis: the common ground', *International Journal of Psycho-Analysis*, 71, 3–20.

——(1995) *The Talking Cures: The Psychoanalyses and the Psychotherapies*, New Haven CT: Yale University Press.

Zetzel, E. R. (1956) 'Current concepts of transference', *International Journal of Psycho-Analysis*, 37, 369–75.

3

WISH FULFILMENT AND THE MASTERY OF TRAUMA

Owen Renik

One of Joseph Sandler's most important psychoanalytic contributions has been his work on the theory of motivation. By following the evolution of his thinking over time as one can, for example, in the cogent and readable summary, 'Towards a reconsideration of the psychoanalytic theory of motivation' (Sandler 1989) it is evident that Sandler has consistently urged analysts away from reductive theoretical assumptions and towards a phenomenological conception of human motivation, especially one derived from observations made in the clinical situation. In this regard, I would like to single out for emphasis two of Sandler's ideas: first, his 1974 recommendation that we consider a whole array of 'peremptory urges' (53) that give rise to conflict, rather than restricting ourselves to thinking exclusively in terms of instinctual drive derivatives; and second, his formulation of a hierarchy of pleasurable and unpleasurable feelings that can act on the psyche as a demand for work (Sandler and Joffe 1966). I would suggest that these two ideas point us towards an expansion of the psychoanalytic concept of *wish* that gives it greater clinical applicability.

My somewhat provocative proposal is that if Freud (1920) had been working with such an expanded concept, he would not have erred as he did in his analysis of post-traumatic dreams and other symptoms in which painful experiences are repetitively re-created. As it was, Freud failed to discern the role of wish fulfilment in these phenomena; and his mistake set the stage for the misconception, still widely held, that wish fulfilment and mastery of trauma are separate, unrelated endeavours. After briefly reviewing the ideas of Freud and those who followed him, I will explain and illustrate the view, consistent with the direction Sandler has taken in his writings about motivation, that wish fulfilment and mastery of trauma are complementary aspects of the same psychic activity.

POST-TRAUMATIC DREAMS

Let us begin with the clinical phenomena at issue. Post-traumatic dreams whose manifest content obviously *alters* traumatic events have never posed a problem for psychoanalytic understanding, because the alterations are invariably found to serve wishful purposes, albeit subtle ones. For example, a woman opened the door to her bedroom one afternoon and was shocked to find her previously healthy young husband sprawled dead on the floor from a heart attack. Following this awful experience, she dreamed repetitively of hearing her husband moaning as she raced up the stairs, terrified, just in time to witness his death agony. These post-traumatic dreams were in many ways just as horrible as the original trauma, except that the shock was made less abrupt which, as it turned out, was of the greatest importance to the woman. For various reasons, the utter surprise she had to endure made her husband's death even more painful. In her dreams, she wishfully gave herself a brief time to prepare herself for the sight of her dead husband, a time of preparation that she was not allowed by the actual events as they really transpired. Similar reports abound in the literature (e.g. Loewenstein 1949; Stein 1961).

The difficulty comes, however, in understanding post-traumatic dreams that depict events exactly as they occurred. The question is, what wish is served by the undistorted repetition of a painful experience? One school of thought has been that the pain of faithful re-creation is linked to deep, covert gratification (e.g. Wisdom 1949; Kris Study Group 1960). However, clinical experience indicates that analysis along these lines generally produces little benefit. Freud (1920), who was well aware of the desire for punishment and other aspects of masochism, could not find compelling evidence for such motivations in post-traumatic dreams that faithfully re-create a disturbing event. He concluded: 'These dreams are endeavouring to master the stimulus retrospectively. ... They afford us a view of the function of the mental apparatus which ... seems to be more primitive than the purpose of gaining pleasure and avoiding unpleasure' (32). It was this line of thought, of course, that led Freud to posit the compulsion to repeat as a basic principle of human motivation.

Thus Freud established the premise that repetition of trauma serves the purpose of mastery. Still, we must ask: how, exactly, does faithful repetition of a traumatic experience help to master it? One explanation sometimes offered is that relief is afforded by 'turning passive into active'. However, evidence in support of this hypothesis is very hard to come by, inasmuch as accurate post-traumatic re-creations are usually every bit as terrifying and are experienced just as passively as the original. Furthermore, interpretation along these lines in the clinical situation does not tend to prove terribly effective.

Now, if we take Sandler's point of view and think of a wish for a state of well-being or safety, we can arrive at an understanding of the function of accurate post-traumatic re-creations. It is an understanding in which wish fulfilment and mastery come together.

Two observations must be taken into account. The first is that post-traumatic dreams that accurately re-create traumatic events are dreamt only by people who have successfully endured narrow escapes. People who have suffered actual harm have post-traumatic dreams in which events are altered so that the harm is repaired: lost loved ones reappear, physical injuries are mitigated, and so forth. It is those individuals who have been badly frightened but have escaped relatively unscathed who dream of events exactly as they occurred. (Balson's [1980] findings concerning the dreams of rescued prisoners of war dramatically confirm this principle.)

The second observation is that dreams that accurately depict traumatic events never include the successful escape from danger. In that sense, we might say that their accuracy is only apparent. The deletion of the happy ending constitutes an important alteration of reality by omission.

These two observations taken together make it possible to see that such post-traumatic dreams have a function similar to the one Freud (1900) elucidated for typical examination dreams. Both types of dreams provide disguised reassurance to the dreamer. Typical examination dreams, it will be remembered, occur when the dreamer is about to take an examination in waking life. He dreams of taking an examination and doing very badly in it. What Freud recognized about these dreams is that the examination taken in the dream is not the same one that is imminent in waking life. In fact, the examination depicted in the dream is one the dreamer has already taken in the past and in which he has done very well! Thus a typical examination dream expresses the dreamer's wish that they will do as well in the examination they are about to take as they have done in an examination successfully completed in the past. However, because, for one reason or another, success in the upcoming examination arouses conflict in the dreamer, the fantasy of success is disguised as a failure in the dream's manifest content.

Similarly, a person who dreams with accuracy of traumatic events they have endured in reality is a person who has been badly frightened and is in need of reassurance that they are safe. They dream over and over of their successful escape, in the same way that a soldier wears 'the bullet that missed' around his neck. Repeated re-experience of the close call is like the handling of a talisman. Because the reassurance sought by the dreamer has become embroiled in conflict, it is disguised in the manifest content of the dream via deletion of the happy ending. The mechanism of disguise in the sort of post-traumatic dream that does not alter the traumatic event is thus precisely the one employed by the typical examination dream (falsification of the reassuringly successful outcome), and Freud would doubtless have recognized it had he been thinking that the wish fulfilled by a dream could be a wish for safety or well-being. As it was, in 1920 Freud was immersed in investigating sexuality and aggression, and, accordingly, he conceived of wishes narrowly in terms of instinctual gratification. Consequently, he failed to see how his own paradigm, the one he had developed in studying typical examination dreams, could be applied to unveil the wishfully reassuring purpose of what he came to call 'dreams from above'.

I have previously discussed how such dreams in their accurate depictions serve to master the effects of disturbing events via reassuring wish fulfilment (Renik 1981). I gave an example of a woman who had been in a railway accident just when she felt guiltily that she deserved punishment for her venomous feelings towards her husband, whom she was in the midst of divorcing. She could hardly believe that a vicious person like herself had been allowed to escape unharmed from a catastrophe when so many others had been injured and killed. To reassure herself, she accurately re-created again and again in her dreams, the circumstances of the accident from which she had emerged unscathed. The reassurance, however, caused her conflict because she felt it was undeserved, and so she always became progressively more anxious and awakened before recalling her arrival to safety. Another example concerned an unusually pretty young woman whose jealous mother had always warned her that her flirtations would lead to trouble. Corresponding all too closely to her mother's dire prediction was an incident in which the young woman went on a date that was interrupted and where she wound up being stripped naked, threatened and robbed. Old conflicts about her fantasy of Oedipal triumph were stirred up. As a consequence, she nightly reassured herself by repeating the successfully negotiated episode in her dreams. Because of her feelings of guilt, however, her dream omitted the fact that she had been rescued, physically unharmed, by the police.

The following vignette illustrates that post-traumatic symptoms other than dreams can also serve the purposes of both mastery and wish fulfilment. The clinical phenomenon on which I focus is the 'flashback', a cardinal symptom of post-traumatic stress disorder. Flashbacks can be conceptualized as waking versions of the sort of reassuring fantasy represented by post-traumatic dreams in which a traumatic event is accurately re-created. Viewing flashbacks well known to be obdurate post-traumatic symptoms as wish fulfilments in the service of mastery can provide a way to approach them therapeutically.

CASE EXAMPLE

A young man came to see me because he was plagued by flashbacks to the point that he was unable to function socially or at work and was seriously entertaining thoughts of suicide. Some months before, he had gone to Asia on a business trip, the last week of which he spent in a beautiful city whose streets teemed with homeless, impoverished people. He was intrigued by the place and made it a point to take a long exploratory walk each day. He saw much that was fascinating, and also much miserable suffering. He was aware of being very moved and impressed at the time, but not terribly disconcerted by his experiences on these walks.

Once he returned, however, he found himself vividly reliving certain episodes from his travels that kept coming to mind unbidden. He saw the faces of beggars who had importuned him insistently, felt them once again plucking at his clothes, and heard their pleas in a language he could not understand but whose meaning was unmistakable. In the recall, he experienced a dread that he had not felt originally. He became distracted, irritable and unable to sleep. At first he attributed his symptoms to travel fatigue, jet lag, or the culture shock of re-entry to the West; but the flashbacks did not go away and he could not seem to pull himself together.

He saw several psychiatrists who gave him a diagnosis of post-traumatic stress disorder. They told him he was going over a bad experience in order to gain control of it, but that made no sense to him because he felt more out of control now than he had in Asia. A series of antidepressants and antipsychotic drugs were given extended trials at therapeutic doses, but with little improvement. He was quite desperate by the time I saw him.

Two points in his history seemed significant: first, the business aspect of his trip had been quite successful, and he now enjoyed considerable financial gain after struggling for some time to get his company off the ground. Second, the patient had a younger brother who was his only sibling, and of whom he was apparently quite fond. The brother was something of a lost soul, though, and he had recently encountered some disappointing reverses in his own career. The patient became teary-eyed when he spoke of his brother.

My approach was guided by the idea that this patient's flashbacks might express a hidden wish for reassurance. I began by pointing out to him the obvious, namely, that his flashbacks and the disorganization they caused threatened to ruin the success he had achieved. When he agreed, I suggested that perhaps he felt he did not deserve his success, especially given the fact that his brother was not equally fortunate. Clearly, the specific scenes he found himself reliving were relevant in this regard; he may have felt guiltier about the beggars than he realized.

These suggestions were not far from his own thoughts. Similar ideas had occurred to him, he said. It was true that he felt uncomfortable being better off than his brother, but he had not connected this sentiment with his flashbacks. Now that I mentioned it, he could see that the beggars reminded him of his brother; in a way in both situations he had the same bad feeling about not being more helpful.

On the other hand, he thought he was entitled to what he had achieved. He had worked hard for it, yet now these awful flashbacks were dragging him down. 'There seems no escape', he said. Focusing on these words, I remarked that it was particularly important that the experiences he had relived in his flashbacks were ones in which there had been an actual danger of being dragged down, but from which in fact he *had* escaped. I noted that the escape was not included in the flashbacks. This observation struck him, and led us to a discussion of how he had come to take long walks alone through potentially dangerous neighbourhoods in the first place. He recognized in himself a certain temptation to flirt with disaster, a difficulty in accepting as real the business success he knew he was in the midst of achieving, and a vague sense that he did not merit such good fortune.

On the basis of all this discussion, we were able to put together an understanding of his flashbacks as an effort to reassure himself that he had indeed escaped a punishment he felt he deserved for superseding his brother. For the same reasons that he did not feel completely entitled to his business success, he also did not feel completely entitled to the reassurance he derived from going over and over his successful escape from danger in Asia, and so he disguised the reassuring memory by deleting its happy ending. Thus, in conscious awareness, he experienced his efforts to reassure himself as if they were submissions to an awful fate. The more he tried to reassure himself, the more doomed he felt; the more doomed he felt, the more he tried to reassure himself. For the moment, guilt seemed to be winning out over self-preservation as the misguided loop went round and round.

This formulation was enormously pleasing to the patient. It gave him an explanation for his symptoms that made sense. In light of it, he could see the flashbacks as something that occurred for a reason, rather than something that just happened and had to be passively endured. He had done well in Asia, which is why being there had felt okay at the time. Remembering this was a positive purpose he could understand.

In subsequent sessions, he reported that he was having flashbacks much less frequently and that they did not bother him as much, because he knew why he was having them. He showed little inclination to look more deeply into his guilt feelings towards his brother and the anxiety against which he needed reassurance. When I invited him to do so, he made it very clear that he was quite satisfied to leave well enough alone. Within two weeks he was off medication, he was having only occasional flashbacks (which did not upset him) and he felt on track again. He was grateful for my help and indicated that he would call me again if he needed to. Over the next few years, I received an occasional holiday card informing me that business was great and that there were no further problems.

Clearly, the understanding of his flashbacks at which my patient and I were able to arrive was only one element contributing to the therapeutic success of our interactions. The limited nature of the investigation we were able to undertake, and the patient's unwillingness to proceed further, strongly indicate that symptom relief depended at least as much on unexamined elements in our relationship as on the conscious insight we achieved.

Our formulation certainly facilitated a measure of intellectualization. Also, I functioned very much as a psychological expert, relying heavily on my own ideas to speak confidently about relatively limited data supplied by the patient. It seems very likely that, among other things, a fantasy of the patient's was evoked in which he submitted to some powerful but benign authority and received expiation and strength. At the same time, it is probable that even if an enactment of this sort did take place, some validity in my view of his flashbacks may well have been crucial to my gaining the position of authority that made the transference cure possible. Furthermore, enactment of a transference fantasy, however powerful its effects, does not *per se* invalidate insights arrived at in the process; nor does the fact that the insights may in part be used defensively. Glover (1931) long ago made clear that successful analytic work usually facilitates repression at the very same time that it permits self-discovery to take place.

CONCLUSION

I have emphasized the complementarity of wish fulfilment and mastery of trauma as psychoanalytic principles of motivation. Freud's thinking took a turn that obscured this complementarity, but Sandler's work helps us identify it. I believe the complementarity of wish fulfilment and mastery is a most important point not only for theory building, but also for clinical work. Post-traumatic dreams that accurately re-create traumatic events, and flashbacks in the waking state, represent attempts at mastery that can be recognized as such only if the wish fulfilments expressed in them are appreciated. A psycho-therapeutic approach based on an understanding of the complementarity of wish fulfilment and mastery of trauma can prove successful, as I have illustrated, with these notoriously refractory symptoms.

REFERENCES

Balson, P. (1980) 'Dreams and fantasies as adaptive mechanisms in prisoners of war in Vietnam', unpublished paper, Palo Alto CA.

Freud, S. (1900) 'The interpretation of dreams', *Standard Edition*, vols 4–5 (1953), London: Hogarth Press, 1–627.

——(1920) 'Beyond the pleasure principle', *Standard Edition*, vol. 18 (1955), London: Hogarth Press, 1–64.

Glover, E. (1931) 'The therapeutic effect of inexact interpretation: a contribution to the theory of suggestion', *International Journal of Psycho-Analysis*, 12, 397–411.

Kris Study Group (1960) 'Contribution to the study of the manifest dream', *Psychoanalytic Quarterly*, 30, 464–6.

Loewenstein, R. M. (1949) 'A post-traumatic dream', *Psychoanalytic Quarterly*, 18, 449–54.

Renik, O. (1981) 'Typical examination dreams, "superego dreams", and traumatic dreams', *Psychoanalytic Quarterly*, 50, 159–89.

Sandler, J. (1974) 'Psychological conflict and the structural model', *International Journal of Psycho-Analysis*, 55, 53–62.

——(1989) 'Towards a reconsideration of the psychoanalytic theory of motivation', in J. Sandler, *Psychoanalysis: Towards the Second Century*, New Haven CT: Yale University Press, 1–296.

Sandler, J. and Joffe, W. (1966) 'On skill and sublimation', *Journal of the American Psychoanalytic Association*, 14, 335–55.

Stein, M. M. (1961) 'Trauma and dream', *Psychoanalytic Quarterly*, 30, 474–6.

Wisdom, J. O. (1949) 'A hypothesis to explain trauma re-enactment in dreams', *Psychiatry*, 24, 329–36.

4

BETWEEN THE BACKGROUND OF SAFETY AND THE BACKGROUND OF THE UNCANNY IN THE CONTEXT OF SOCIAL VIOLENCE

Yolanda Gampel

In this chapter I shall discuss Sandler's concept of the background of safety and suggest its applicability to clinical theory and technique when practising psychoanalysis with patients who have experienced man-made disasters or extreme social violence, such as war. Freud began to be concerned about the effects of war during and after World War I. In 1915 he wrote:

> It [war] tramples in blind fury on all that comes in its way, as though there were to be no future and no peace among men after it is over. It cuts all the common bonds between the contending peoples, and threatens to leave behind a legacy of embitterment that will make any renewal of those bonds impossible for a long time to come.
>
> (Freud 1915a: 65)

The fury and embitterment that Freud was concerned about have continued throughout this century; the power of these destructive forces has appeared repetitively and unequivocally both in the individual and in society.

It is difficult to speak about war from a purely theoretical point of view without relating to its concrete reality and manifestations. It is also difficult for psychoanalysis, which focuses primarily on the internal world, to function in a context of violence and war. The technical difficulties involved in continuing psychoanalysis during extreme external circumstances will also be discussed in this chapter.

Today more than ever before, we find ourselves treating more and more patients with disorders that turn out to be linked to a background of trauma due to social violence. Where and how does the social violence that occurs in reality show itself in the clinical material? This question is particularly relevant today when many treatments are taking place in countries where war and social violence are occurring at the same time. In fact, we are faced with a series of questions: how has social violence affected the mind? Can we apply the same theory of personality development in treating people who in childhood and adolescence experienced terrible traumas due to social violence? How should psychoanalysis be practised with such people?

Freud never ceased to maintain that mastery of psychoanalytic technique could be achieved only through clinical experience rather than through purely theoretical and intellectual approaches. He pointed out that the theory of psychoanalysis is an effort to make transference and resistance understandable, and that both transference and resistance are results of repression based on the processes of remembering and forgetting.

To grasp these concepts clearly and to understand their meaning in connection with new developments in psychoanalytic technique, we must find more subtle terms for conceptualizing these techniques. Melanie Klein's theoretical contributions and her primary interest in primitive anxieties resulted in the expansion of the repertoire of psychoanalytic technique. Yet another theoretical focus involved working with the concept of the loss of reality (Freud 1924) in cases of neurosis and psychosis. Based on Freud's writing in 'Loss of reality in neurosis and psychosis' (1924) and 'The two principles of mental functioning' (1911), Bion (1967) developed ideas that were supported by his considerable experience with psychotic patients. He elaborated on the findings sketched out by Freud, and suggested modifications to Freud's descriptions that affected later theory and practice.

For Sandler and his colleagues (1969), transference as a clinical concept can also be seen as a dimension of object relationships in general. He developed the concept of the representational world and of the complex self- and object-representations at play within it, as the ego constantly attempts to balance the press of anxiety and the search for conditions of safety. Sandler conceptualized the principle of safety and pointed to the individual's striving for a background of safety. For Sandler, this background of safety is a dialectical counterpart to anxiety.

THE CONCEPTUALIZATION OF
TWO BACKGROUNDS

I wish to identify two polar concepts, the 'background of safety' and the 'background of the uncanny'. Both lie within the individual who is experiencing and living in the context of social violence.

The concept of 'the background of safety', as Sandler (1960) introduced it, emphasizes the notion of safety as a feeling or state quite distinct from the feeling of sensual pleasure. Sandler uses perception as an example of an activity that can generate feelings of safety. He (1960: 353) stated that the act of perception is an act of ego mastery through which the ego copes with excitation, that is, with unorganised sense data, and is thus protected from being traumatically overwhelmed; that the successful act of perception is an act of integration that is accompanied by a definite feeling of safety – a feeling so much a part of us that we take it for granted as a background to our everyday experience.

In working with Sandler's concept, I wondered about the opposite of the background of safety. All the terrible spectacles of war and social violence, with all their pain, call into question our apparatus for perception and their representations. Overwhelmed and sometimes destroyed because of the power of these forces, our capacity for symbolization is paralysed. What happens when the perception of safety given by social context is lost? What occurs when horror, violence and torture force distortions of reality on the individual? Freud's idea of the 'uncanny' may suggest an answer.

Freud (1919) introduced the term 'uncanny' in an attempt to conceptualize qualities of feeling that arouse dread and horror. Although Freud recognized its undoubted connection to that which excites fear, he wished to distinguish, within the field of what is frightening, a special core feeling of uncanniness. The uncanny is not a symptom, behaviour or neurotic organization. It is a lived experience ('erlebnis'), without significations, which cannot be translated into words. At the same time that the uncanny is familiar ('heimlich', 'belonging to the house or family, intimate, friendly, comfortable'), the 'unheimlich' is the opposite, referring to what remains hidden, 'concealed, kept from sight, withheld from others'. To the notion of the hidden, Freud (1919: 222–4)) added the idea of the dangerous, 'eerie, weird, arousing gruesome fear'. However, as Freud explained, the uncanny represents something primary that has already been experienced. It is as if the experience of the uncanny is a sort of dialectic between reminiscence and forgetting.

Thus I suggest expanding the term 'uncanny' to describe precisely those experiences that cannot be expressed in words, in particular, memories of dread and horror aroused by experiences of extreme social violence, and not just repressed primary infant experiences. Furthermore, within the social historical context, the uncanny – the dread and horror of social violence – is something primary, already experienced in the history of our century, that belongs to the familiar and is yet hidden and dangerous, having been transmitted from generation to generation. This is inscribed in the trans-subjective space.

Experience of such horror and violence can lead to the blurring or destruction of the distinction between the impossible and that which might indeed come to exist. Such an assault on the boundary between fantasy and reality becomes traumatic in itself and leads to great fear of one's thoughts and expectations. Thus a 'background of uncanniness' is created. It is as if the uncanny feelings become an organized structure; the uncertainty, the state of disorganization, becomes framed and becomes part of the person.

I contend that one of the ways of coping with a traumatic past induced by social violence is to live between the two poles – between the feeling of safety and the uncanny feeling. The background of safety originates from a sense of safety that develops in the primary background object of primary identification. The infant is helpless. It is primarily the adult caregiver who provides the context of the infant's experiences. Normal development is determined by the fact that the external world, represented initially by the parents, allows for neutralization of aspects that are aggressive, fearful and anxiety-producing. In such circumstances, the external world reveals giving, accepting and peaceful behaviour to the child. This structure is consolidated within an individual in an organized family and social context where the norms and ethical and moral customs, traditions and rules were clearly transmitted and experienced as such.

Conversely, when this organized world is disrupted because of social violence, the terrible perceptions of anger, death, torture and destruction bring about the feeling of the uncanny. All these experiences and feelings become a background that I suggest we call the background of the uncanny, which is the opposite of the background of safety.

We are faced with two opposites that exist within the individual. One is a feeling of safety that arises out of a constant affective background we can describe as a continuity of being in a constant social context. The other is a feeling of uncanniness caused by a fragmented, violent social context. The latter is without continuity and transmits extremely paradoxical messages. I will make a distinction between individuals who are living in such a context or who have suffered direct trauma, and those who are only spectators to social violence.

Thus one can assume the existence of both backgrounds – the 'background of safety' and the 'background of the uncanny' – working at different levels and at different moments. While one of them is acting in the foreground, the other lies in the background, and vice-versa. Although all individuals harbour within themselves a silent and hidden legacy of aggression, it is important to underline that individuals who have gone through violent social traumas were forced into acquaintance with terrible aggression by a brutal, external world and not because of their own hidden aggression.

The different modes of coping with knowing and not knowing about massive trauma have been recorded. People who have experienced a trauma – the most unthinkable nightmarish occurrence – can deal with the return of a perception of horror consciously and unconsciously through different defence mechanisms, such as affective anaesthesia (Minkowski 1946) and psychic numbing (Lifton 1967), or by consciously removing themselves from the perception of violence, choosing not to read, listen to, or watch anything related to their trauma.

Nonetheless, one can speculate that the perception of violence has already entered like radioactivity (Gampel 1993a, 1993b) and has made its way into the psyche, touching the three psychic spaces and their representations (Puget 1989), the intra-, inter- and trans-subjective spaces. The intra-subjective space is the space of what is most privately individual (instincts and instinctual representatives); the inter-subjective space is the linkage space (object relationships); and the trans-subjective space is the social and cultural space – each with its own laws and modes of functioning.

In the case of survivors of extreme traumatic social violence, such as people who were children or adolescents during the Holocaust (see following examples), we can assume that the uncanny background cannot be assimilated, nor can it be integrated into pre-existing structures or into present experiences. This uncanny background, living side-by-side with the safety background, leads to a world of estrangement.

CASE EXAMPLES

This is an excerpt from a meeting in the third year of a group composed of survivors who were children during the Holocaust. The group provides a framework of dialogue through which people can talk about their personal traumatic history and highlight episodes previously forgotten or disregarded because the affect that they create is so violent that it exceeds the ego's capacity for regulation.

Mr Y

Mr Y, who was eight years old when he was taken to Terezenstadt with his mother, commented on a statement by Mr B who was in the Lodz ghetto until aged eighteen, then in Auschwitz from age 18 to 19. Mr Y said: 'About the subject that's just been raised, it's interesting, I've been thinking about it at home. We're talking here about all sorts of things, but where is the everyday, where is the always, where is the all the time? I want to tell you that I'm a lot younger than you are – it looks that way – and I still work full time and haven't read any Shoah literature recently. Let's say, too, there's always a TV program on the Shoah. Well, I haven't been watching them recently. But these feelings you just told us about ... it's as though it was me talking, because that's exactly how it is. You don't know where it comes from. Suddenly, it's there. It can be with anything at all.'

Then Mr Y went on to tell a story from his childhood:

I was maybe fifteen then, in a Kibbutz, in a 'mobilization', where everybody is organized to work together in the fields. We were gathering sugar beets. Farmers. A tractor was moving along, taking out the sugar beets. I went along and gathered them into stacks. I was going along, I picked up one sugar beet and threw it onto that stack of beets and it went 'pphht', and I just stood there. That's it.

With that stack of sugar beets, I saw pictures, white stacks going 'kchch', another one comes and goes 'kchch', and I stood there. And listen, that picture, let me tell you it was the first of my flashbacks, of these things that keep coming back every time. One time I said to my wife: 'I'd define it like a library, a filing cabinet, there's some sort of cabinet of drawers there, suddenly a drawer opens, something pops up out of it, and it closes'.

(Gampel 1992a: 47)

Through this excerpt, we can see how the two backgrounds are separated. The survivors have to put the uncanny background into a 'filing cabinet', and they try to keep the drawers locked so that nothing pops out suddenly. They are consciously aware that when the drawer opens up suddenly, they are faced with very concrete memories that come through sensory impressions. These concrete sensory memories cannot be transformed in dreams or thoughts, because these phenomena arise from living a terrible reality. They are the concrete metaphor for these horrors. The lived reality and the transformation of emotions occurred simultaneously, and the mind is saturated. This saturation of the mind hinders the stimulus of current perceptions.

Both these backgrounds exist in the preconscious, and therefore they are not repressed but are suppressed. Suppression is seen as a conscious mechanism working on the level of 'second censorship', which Freud places between the conscious and the preconscious. Suppression involves an exclusion from the field of consciousness, not a translation from the preconscious system to the unconscious system (Freud 1915b, 1915c).

From my clinical experience working with survivors who were children growing up in the Shoah, it appears that the two backgrounds do not always remain side-by-side. A part of the uncanny background appears to seep into the safety background, and an area of ambiguity is created that is characterized by confusion, nightmares, somatization, discomfort and disbelief. If the uncanny background covers a larger part of the safety background, then we are faced with more serious symptomatology. In extreme situations, the uncanny background covers the safety background almost completely (see following example and Figure 4.1).

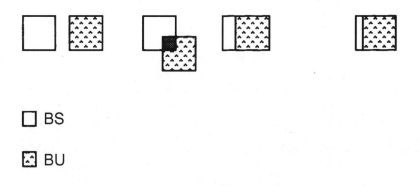

☐ BS

▨ BU

Figure 4.1 The different backgrounds

Mr D

Over the past thirty years, Mr D has spent more time hospitalized on the psychiatric ward than living in the outside world. He is quiet, gentle, and well spoken. One day a nurse who had come from Russia began working on the ward. After she was introduced to the patients there, Mr D turned to her and said, 'You came here for them to take away your virginity'. This uncharacteristic comment took the staff by surprise. The staff members believed that something new was happening to him, and they were searching for the meaning of his comment. They knew very little about him except that he was unmarried, without any family, and very lonely. When Mr D was 12 or 13 years old, he had been at Auschwitz. From the testimonies of other children and adolescent survivors there, we know that many of them were forced to carry out homosexual activities. The staff had picked up some clues from Mr D's history and behaviour that led us to hypothesize that perhaps he had undergone experiences similar to those of other children.

Violated, he remained alive; his body was living, but his mind, cognition, and capacity to remember were not with him. Through the stimulus of a newcomer and a stranger, he had come into contact with the uncanny background that had been obliterated by his psychotic state. We may assume that the psychotic state prevented him from coming into contact with the terrible uncanny experience. The hospital became a sort of safety background to his psychotic state. Through the new young nurse who was a stranger, something of the uncanny was revealed in the background of safety that he had created in the hospital.

Mrs GS

The case of Mrs GS illustrates the second way that the uncanny background can seep into the safety background. This clinical case presents a single moment in an ongoing psychoanalytic treatment (Gampel 1990).

Mrs GS, a fifty-three-year-old woman, saw her parents for the last time at the age of six when she was transferred to a church orphanage and later to a convent. She is married and the mother of two daughters, one of whom has been in psychotherapeutic treatment for four years. Mrs GS came for treatment herself because of her depressive state and her phobic and obsessive tendencies. At times she would be in such a severe anxiety state as to be unable to cope with daily life. It was as if the uncanny took over all of her safety background, temporarily paralysing her.

In one session in the fourth month of her psychoanalytic treatment Mrs GS had thought about many things since the previous session and was very angry at herself for not being able to get rid of a thought once it entered her mind. She was always at war with herself, and she could not forgo the battle.

In her craziness, everything always has to be in order, in its proper place. She talks about amazingly organized and tidy closets and about the immense energy she invests in neatness, unable to restrain herself.

When asked to give an example of a thought that does not leave her mind, she talks about her husband's trip abroad. With a smile, she says that the trip took place eight years ago. Despite her anger at his departure, she tried to enjoy her own vacation. At that time, she still drove a car and she would go down to the beach. But instead of enjoying the sun and relaxing, she was bothered by worrisome thoughts: Why did he go? Why did he leave me? And so forth. She asks what she should do with these kinds of thoughts.

While listening to her, I feel anger towards this resentful woman who continues to bear grudges after so many years. I think how evil and aggressive she is. At this moment, I, too, dislike her and feel rejecting towards her. These feelings arouse discomfort in me. How can

I have such strong negative feelings towards this woman who has suffered so much?

I relate not to her thoughts, but to her feelings of anger, revenge, resentment, jealousy and envy. I tell her that we have to work out these feelings and not the thoughts. Mrs GS looks at me with surprise, uneasiness and embarrassment, because it is not easy to relate to these feelings. She asks whether she actually has any connections to the feelings I have described. I tell her that in order for her to be in contact with these feelings, she would have to relinquish the place of the victim and the sufferer and come into contact with her own aggression. She remains silent. She then says that she feels as if she is in a total blackout – she cannot think of anything. Again, she is quiet.

Mrs GS tells me that on the bus on her way to the session, she wondered what she would talk about. On the bus, she felt a strong feeling of envy towards all the children going to school. She adds quietly that her own children do not want to study. I mention that I knew that she used to drive but did not know she had stopped. She responds that the traffic in Israel is so volatile, and the drivers are so aggressive; she is so tense when she drives that she is afraid that she will fail to react in time because of her slowness. This worries her because it is a matter of life and death.

I think about how clearly she offers up her fears of losing control and her feelings of jealousy, envy, frightening aggression, and the obsessive mechanisms she uses. Gradually, my antipathy towards her begins to fade and I become capable of thinking about her as a young child living in a monastery.

Without being personally familiar with the atmosphere of a monastery, I try to enter her background during her childhood through her recollections: a world of self-restraint, order and cleanliness. I also think of the extreme loneliness she must have felt as a child living in a monastery, a place in which, perhaps, her only outlet was her thoughts. We both turn inward, each absorbed in her own thoughts.

After several moments of silence, I ask her if she has dreamt anything since our last session. Mrs GS nods affirmatively but says that she does not remember the details, just the theme. In her dream, her older daughter was five years old and was killed. She tells me this in a detached manner, without any affect. Again, I feel anger on thinking about what she has done to her children. At this moment, I am highly identified with her children. Together with the anger, I feel compassion and a profound sadness.

Mrs GS's associations to the dream are that maybe her daughter is really herself. She continues to associate in a most intellectual manner. I ask her to tell me about her daughter when she was five or six years old. She describes her as a good girl who did not cause any problems, and who did not have separation difficulties when entering kindergarten or first grade. Today, her daughter is under psychiatric care and, although twenty-nine years old, acts like an adolescent, incapable of completing anything and unable to hold down a job. Mrs GS continues to say that she never let either of her daughters bring home friends. She does not like people – they bother her. She prefers to be alone. The truth is that she did not want them to 'mess up the house'. She wanted everything to remain in its proper place.

I feel constricted and identify with her daughters. (Mrs GS did not give them the possibility of developing their own background of safety within the present reality.) Like them, I feel that she does not leave me room to live, develop and create.

I tell her that I am thinking about how at the age of six, when she lost her parents and remained alone, something inside her died. From that point onward, she learned that everything had to be very organized, as the nuns in the convent taught her, so that nothing will ever change again.

She looks at me with great surprise and says that she never connected her orderliness and cleanliness with her education in the convent, but how true it is. (Here in her memories, one background had seeped into the other. Later in her therapy, her compulsive, orderly personality was also attributed and related to her home and parents as she recalled them. She particularly recalled her very clean and orderly home and her mother's demands for neatness and precision.)

Another time, Mrs GS described a different version of how she was taken from her home. This time she says that she was seven years old. The laundress took her to her own home, where she had to stand in total silence behind a closet hidden behind stairs so that she would not be found. Mrs GS begins to cry. She does not understand why she is crying now, because she had already told me all of this. She cries for a long time, then continues the story. She was transferred to an orphanage in a convent, which was absolutely terrible. Today she mentions that she had been there for a year, whereas last time she said she had been there for only one month.

From there, she was taken to a distant convent on a mountain, among several villages, a place where she was the only child whom everyone spoiled. She describes the convent, the landscape around it, the silence and the order. Each day she knew exactly what to expect, because each day was a copy of the previous one. She remembers this period with great pleasure. She would have liked to remain there. What a pity that she had to go through so many changes once they took her away from the convent – changes of landscape, country, language and religion. I suggest to her that, for her, maintaining order and remaining alone with the order is like holding the convent within herself and at the same time continuing to live inside it.

The session is coming to a close. The room is filled with silence – not a tense silence but one of work. I am very much with her, without anger and anxiety.

(Gampel 1990)

This case illustrates one way of dealing technically with the seeping of the uncanny background into the background of safety within the therapeutic hour. It exemplifies some technical problems in the practice of psychoanalysis that arise in working with child survivors. Two aspects in particular are important to focus on: first, the survivor's difficulty in accepting her own internal hatred, cruelty, violence and aggression, which are directed both towards herself and the people she loves, becomes evident during the session. It is very difficult for the survivor to take responsibility for this side of her nature, which she views as undermining her capacity to love and be constructive. And second, at the same time, it is most difficult for the analyst to point out these emotions to the survivor, for whom aggression, hatred and sadism are tantamount to Nazism. In turn, the countertransferential feelings of resentment and rejection towards the patient elicit shame and guilt feelings in the analyst.

THE PRACTICE OF PSYCHOANALYSIS IN THE CONTEXT OF SOCIAL VIOLENCE

The uncanniness created by war or other forms of social violence raises a series of questions concerning the role and practice of psychoanalysis. The psychoanalytic work exposes the analyst to the depths of the internal currents of another person's mind, and stirs up similar currents within the analyst's own internal depths. What happens when both patient and analyst are exposed, at the same time, to extreme external circumstances? How is this 'actuality' introduced into the special space of the psychoanalytic session? How is the analyst to deal technically with this actuality? We can relate to events happening in the external world that cause an eruption in the expected, normal life, when patients and analysts are immersed in the same social context (Gampel 1992b).

I suggest that analysts try to understand the actual eruption as well as its symbolic value or meaning for the patient, through awareness of the analytic setting and understanding of the transference. To allow such processes to occur, the analyst must maximize her countertransference readiness, listening to the patient who is using her. It is therefore critical to not confuse the past infantile unconscious with the present unconscious (Sandler and Sandler 1983). The experience of extreme violence must be placed within the temporal and spatial context of the patient's present life.

We who live in countries exposed to social violence, even if we are not directly involved, are affected by infiltration through the senses and perceptions. In addition, people are exposed through the media to terrible social violence that arouses feelings of uncanniness. We live with a background of safety, but within it appears a shadow of uncanniness.

My background of safety includes my home, my consulting room and my schedule. It also includes my comfortable armchair where I am seated looking at a patient who is lying on the couch. With one ear, I am hearing his words – the manifest content of his narration – and with the other 'ear' I hear the latent content of his discourse. He talks about a dream, about aggression, about incestuous desires, about his passions and temptations, about his love and hate, and his libidinal and sadistic fantasies. I finish the hour at eight o'clock in the morning, and enter the kitchen to make coffee. I have twenty minutes until the session with the next patient.

I open the newspaper and I read about Gaza, about Yugoslavia, about Germany and Somalia, and I come into contact with the domain of uncanniness in daily life. It is the manifest discourse of violence, hate, death. This is actuality, this is reality, not the internal reality I was dealing with some moments before. The print spread before me is a symbol of our time, culture and civilization. It is the concrete metaphor. What I have heard in the previous hour is related to the internal world and internal vicissitudes. I think I can deal with these internal vicissitudes through psychoanalysis in my relatively comfortable and safe technical and theoretical background. However, the newspaper forces the external reality of our world upon me, and I feel helpless.

The session with the next patient is about to begin. When I open the door to the patient, these external realities and the feelings and thoughts that they arouse are running through my head. I try to get rid of these intrusions of sadness and helplessness, to put them aside, to suppress them from consciousness, and to be with the patient without the infiltration of the uncanny.

However, later the same day, in a session with a six-year-old child, reality intrudes through the patient:

E charges in and moves around the room restlessly. He says, 'Mother bought me a boxing bag. It's a present that Grandmother promised me, and Mother bought it'. Jumping up and down with his hands waving in the air, he declares that he has two pairs of gloves, and how he hits with them!

I comment: 'Your mother must be very pleased with the present you got, you can beat the boxing bag as much as you like, and not hit and annoy your brothers'.

E looks at me in surprise!

Introducing his external reality into the session, I explain: 'Your mother telephoned me and told me that she had a very difficult time with you, and that she wanted to send you away from home'.

E objects: 'She would never do that, and I am going to keep on doing what I want'.

I respond: 'We should try and look at this need to be in such a role at home'.

E doesn't want to talk about it and puts his hands over his ears and closes his eyes. When he takes his hands off, I ask him: 'How is this related to your father being in the reserve duty in Gaza now? Perhaps you are worried about him?'

E vehemently objects: 'What, can't I miss Father? I miss him, and that's all!'

He collects the cushions from around the room, lies down on them, and goes to sleep for about five minutes. He then gets up and says: 'I'm going to put on a play for you'. He turns off all the lights, sits in a chair in the corner of the room with his finger in his mouth, and cries and cries and cries.

E then says: 'The first play is over!'

I ask him: 'Can you tell me the content of the play?'

E replies: 'A baby is sleeping, and they left the window open, and his back is cold, and he is crying'.

E then acts out another scene, in which a baby is crying as well because it is uncomfortable and nobody comes to help.

I explain: 'You are telling me that as well as the E who hits his brothers and is naughty, there is an E who feels like a little helpless baby who is uncomfortable and miserable and then he cries and cries and there is nobody to make him feel better'.

Calmer, E turns the lights back on. From the game that develops afterward, it seems that he feels held and contained.

This session made me face a technical problem related to the intrusion of external events into the session. The day before, the mother had called to tell me that her son had been behaving terribly over the previous two days. She was alone with the children because her husband was on army reserve duty and would be serving in Gaza over the next two weeks. I connected the son's bad behaviour to the absence of the father and the fact that the wife and the children were worried about him because the situation in Gaza was dangerous.

I believed that this external situation of violence was mixed up with E's Oedipal conflicts, but first of all it was necessary to clarify the external situation and to take it into account before I went on to analyse his internal conflicts. It is interesting that in E's play, the fantasy was of an open window that allows what is happening in the outside world to seep in, and nobody came to close this window.

I think that in the current reality in Israel, the safety background of the session and treatment is continuously being threatened by the background of violence, and it is very difficult for the psychoanalyst to close the window on the external violence, which may create a domain of uncanniness. This violence infiltrates not only the patient but also the analyst. Thus, as analysts, we have to take a very difficult path, like someone walking a tightrope: being attuned to the unconscious, internal world of the patient, yet at the same time taking into account the infiltration of the social violence into the clinical material. Only after understanding these two realities can we continue our regular work of interpreting the here-and-now in the transference.

We can assume that every actual situation may be linked in a symbolic manner to internalized figures and events of the past. How can we relate to both the past and the present, to the external and the internal, without giving up either of them?

Taking into account the external and historical events in reality brings us back to 'Constructions in psychoanalysis' (Freud 1937). To interpret only the inner world, as it reveals itself in the transference, ignores and violates the personal history, the historical events and the process of history-making that ensure the continuity of life. When the patient confronts the analyst with external events, the analyst is faced with what is known. Patient and analyst thus share a common external reality and are faced with the phenomenon of overlapping worlds (Puget and Wender 1982). However, each external reality has a particular meaning for the individual, and it is here that we enter the unknown. By relating to the shared external reality, the analyst slowly helps transform the external impersonal event into an experience with a particular quality for the subject. Thus the analytical framework maintains a dialectical process between internal and external reality.

SUMMARY

This chapter discusses certain theoretical and practical problems of practising psychoanalysis when working with people who have lived through or who are living in situations of extreme social violence.

In the model presented, two backgrounds are taken into consideration: the background of safety and the background of the uncanny. The proposed hypothesis is that people who have experienced extreme traumatic and violent situations need to dissociate these two backgrounds to survive without being engulfed by their past.

An example from group meetings of child survivors exemplifies the concept of working with people who have dissociated the two backgrounds and have attempted to forget what they are remembering. What they remember is not through screen memories; instead, their recollections emerge as raw and real – concrete memories of a terrible reality they suffered but are unable to disguise – and that they cannot integrate with the everyday reality of their present life.

I have also pointed out what happens when the two backgrounds come into contact and when, in the more extreme situation, the uncanny seeps into or engulfs the safety background. These different modes are illustrated with clinical material, and the technical difficulties that arise in psychoanalytic practice are considered.

Furthermore, the practice of psychoanalysis in an actual situation of war and violence is discussed. The role of reality is examined within the context of an analytic session.

When terror and social violence exist in the patient's and analyst's environment, should the analyst introduce this external reality into the session even if the patient does not make any associations that connect with what is going on outside? Can we continue to maintain the neutral analytic setting and ignore or deny external reality? These questions are very relevant in Israel, where internal themes of anxiety and aggression and traumatic events in individual and family histories are so deeply intermingled with external reality.

REFERENCES

Bion, W. (1967) *Second Thoughts*, London: Maresfield Reprints.

Freud, S. (1911) 'Formulations on the two principles of mental functioning', *Standard Edition*, vol. 12 (1958), London: Hogarth Press, 213–26.

——(1914) 'On the history of the psycho-analytic movement', *Standard Edition*, vol. 14 (1963), London: Hogarth Press, 1–66.

——(1915a) 'Thoughts for the times on war and death', *Standard Edition*, vol. 14 (1963), London: Hogarth Press, 273–302.

——(1915b) 'Repression', *Standard Edition*, vol. 14 (1963), London: Hogarth Press, 141–58.

——(1915c) 'The unconscious', *Standard Edition*, vol. 14 (1963), London: Hogarth Press, 159–215.

——(1919) 'The "uncanny" ', *Standard Edition*, vol. 17 (1955), London: Hogarth Press, 217–56.

——(1924) 'Neurosis and psychosis', *Standard Edition*, vol. 19 (1961), London: Hogarth Press, 147–53.

——(1937) 'Constructions in analysis', *Standard Edition*, vol. 23 (1964), London: Hogarth Press, 255–69.

Gampel, Y. (1990) 'Some reflections on counter-transference in psychoanalytical work with Shoah survivors', presented at the conference 'Children in War', Sigmund Freud Center, Jerusalem.

——(1992a) 'Thoughts about the transmission of conscious and unconscious knowledge to the generation born after the Shoah', *Journal of Social Work and Policy in Israel*, 5–6: 43–50.

——(1992b) 'Psychoanalysis, ethics, and actuality', *Psychoanalytic Enquiry*, 12 (4), 526–50.

——(1993a) 'From the thing in itself by modelling through transformation by narration in the therapeutic space', *British Journal of Psychotherapy*, 9 (3), 280–90.

——(1993b) 'Taking leave of one's grandparents' past', *Cuadernos Clinicos, Revista de Psicoanalisis con Niños y Adolescentes*, 6, 23–34.

Lifton, R. J. (1967) *Death in Life: Survivors of Hiroshima*, New York: Random House.

Minkowski, G. (1946) 'L'anesthesie affective' ('The affective anaesthesia'), *Annals Médical Psychologiques (Annals of Medical Psychology)*, 104.

Puget, J. (1989) 'Un espace psychique ou trois espaces? Sont superposés?' ('One psychic space or three spaces? Are they overlapping?'), *Revue de Psychotherapie Psychanalytique de Groupe (Review of the Psychoanalytic Psychotherapy Group)*, 13.

Puget, J. and Wender, L. (1982) 'Analista y paciente en mundos superpuestos' ('Analyst and patient in overlapping worlds'), *Psicoanalisis (Psychoanalysis)*, 4 (3), 503–22.

Sandler, J. (1960) 'The background of safety', *Journal of Psychoanalysis*, 41, 352–65.

——(1989) *From Safety to Superego*, London: Karnac Books.

Sandler, J. and Sandler, A.-M. (1983) 'The "second censorship", the "three box model" and some technical implications', *International Journal of Psycho-Analysis*, 64, 413–26.

Sandler, J., Holder, A., Kawenoka, M., Kennedy, H. and Neurath, L. (1969) 'Theoretical and clinical aspects of transference', *International Journal of Psycho-Analysis*, 50, 633–45.

5

SOME REFLECTIONS ON THE CONCEPT OF ENACTMENT

Roy Schafer

The concept of enactment is currently very much in the psychoanalytic air. Indeed, it qualifies as a 'buzz word'. That is, using it establishes the analyst as up-to-date, if not avant-garde – or so the analyst hopes. This being so, some conceptual working through is called for; otherwise 'enactment' may lose its value in the psychoanalytic vocabulary. I shall begin with a much-needed discussion of the conceptual boundaries of enactment; then describe its clinical manifestations, overuse and vicissitudes in different schools of psychoanalytic thought; and conclude with some summarizing comments. My goal is to provide a step towards clarification and consistency of discourse, not to attempt the final word on the topic. In psychoanalysis, as in all other disciplines, there never has been, and never will be, a final word on any topic.

ON CONCEPTUAL BOUNDARIES

It is most useful when enactment is not considered just another term for what Freud called acting out, or for what is sometimes called acting in when referring to events within the analytic session. Freud (1914) used 'acting out' to refer to instances when memories were performed in current life rather than remembered. He saw this performance as a sign of resistance on the one hand, and of the need to repeat on the other.

Freud emphasized the therapeutic importance of recovering early patho-genic memories. That recovery was to be effected by reducing infantile amnesia through the analysis of resistance (Freud 1912). Freud never relinquished this emphasis on the curative power of remembering. His topographic model of mental functioning, neurosogenesis and the analytic process had a permanent, although not exclusive, hold on his thinking (see for example his 'Outline of psycho-analysis', 1940).

Later on, 'acting out' has been carelessly used by some analysts and others to imply being bad, specifically by getting oneself, the analyst or the analysis into administrative, emotional or legal difficulties. On the whole, this corruption of analytic meaning does not seem to have affected the current usage of 'enactment' – although history warns us to be ready for that eventuality.

The vocabulary of enactment is also not identical with others that have developed around well-established psychoanalytic concepts. One of these concepts is 'character', when the word is used to refer to habitual modes of action that will show up in the analytic relationship as they do elsewhere. 'Character', however, is a rather general term; in addition, unlike enactment, it refers to established traits rather than to processes, positions, or scenarios that are constantly in flux. Thus it does not address itself as finely as enactment to the nuances of the immediate give-and-take in the analytic situation.

Another well-established term to consider here is 'repetition'. This term, however, tends to be so centred on the idea of an independently operating compulsion that it, too, can blur the analytic focus on the complexity of the here-and-now engagement of the two parties to the analysis. Still another term, 'compromise formation', is oriented far more to impulse–defence conflict and its outcome within the mind than it is to the object-relational playing out of issues.

Then there is 'nonverbal communication': used especially by the Kleinian analysts to characterize many enactments, this term sometimes seems to have been extended too far, in that it considers occurrences that have never been established in the analytic dialogue as having the intent of communication. In these instances, the phenomena are interpretable enough to be brought into the analysis by the perceptive analyst; however, it does not make matters clearer when we equate the interpretability of nonverbal phenomena with communicative enactments.

Enactment is perhaps closest to the idea of participation. 'Participation' implies that, even when analysands seem most unresponsive or uncommuni-cative, they may still be viewed as participating in the analytic process. For example, instead of thinking that analysands are psychically dead, or too resistant to do analytic work, or simply paralysed by anxiety – any of which is a static and probably essentialist trait characterization – the analyst may view them as participating in the analysis in a manner that is deadening, restrictive or frightened to the extreme. In other words, they may be viewed as engaged in actions relevant to the treatment even when they are most inactive. This perspective is analytically affirmative rather than negative, and is frequently more effective in initiating and sustaining collaborative analytic work (Schafer 1976, 1983).

ON IDENTIFYING ENACTMENTS

The analyst identifies enactments through close analysis of the moment-to-moment interplay of language, physical movement, emotional expression, associative content and already established dynamic context. Correlatively, the interpretation of enactments is oriented primarily to the present rather than to the past. This way of working defers explicit interpretations about the past and does not necessarily cast present-oriented interpretations in language that refers to typical infantile prototypes, such as the Oedipal triangle. To begin with, the analyst might refer only to an emotional atmosphere of coldness or defensiveness or solicitousness. It is the phenomenology far more than the explanation or cause that is to be worked out as fully as possible before going any further. The analyst does not want to presume too much or get too far ahead of the analysand, and certainly the analyst wants to avoid playing the role of the omniscient healer. Thus the idea of enactment is that of a vehicle for always keeping alive the questions:

- What is going on here right now?
- What am I being told indirectly or being shown concerning the patient's way of experiencing this moment in the analytic relationship or of trying to structure it?
- How might I be stimulating or supporting that performance?

The analyst, of course, always makes his or her own contribution to any countertransference enactment, and, in extreme instances, that contribution may far outweigh the analysand's and therefore not lead to understanding and useful interpretation. In the main, however, the analyst is regarded as a sensitive, responsive listener in whom a variety of reactions may be stimulated and who can observe these reactions and put them to good interpretive use by clarifying the analysand's role in bringing them about. In this latter regard, the analyst's countertransference enactments have been attributed either to the analysand's projective identifications (a Kleinian emphasis) or to what Sandler (1976) called role-responsiveness, regarded as the analyst's participation in 'actualizing' unconscious phantasies (1987). In either case, the analyst may be viewed as complying with an unspoken need for manipulation; both the need for manipulation and the response to it take place more or less unconsciously.

With this general understanding, the analyst is technically prepared to identify enactments. And the heightened attention to the present moment works against untimely, exclusive, possibly avoidant and intellectualized preoccupation with the past or with current matters far removed from immediate transference–countertransference interactions.

We cannot, however, fix 'enactment' in one place for ever. It is not possible to establish permanently the meaning of any psychoanalytic term, or of any other term for that matter. Meanings evolve in psychoanalysis as they do in law: terms take on meaning as cases are processed and decisions rendered; to begin with, they are virtually empty vessels waiting to be filled and refilled by a more or less changing history of usage and challenge.

Consequently, both what I have already summarized about the meaning of the term 'enactment' and what I shall go on to say about it cannot claim to settle anything permanently.

Nor can a term be fixed in just one place, even at a given moment. As soon as we reflect on what is being enacted, we come face-to-face with the recognition that what seems to be a simple matter of perception is controlled, even if not fully determined, by preferred interpretive storylines (Schafer 1992). These storylines, derived from master narratives, tell us how to conceive of unconscious mental functioning and unconscious intersubjectivity. For example, we may prefer to think in the traditional metapsychological manner of defences struggling to ward off impulses and ending up in compromise formations; we may prefer to think of shifts between paranoid-schizoid and depressive positions (Segal 1964), of fluctuations in the states of cohesiveness of the self (Kohut 1977) or of changes in the 'representational world' of self, objects and their relationships that the ego, as one of its functions, builds up and then uses in constructing all-new emotional-cognitive experience (Sandler and Rosenblatt 1962). When we do confront this recognition, we realize that we must give up the assumption that what we do when we analyse is *un*cover or *dis*cover or *re*cover what is already there in fully developed form. Instead, we are prepared to assume that there is little or nothing that exists 'out there' in a well-formed manner. It does not exist until it is brought into being and given a shape by an act of naming and characterization within some kind of psychoanalytic context and ongoing dialogue. For example, the analytic observer, in dialogue with the analysand, constructs a version of the analysand's representational world and its constructive principles.

Thus, as analytic data, enactments must be regarded as constructions. One analyst might say to an analysand who, at that moment, is acting in a clinging manner, 'You are showing me your anxiety about not controlling me totally'; another might say about that same moment, 'You are frightened that I may try to seduce you if you appear more womanly to me'; a third might say, 'You are building a wall of anxiety around yourself to preclude, through your appearance of fragility, yet another shattering experience at my hands'; while a fourth might say, 'You must be seeing yourself as altogether helpless in relation to me right now'. All four are interpretations of one enactment – a clinging manner – and each may elicit a different response that further defines or clarifies all that is being enacted in that analytic moment.

Viewed in its most general sense, enactment has always been a significant item in psychoanalytic interpretation. In his early writings, for instance, Freud discussed the motoric betrayal of secrets by patients (Breuer and Freud 1893–5). Yet there has been an evolution in understanding and technique in this respect. Now there are many more options regarding how to interpret enactments and how much emphasis to put on them. In other words, as we attempt to develop or drive home an interpretation and then to work it through, we know and accept that we have available different ways of characterizing the momentary total situation and relationship. We are always engaged in construction.

Perception itself is a constructive activity, so that what people say they see, however well their seeing conforms to convention, is no more than one possible version, and there is no final answer to the question of what it is a version of because any other statement is itself a version. Even what I called 'clinging' in my earlier example is a version; it could have been put otherwise, as we see when we consider the kinds of redescriptions that the analyst's comments imply. There is no perception, therefore, that can escape this constructivist viewpoint. The case is the same and even more compelling when we think of interpretation. On this basis, we are better prepared now to show how, again and again and in many modalities, the analysand is showing as well as telling (or showing instead of telling) the same conflict, the same feeling of alienation, the same compromise, or whatever. We do strive, of course, to be in tune, but we do not idealize exactness or exclusiveness once we understand that we are working with only one of a number of possible versions of what is taking place.

ON THE OVERUSE OF 'ENACTMENT'

It is possible to overemphasize both transference and countertransference enactments. Enactment is sometimes used in relation to the analysand as though it applies to any analytic material that can be interpreted as having transference significance. That this amounts to overuse can be recognized once we realize that it renders the term superfluous, if not meaningless; enactment then has become a synonym for being in analysis. When things reach that pass, one knows that the analytic discourse is being controlled by fashion rather than by thought-through understanding. Certainly, a dream, a memory or a comment about the analyst can be part of an enactment, but it can be more useful in many instances when viewed simply as additional analytic material available for understanding and interpretation.

With regard to countertransference, similar problems arise, although with an added problematic twist. For sometimes analysts seem to feel licensed to be freely and demonstratively responsive to an analysand's manipulations; they participate in this way on the assumption that this is what analysis is all about and that it can be made into a valuable source of information and remediation through later understanding and interpretation. What may happen instead, however, is that the analyst's loose rein on his or her acting out (in the old sense) confirms the analysand's unconscious fantasies to such an extent that subsequent interpretation will seem to the patient to amount to little more than a confession of guilt, an attempt at further seduction, a cover-up, or something that extends the enactment rather than explains it.

Whatever the case may be, then, interpretation becomes progressively less influential. Too much reality confirmation cannot be undone by interpretation, and by 'too much' I refer not only to numerous instances but also to one serious or traumatic enactment, of the order of a sexual approach or a scathing denunciation.

ON BEING COMMITTED TO ONE SCHOOL OF THOUGHT

The emphasis on countertransference enactment has developed particularly in connection with attempts to begin and continue analytic work with exceptionally difficult cases. These cases may be those that are either stagnating or, frequently, in explosive or life-threatening states. Once we have been trained and have gathered some experience, however, we are never entirely without interpretive resources or the capacity for suspended judgement. Our analytic resources are embodied in expectations of what we are likely to encounter, in the sense of readiness to articulate or modify these expectations step-by-step as the analytic work proceeds, all with a reasonable sense of assurance that it will be possible to do further sorting out of the important issues later. In these ways, analysts never approach a clinical situation from scratch. At the same time, the history of our field shows that these aspects of preparedness do not preclude surprise, revision, or the development of new ideas and techniques.

An essential resource in this regard is one's readiness to orient oneself on the basis of commitment to a single school of analytic thought. The school of thought provides the theoretical guidelines or the interpretive storylines of analytic work. The boundaries between schools of analysis are not altogether sharp, but neither are they unknown or easily breached in either direction. Some analysts have played down the importance of these guidelines or storylines and these boundaries, so that they draw on a number of schools of thought in interpreting enactments. Their doing so gives some cause for unease, for they may be manifesting a form of intellectual claustrophobia, rebelliousness or confused understanding, and dressing it up as an assertion of flexibility, spontaneity, and even an implied assertion of romantic individualism. It then begins to seem that doing analysis is perhaps being equated with one's own lifestyle.

This questionable free-spiritedness raises an epistemological and methodological set of problems, too, for it is inherently positivistic in a naive way. In effect, it asserts the outmoded idea of being 'natural'. This idea depends on the notion that there are essences out there that are simply waiting to be uncovered, discovered or recovered, and that they are better revealed when there are no strong pre-existing commitments to get in the way. Acceptance of the ideas of the constructivist nature of perception and interpretation and of the multiple options available for developing one or another version of the analytic moment, does not allow any implication that one truly gets at the essence of the one-and-only reality that there is to deal with (Schafer 1992).

CONCLUDING COMMENTS

The long history of the term 'enactment' within psychoanalysis has been registered under a variety of partly overlapping names and has been placed within a variety of overlapping contexts. Analysts have always been interpreting enactments, although less so on the side of countertransference in the past than they do now. At least they have been in a position to interpret both types of enactments (see for example Fenichel 1941).

Changes have taken place, however, most particularly:

1   Closer attention is paid now to how, unconsciously, the analyst may be drawn into an enactment through changes in the countertransference that have been more or less induced by the analysand.

2   Greater emphasis is usually placed on the present moment than on reconstruction.

3   There is greater acceptance of the idea that the analyst's participation in enactments is an inescapable part of any analytic endeavour, although it is not, on that account, to be recommended or treated casually.

4   It is more clearly recognized that, inevitably, the specification of what is being enacted or jointly enacted is strongly influenced by the interpretive story lines of the school of analysis to which one is primarily allied.

5   Analysts who freely shift among the interpretive lines of different schools of analysis arouse three sets of suspicions:

    (a) their demonstrations of learnedness and authenticity may amount to little more than intellectualized expressions of claustrophobia, rebelliousness, or confusion;

    (b) they are subscribing in an epistemologically naive way to a simple form of positivistic thinking that is allegedly theory-free; and

    (c) they have an inadequate grasp of the entailments, the more or less well-defined and system-bound theoretical and technical terms and tactics. On whatever basis, one must consider whether some countertransference enactment is involved in this allegedly free-spirited flexibility. Admittedly, it is not always easy to differentiate analytically what is excessive from what is different, unexpected, or creative work in a new mode. Here again we should not rush to analytic judgement.

REFERENCES

Breuer, J. and Freud, S. (1893–5) 'Studies on hysteria', *Standard Edition*, vol. 2 (1955), London: Hogarth Press, vii–xxxi, 1–311.

Fenichel, O. (1941) *Problems of Psychoanalytic Technique*, New York: Psychoanalytic Quarterly Press.

Freud, S. (1912) 'The dynamics of transference', *Standard Edition*, vol. 12 (1958), London: Hogarth Press, 97–108.

——(1914) 'Remembering, repeating, and working-through (further recommendations on the technique of psychoanalysis II)', *Standard Edition*, vol. 12 (1958), London: Hogarth Press, 145–56.

——(1940) 'An outline of psycho-analysis', *Standard Edition*, vol. 23 (1964), London: Hogarth Press, 139–207.

Kohut, H. (1977) *The Restoration of the Self*, New York: International Universities Press.

Sandler, J. (1976) 'Countertransference and role-responsiveness', *International Review of Psycho-Analysis*, 3, 43–8.

Sandler, J. (ed.) (1987) *Projection, Identification, Projective Identification*, Madison CT: International Universities Press.

Sandler, J. and Rosenblatt, B. (1962) 'The concept of the representational world', *Psychoanalytic Study of the Child*, 17, 128–45.

Schafer, R. (1976) *A New Language for Psychoanalysis*, New Haven CT: Yale University Press.

——(1983) *The Analytic Attitude*, New York: Basic Books.

——(1992) *Retelling a Life: Narration and Dialogue in Psychoanalysis*, New York: Basic Books.

Segal, H. (1964) *Introduction to the Work of Melanie Klein*, New York: Basic Books.

6

IMPORTANCE OF NARCISSISTIC CATHEXES IN THE EARLIEST ASPECTS OF THE OBJECT RELATIONSHIP

Serge Lebovici (translated by Philip Slotkin)

THE GENESIS OF MENTAL REPRESENTATIONS

The latest clinical and psychoanalytic research shows that the early develop-ment of mental representations can be understood only in terms of the competence of newborn babies and of very young infants to form for themselves a representation of the maternal care they receive. In particular, they draw on a rich, if dispersed, sensoriality, which tends to become bound up in the repetition of daily experiences charged with emotional exchanges (Lebovici 1983; Sameroff and Emde 1989; Stern 1985).

The basis for this understanding, it will be seen, is a body of research whose fundamental hypotheses diverge from Freud's theory of the genesis of the representation of the object. The basic hypothesis of classical analysis is the oral dependence of the neonate, whose initial helplessness ('Hilflosigkeit') demands the assumption of the child's complete union with the maternal caregiver. For Freud, this union is quickly called into question: the baby is confronted with mini-separations, with which it copes by means of oral autoerotism, thereby reactivating the memory traces laid down as engrams stemming from experiences of the satisfaction of feeding needs. The lack of a breast creates the wish for a breast: the baby hallucinates the pleasure before forming a representation of the desired breast. As Freud wrote in 1925, 'There are [thus] good reasons why a child sucking at his mother's breast has become the prototype of every relation of love. The finding of an object is in fact a refinding of it' (Freud 1905: note in the 1925 edition, 222). To illustrate my own conceptualization of the genesis of mental representations prior to the perception of objects for the purpose of representing them, I wrote that the mother is cathected before she is perceived (Lebovici 1960). This has often been quoted in the French literature.

The thesis that a theory of development attempts to illustrate is, in fact, based on the theory of the mutual attachment between the baby and its caregivers. Bowlby showed the importance in all mammalian species of the urge for close physical contact between the young and their caregivers. This interaction assumes meaning through the relationship that gives rise to object representations, by virtue of the remarkably early representations of care received, facilitated by the mother's premature interpretation. This occurs, for example, when a three-week-old baby stretches out his arms to his mother, who brings him close (a foot away) so that he can see her. The mother takes the baby in her arms because she thinks (premature interpretation) that this is what the infant wants. Nothing of the sort, comments Bowlby, who describes the baby's reaching movement as a mere phylogenetic survival response harking back to the way a young primate runs to its mother or mother substitute and clings to her fur. This movement, interpreted by mothers whose babies are by nature unable to move, constitutes a paradigm of Imre Hermann's (1943) thesis concerning the clinging instinct. The essential point seems to be that, three weeks later, babies will stretch out their arms to their mother when they hear her voice, thereby demonstrating ability to combine different sensory representations of maternal care.

So it is, then, that the fabric of mental life is woven through interactions. For the time being, we shall merely show that these representations of care accumulate, eventually constituting − especially during the baby's calm waking periods − representations of the mother, whose degree of elaboration increases as such exchanges are encouraged by their frequency and regularity, particularly when they take place in a climate of 'affective attunement' (Stern 1985). We shall also see how, by virtue of the meaning of the care she supplies, the mother is also concerning herself with a child that she imagines: her imaginary child of fantasy (Lebovici 1983). In other words, the 'eventualities' that occur during the course of this care take on the significance of events that constitute the first scenarios (or 'scripts') that might become the subject of subsequent narrations by the person who was that baby.

However, before embarking on this description, whereby an intersubjective and intrasubjective meaning will be conferred on this interactive life, we must try to determine the baby's active role in the genesis of mental life through his own actions − in my view, the essence of his contribution. In other words, we shall attempt to show that a baby's activity also tends to 'parentalize' the parents. I would now add the following phrase to my 1960 aphorism: 'and the baby thereby *makes* of his mother a *MOTHER*'.

A good paradigm for our purposes is Winnicott's (1967) paper, 'Mirror-role of mother and family in child development'. He writes (112):

What does the baby see when he or she looks at the mother's face? ... Ordinarily, what the baby sees is himself or herself. In other words, the mother is looking at the baby and what she looks like is related to what she sees there.

A few pages later, Winnicott says (114):

I refer here ... to the exasperating and skilful and challenging artist of our time [Francis Bacon] who goes on and on painting the human face distorted significantly. From the standpoint of this chapter, this Francis Bacon of today's date is seeing himself in his mother's face, but with some twist in him or her that maddens both him and us.

A few lines earlier, he had written (113): 'when the average girl studies her face in the mirror, she is reassuring herself that the mother-image is there and that the mother can see her and that the mother is *en rapport* with her'.

We customarily assign emblematic value to this paper by Winnicott, which I suggest can be summarized as follows: *When a baby looks into his mother's eyes, he sees two things: first, the mother's pupils; second, the mother looking at him. In other words, the mother sees her baby and looks at her baby looking at her, hence proclaiming her to be mother.* This allegory, with its emblematic and paradigmatic value, poses the problem of the being in the world that this baby is, and induces us to inquire as to the origin of the baby's activity – that is, the nature of its self.

THE GENESIS OF THE PROCESS
OF SUBJECTIVIZATION

Freud urged us to study the psyche in topographic terms; in his second topography – which American authors call the structural version and which is composed of the three agencies of the id, the ego, and the superego – there is no need to invoke the 'subject' of one's acts or thoughts. Oddly enough, however, Freud had suggested to 'his Princess', his favourite student and follower in France, Marie Bonaparte, that she should recommend to the nomenclature committee of the Paris Psychoanalytical Society that the German word *Ich* be translated by *Moi* and *Es* by *Soi*.[1] French psychoanalysts have, in fact, recently begun to distinguish between the *Moi* and the *Je*: the former denotes the ego of the second topography, while the latter seems equivalent to the self (*Soi* in French) – that is, the subject, the actor of one's thoughts or actions. Sandler (1987: 82) also discusses the semantic problems presented by Freud's use of the concept of the 'ego ideal':

James Strachey, in his editorial introductions to 'On narcissism' and *The Ego and the Id*, points out that the meaning that Freud attached to *das Ich* underwent a gradual modification: 'At first', says Strachey, 'he used the term without any great precision, as we might speak of "the self" '. Strachey also points out, in his introduction to the later paper, that 'it seems possible to detect two main uses, one in which the term distinguishes a person's self as a whole ...'

Sandler (1987: 77–8) therefore first demonstrates the relative ambiguity of the concept of the ego ideal:

> In 'On narcissism' (1914) and the *Introductory Lectures* (1916–1917), the term was used to refer to the individual's ideal for himself, constructed as a consequence of his efforts to regain infantile narcissism. It was here distinguished from the self-observing and critical agency, the conscience.

Sandler continues (78):

> In the *New Introductory Lectures* (1933), the superego is referred to as the 'vehicle of the ego ideal'. This usage was foreshadowed in 1924 in 'The economic problem of masochism', in which Freud noted that 'the ego reacts with feelings of anxiety ... to the perception that it has not come up to the demands of its ideal, the superego'. The use of the term 'ideal' here refers to the ideal parents as embodied in the superego.

The concept of the 'self' has indeed been used in two senses in the English-language psychoanalytic literature:

1   The American ego-psychology school (H. Hartmann) grew out of Anna Freud's studies of ego development: the ego, like the id, stems from a common source, the self in which the primitive unconscious and its three agencies, the id, the ego, and the superego, are organized.
2   Winnicott was probably the first to use the term 'self' in a different sense from the American school. For him, the psychic object exists both in its perceived reality *and* in its unconscious representations and the fantasies that represent it.

Although differing from Melanie Klein, Winnicott does not confuse the object with the scenarios in which it is evoked, but tends rather to contrast self and object. The self, in his view, is constituted because the attacks on the object also give rise to a depressive state (rather than a depressive stage). This state, he holds, convinces the child of her existence and helps to enable her to achieve a sense of continuity of psychic life; it is an unconscious state. I do not wish to give an excessively personal interpretation of Winnicott's theories, which are elastic enough to permit many readings, but, as is so often the case, it must be acknowledged that the avenues opened up by Winnicott were promising.

When Kohut developed his theory of the self in the United States, it caused a scandal. He believed he could show – initially for technical reasons – that the Oedipal interpretation of transference conflicts might prove fruitless because of 'grandiose' narcissistic cathexes (Kohut 1971). Although this first book interested many analysts, it must be admitted that the technical considerations developed in his last work are difficult to follow and seem tantamount to an abandonment of psychoanalysis (Kohut 1984).

Be that as it may, Kohut proposed that cathexis of the object should be distinguished from that of the self or, in his terms, of the 'self-object'; this term was intended to denote the cases in which the object of the self is the self itself. This notion is surely not far from Freud's own idea, developed in his study of secondary narcissism (Freud 1913) in which he assigned different fates to the libido according to whether it invested the object or was turned back on the ego. However, Freud admittedly retained the opposition between the libido and the ego instincts. Freud's theory describes, first of all, primary narcissism, a boundary concept postulated on the initial helplessness of the newborn infant, who is totally dependent on maternal care, and whose union with it causes the baby to disregard anything in his body that is distinct from that care. This situation gives rise to a feeling of omnipotence that combines total impotence with the self-sufficiency of a living being who does not experience any need external to himself. To this concept of primary narcissism, clinical and therapeutic experience opposes secondary narcissism, which invests the subject with wishes or turns back on itself. The sequence corresponding to this theory may be described as follows: from primary narcissism to autoerotism to secondary narcissism.

Later, seeking greater consistency in his hypotheses on the role of the erotogenic zones that reactivate the memory traces of experiences of need satisfaction so as to allow the hallucination of pleasure, Freud came to place the autoerotisms at the root of narcissism and of object cathexis, as illustrated in Figure 6.1.

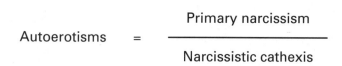

$$\text{Autoerotisms} \quad = \quad \frac{\text{Primary narcissism}}{\text{Narcissistic cathexis}}$$

Figure 6.1   The relationship of primary narcissism and narcissistic cathexis

In the context of these successive descriptions, Green (1983) used the term 'antinarcissism' to describe the situation when the libido turns back on the ego, and contrasted the 'narcissism of life' with the 'narcissism of death' (or negative narcissism): 'Unlike the former, whose aim is the fulfilment of the ego, the latter tends to abolish the ego in its aspiration to nothingness' (Green 1983: 4).

For their part, Sandler's contributions (1987) emphasize the relationships between the self ideal and persons encountered in life, but, of course, in the form of identification with an ideal, admired object (or a feared object, as in the case of identification with the aggressor). Here the admired object may be internalized or met with in the present environment; it may be a child as desired by the admired objects; or, finally, it may be the self ideal as constructed in the past. These proposals are clearly consistent with the development of Sandler's thought, as featured, for example, in contributions dating from 1986 and 1987, wherein he asserts that we have not only an unconscious structure founded in the past, but also an unconscious structure oriented towards the present.

Nevertheless, the kinship between what cannot possibly be classified among the psychic agencies and secondary narcissism once again appears clear and indeed obvious; there is no point in adducing large numbers of confirmatory examples. What we need to examine is the particular slant of the 'self' of the American school of psychoanalysts. This is most clearly reflected in the work of Sameroff and Emde (1989). For these analysts, steeped in experimental research, the self is another unconscious that characterizes the functioning of our nervous system; it is the 'third unconscious', in addition to the unconscious system and unconscious acts and thoughts. The unconscious system is characterized by the fact that our nervous and cognitive functioning is *not conscious*. It is true that our thought operations are not organized in clear consciousness. Emde (1988) often refers to the programmed aspects of this system, which he describes as being rooted in the earliest social relationships; this leads him to refer to early morality and the sense of 'we-ness', which, in his view, ought to be studied along with the first rudiments of ego. It is perhaps legitimate to think that Winnicott might have accepted such proposals when he described the self as a sense of the continuity of existence. Perhaps Freud himself would not have rejected these views, considering as he did that the ego was initially established on bodily foundations.

However, some authors describe the organization of the nervous system on the basis of its self-organization, and consequently invoke a biological self: each individual confronts biology with the question of the influences determining the selection of potentialities on the level of the nervous system and the cognitive apparatus. The specific activity of the system brings about a selection of synaptic functioning (Changeux and Danchin 1976). This 'selectionistic' model postulates the existence of a direct relationship between nervous activity and the way it organizes the maturation of the brain.

> This would lead to the hypothesis that the individual constructs himself biologically (and psychologically) by his own activity from the material supplied at birth. This hypothesis of a *self-organization* (in the sense of a self-selection) could constitute an approach to the relations between biology and psychology.
>
> (Hochmann and Jeannerod 1991: 127–8)

Of course, such an hypothesis does not reveal the nervous system's motive for seeking to achieve efficacy. Many years ago Mourgue and von Monakow (1928) proposed a quasi-Freudian hypothesis to the effect that the organism expresses itself by 'instincts', which pursue often-unconscious tendencies towards creation: the 'formative' instinct, which protects the organs of our body; the instinct of preservation, which protects the child's interests; the sexual instinct, which protects the interests of the family; and the social instinct, which protects the interests of humankind.

These speculations are connected with my own concerns in the study of the self, developed here, suggesting possibilities of transduction between theories of the self-organization of the nervous system and of the psyche. These theories are helpful today when we attempt to understand the genesis of intersubjectivity, which the cognitivists explained by the theoretical invocation of the theory of mind (Baron-Cohen, as quoted in Frith 1989). A theory of this kind assumes that the process of subjectivization includes a decisive moment, when the young child ascribes mental functioning to the other – a cognitive capability lacking in an autistic child. This paradigm of autism may be a meeting point between the cognitivistic approach and the psychoanalytic study of access to symbolic thought. We shall return later to the form assumed by the beginnings of intrapsychic and intersubjective mental life, which is, of course, a decisive moment in the evolution of the process of subjectivization. For the time being, we need stress only that the description of a biological self (or biological unconscious) is not inconsistent with the biological and cognitivistic approach to psychic life.

Similar hypotheses can be found in Jung's theories (see Fordham 1969) on the role of what he also calls the self, the dynamic organization of the foundations of mental functioning examined from the point of view of what is intuitive and thought.

Hence all theoretical studies of the genesis of mental life invoke a system of subjectivization, the self, which is not an agency as described by Freud[2] but rather the subject of action and thought as opposed to the object. It is not only a modulator of narcissism, but also a force that prompts acts and thinking. Nor shall we dwell on the fact that Winnicott considered the self to be revealed only by its expression in the 'false self', whose clinical manifestations reflected its submission to the maternal object cathected by the wish, not to conquer it, but to respond to its care by submission (Miller 1981).

Other authors have made clinical contributions to this study as well. In regard to the kinship between borderline pathology and the tribulations of narcissism, Cahn (1991) described the pathology 'of the subject'; Misès (1992) published a book on borderline states in children; and McDougall (1985: 12–13) warned that

> failures ... are sometimes due to the far-reaching effects of parents' unconscious problems, as well as inherent fragilities in certain children. If parents' internal dramas drive them to use their children – either their bodies or their minds – to settle scores with the past and repair their own narcissistic images or damaged libidinal relationships, the megalomaniac small child is not likely to receive the help required to find solutions to the inevitable traumas of human life. For it is parents who give their children a sense of self, enjoyment in their individuality, masculinity and femininity, and the right to enjoy as fully as possible all aspects of adult life.

These few lines invite us to take a closer look at the process of subjectivization.

THE PROCESS OF SUBJECTIVIZATION

Our task is ultimately to understand the fate of narcissistic cathexes in the evolution of the transactions between the baby and those who raise him or her.

Mother (or father)

The 'carers' act in a climate charged with emotions that are often in harmony; they hold in their arms an 'imagined' child, which involves their preconscious lives and the reveries therein rendered latent by their wish for pregnancy: the child has already been seen in ultrasound scans; in 75 per cent of cases, the gender is known; and the chosen first name is meaningful in terms of intergenerational transmission. The other child is the 'fantasy' child that is the product of the wish for motherhood and the wish for a child; it reflects the unconscious residues of infantile conflicts (Lebovici 1983). Laplanche (1991) mentions a generalized seduction by the mother in the course of her caring for the child. He considers that she introduces her infantile sexuality (and her culture) into her caring activity in the form of what he calls 'enigmatic signifiers'. Freud had emphasized the mother's narcissistic cathexis of her baby: the mother, especially during her first pregnancy, needs first and foremost to proclaim that she is proud of having fulfilled her wish for pregnancy, during the first three months of which obscurity reigns and the imaginary child is not yet cathected narcissistically. However, everyone knows how essential this narcissistic cathexis is as an aspect of both parents' love for their child; it protects them from their ambivalence towards the third baby they are carrying in their bodies, and later in their arms, which their narcissistic cathexis makes more acceptable: namely, the child of reality.

Baby

Pre-perceptions arise by virtue of the baby's competencies, which she acquires by use of proprioception (Stern 1985). However, as we have seen at length, the infant deploys narcissism (her self) on her parents and then recathects herself, for example in sleep, replete with the satisfactions received: the baby can dream and wake up 'calm and peaceful', ready to engage in new performances, which are interpreted prematurely by the mother in the deployment of her own narcissism. We therefore consider it reasonable to emphasize the role of narcissistic transactions in the interactive process.

As we have seen, the baby's self reflects the parent she 'sees': during the first weeks of life, babies whose heads are no longer supported by their parents as a precaution fix their own eyes on their mother's eyes, which they 'see' before them at a distance of one foot: they see their mother's pupils.

From the age of three months, interpersonal relationships may be said to exist between a self and maternal care: babies see their mothers looking at them. The child then perceives the specificity of the person of the mother; he gives her a role and ascribes intentions towards himself to her (theory of mind): the child sees that his mother is looking at him; his representations of the mother allow him to move on from the triadic situation of semantic and procedural memory[3] to the beginnings of Oedipal triangulation – the mother has a love object other than the child, namely the mother's husband, the father (phobia of the stranger's face). Symbolic thought is now in operation. Mental and psychic life may be said to exist in terms of the three agencies of Freudian metapsychology and of intersubjective relationships.

In my view, however, these interactive transactions must also be charged with fantasies ('fantasy interactions', Lebovici 1983). The interactions become charged in their monotony with 'scenarios', in which 'eventualities' take on the significance of 'events', which will constitute the foundations of what Stern (1993) suggests should be called 'proto-narrative envelopes'. These will call on the resources of semantic memory and procedure. These scenarios will contribute to the creation of unconscious or preconscious fantasies.[4]

In a later psychoanalysis, these narrations would appear as evidence of the power experienced by the baby to influence her parents; the self could thus be likened to an interactive network constructed through narcissistic exchanges. Another hypothesis is that changes in narcissistic cathexes are the fruit of interactions.

Even if the self appears as the fruit of the self-organization of the functioning of the nervous system and of psychic life, it appears, too, as the fruit of the expansion of the parents' narcissism – the fruit of an encounter. Jeammet (1993: 87) tells the story of Moses' quest for God as interpreted in the Talmud, which, in my view, is an image of narcissistic interactive relationships:

> Every encounter changes us, causing a little of the other to enter ourselves; it renews our vision, increasing our capacities for openness and desire, telling us, every time in slightly different terms, of an Other, whose absence is experienced more and more clearly as close to the image of a presence.

Jeammet adds: 'Moses says to God: "Who am I?", to seek Pharaoh and to allow the Children of Israel to depart from Egypt. God says: "I shall be with you" ' (98).

God also says: 'I am that I am.' 'However accurate and important it may be, this translation, which overvalues transcendental immutability, becomes, when understood as one of the aspects of the Name, a pure misinterpretation when divorced from a relational perspective' (Jeammet 1993: 111).

This allegory speaks eloquently: Moses looked for God and made him into God. But God had chosen Moses. The baby sees her mother, Winnicott tells us; but the mother's face is looking at her (the baby). The baby sees her mother looking at her (she found a mother because she sees her mother looking at her), but proclaims her to be mother *because the mother sees that her baby is looking at her seeing the baby looking at her.*

WHAT ABOUT ME, OR I MYSELF?

'What about me?', demands a child who feels neglected.

'I myself', interjects a French colleague in a discussion to which he is eager to contribute.

In both of these situations, the person speaking obviously wishes to manifest his presence and hence his existence. In this chapter, I have sought the origins of this demand to exist. I have tried to show that this demand is less necessary the more each person's existence is assured by the acceptance of the other, who is himself allowed to exist by virtue of the existence of his self, a self that enables him to facilitate the existence of whoever asks him to be allowed to exist. But anyone who makes the demand 'What about me?' has a sense of his own existence only if he sees that existence acknowledged in the mirror held up to him by the other.

This mirror game reminds us of the nymph Echo, reduced to turning herself into a rock that sent back the voice of Narcissus, who, gazing at himself in the water where he claimed to be seeking her, could see only his own reflection. Admittedly, Narcissus perished, lost in contemplation of himself.

An illuminating scene in Gaston Chéreau's Bayreuth production of *Die Walküre* is when Wotan has had to yield to the mundane demands of his wife Fricka and abandon the defence of his son Siegmund. Wotan gives an account of his life to his daughter Brünnhilde, to whom he must explain his abdication, but instead of speaking to her directly, he tells his story in front of a mirror, in which he can see not only her but also his own decrepitude.

The three-year-old who demands 'What about me!!?' must have passed through many relational and cognitive stages before he is able to insist on his place in the sun. He has to be sure of his ability to identify with his self ideal and his 'aggressor'. However, with the limitations of guilt and shame, he knows that the future can belong to him. He also requires an assured foundation of narcissism in order to have laid down a self and a subjectivity for himself. When assured of his identity, he will be able, not to demand, but to request: 'What about me?'

An adult who says 'I myself' demands everything here and now, everything right away and on the spot. He is surely suffering in his narcissistic assurance; his process of subjectivization has been disturbed in the narcissistic interactions and transactions with parents whose unresolved infantile conflicts have made sure of the intergenerational transmission of this wounded narcissism: their *arbor vitae* (tree of life) gives rise to a verticalized filiation, which stands in the way of an assured affiliation to their culture.

I wonder whether social peace throughout the world might not be better achieved through the preventive measure of bi-generational exchange in all cultures, whereby parent and child confront the infant's narcissism within each culture. Such a perspective might be preferable to the present focus on multiculturalism, whereby each culture is, in theory at least, encouraged to retain its own identity (cf. Lebovici 1993).

NOTES

1 Freud's paper 'Das Ich und das Es' was therefore first translated into French as 'Le Moi et le Soi', before this was corrected to 'Le Ça et le Moi'. On this point, Laplanche and Pontalis (1967: 58) write: '*Das Es* is rendered in the first French translations as *le Soi*. This translation also appears, albeit more seldom, in the work of certain French authors; the word *soi* tends to be reserved for the English *self* or the German *das Selbst*'.

2 Grunberger (1971), however, makes narcissism the fourth agency.

3 Long-term memory includes two mechanisms: semantic memory and procedural or episodic memory. The latter includes more events in time and space with an important affective connotation; the former is linked more to general knowledge,

is less connected with the personal past, and is essentially based on cognitive aptitude.

4 Those that Sandler would presumably classify among the fantasies of the past, which must be reconstituted, and those of the 'present unconscious'.

REFERENCES

Cahn, R. (1991) 'Du sujet (rapport au 51ème Congrès des psychanalystes de langue Française des Pays Romans)' ('On the subject [lecture given at the 51st Congress of French speaking psychoanalysts of Roman Countries]'), *Bulletin de la Société Psychanalytique de Paris* (*Bulletin of the Paris Psychoanalytic Society*), 19, 1–103.

Changeux, J. P. and Danchin, A. (1976) 'Selective stabilization of developing synapses as a mechanism for the specification of neuronal networks', *Nature*, 264, 706–12.

Emde, R. N. (1988) 'Development terminable and interminable: innate and motivational factors from infancy', *International Journal of Psycho-Analysis*, 69 (1), 23–42.

Fordham, M. (1969) *Children as Individuals*, London: Hodder & Stoughton.

Freud, S. (1905) 'Three essays on the theory of sexuality', *Standard Edition*, vol. 7 (1953), London: Hogarth Press, 123–245.

——(1913) 'On narcissism: an introduction', *Standard Edition*, vol. 14 (1953) London: Hogarth Press, 69–102.

Frith, U. (1989) *Autism: Explaining an Enigma*, London: Blackwell.

Green, A. (1983) *Narcissisme de Vie, Narcissisme de Mort* (*Life Narcissism, Death Narcissism*), Paris: Editions de Minuit.

Grunberger, B. (1971) *Le Narcissisme*, Paris: Payot.

Hermann, I. (1943) *L'Instinct Filial*, Paris: Payot, 1971.

Hochmann, J. and Jeannerod, M. (1991) *Esprit, Où Es-Tu?* (*Mind, Where Are You?*), Paris: Odile Jacob.

Jeammet, N. (1993) *Les Destins de la Culpabilité* (*The Fates of Guilt*), Paris: PUF.

Kohut, H. (1971) *The Analysis of the Self*, New York: International Universities Press.

——(1984) *How Does Analysis Cure?* (ed. A. Goldberg), Chicago IL: University of Chicago Press.

Laplanche, J. (1991) *Nouveaux Fondements pour la Psychanalyse* (*New Foundations for Psychoanalysis*), 2nd edn, Paris: PUF.

Laplanche, J. and Pontalis, J.-B. (1967) *Vocabulaire de la Psychanalyse*, Paris: PUF.

Lebovici, S. (1960) 'La relation objectale chez l'enfant' ('The object relation in the child'), *Psychiatrie Enfant* (*Child Psychiatry*), 3 (1), 147–227.

——(1983) *Le Nourrisson, la Mère et le Psychanalyste*, (*The Infant, the Mother, and the Psychoanalyst*), Paris: Le Centurion.

——(1993) 'On intergenerational transmission: from filiation to affiliation', *Infant Mental Health Journal*, 14 (4), 260–72.

McDougall, J. (1985) *Theaters of the Mind: Illusion and Truth on the Psychoanalytic Stage*, trans. J. McDougall, New York: Basic Books.

Miller, A. (1981) *The Drama of the Gifted Child and the Search for the True Self*, trans. Ruth Ward, New York: Basic Books.

Misès, R. (1992) *Les Etats-limite chez l'Enfant* (*Borderline States in the Child*), Paris: PUF.

Mourgue, R. and Monakow, C. von (1928) *Introduction Biologique à la Psychopathologie*, Paris: Félix Alcan.

Sameroff, A. J. and Emde, R. N. (eds) (1989) *Relationship Disturbances in Early Childhood*, New York: Basic Books.

Sandler, J. (1986) 'Reality and the stabilizing function of unconscious fantasy', *Bulletin of the Anna Freud Centre*, 9, 177–94.

——(1987) *From Safety to Superego*, London: Karnac.

Stern, D. (1985) *The Interpersonal World of the Infant: A View from Psychoanalysis and Developmental Psychology*, New York: Basic Books.

——(1993) 'L'enveloppe proto-narrative' ('The proto-narrative envelope'), *Journal de la Psychanalyse de L'Enfant* (*Journal of Child Psychoanalysis*), 14, 13–66.

Winnicott, D. W. (1967) *Playing and Reality*, London: Tavistock. Originally published as 'Mirror-role of mother and family in child development', in P. Lomas (ed.) (1971) *The Predicament of the Family: A Psycho-analytical Symposium*, London: Hogarth Press and the Institute of Psycho-Analysis, 26–33.

7

WHAT IS AN OBJECT?

The role of perception[1]

Hanna Segal

What is an object? In ordinary speech, an object is anything that has material existence in the world. It is usually inorganic and most often man-made. That, of course, is not what psychoanalysts mean by an object. Our use of 'object' is based on the grammatical distinction between a subject and an object. The object is what the subject relates to, whether in the accusative, the dative or the ablative form. Almost in defiance of usual associations to the word, the psychoanalyst's object is human and, to make matters worse, it can also be immaterial. Our internal objects are thoughts, not things.

What does a psychoanalyst call an object? I think the object is something that is cathected by the subject. Originally Freud thought of an object as an object of instinct. I think that more commonly now we see the cathexis as not being purely instinctual. We see the infant as having emotional as well as biological or physical needs, and the object as an object of the infant rather than an object of the infant's instincts.

I think an object in the psychoanalytic sense is someone, or something, that has an emotional meaning for the person. It is needed or loved, hated or feared. Of necessity, it is an object of perception; you cannot relate to what you do not perceive. So the theme that is proposed to us, 'What is an object?', is enormous. It is almost the totality of our emotional experience. I shall therefore confine myself to one aspect of the topic: the role of perception in relation to external objects and to the creation of internal ones.

I shall begin, boldly, by assuming that human beings have inborn mental structures based on biological needs (in humans, this includes psychological needs as well), which become activated at various times of maturation. In my view, these structures are related to phantasies of the self and its basic relation to primary objects. Freud (1911) had assumed inborn phantasies, such as castration phantasies, arising out of our common prehistoric past. Klein and Isaacs (see Isaacs 1948) related them to the operation of instincts. I follow Bion (1963) and Money-Kyrle (1968) in believing that we have inborn phantasies relating to basic biological functions, such as feeding and intercourse, providing a basis that Bion calls preconceptions and that become realized, on meeting reality, to become a concept. I would add that the concept is that of an object.

What I am saying here parallels Chomsky's (1968) view of the development of language. I am always struck by how near he is to a psychoanalytical viewpoint. For instance, he emphasizes that language is not merely a habit or skill to be taught and learned, but that it is always a creative act. He assumes, and indeed demonstrates, that there is an inborn grammatical structure that does not need to be learned. Instead, this structure meets the external world, which provides a vocabulary and grammatical forms, and interacts with the vocabulary and forms to create a language. It is indeed because learning a language is a creative activity, with internal sources and parameters, that Chomsky, one of the fathers of cognitive psychology, is such a formidable opponent of behaviourism. Having an inborn grammatical structure and yet being able to acquire the different grammars of different languages are not contradictory. It is like our view that there is an inborn structure of an Oedipus complex but its actual realizations may be different in varying cultures. Patient A's material illustrates my point.

PATIENT A

Ms A started the session by telling me that she had two very tiny fragments of a dream. In one, she saw me surrounded by middle-aged, stupid, altogether despicable men. Of the second fragment, she could remember only that it had something to do with African land and African people. The first dream seemed to both of us pretty obvious, with an impending long weekend. But the hardly remembered fragment of a dream brought surprisingly rich associations. To begin with, she expressed again her horror of racial prejudices that she cannot free herself from, and that she detests in herself. This comment seemed to provide a link between the first dream about men I may spend my weekend with, and the second about the Africans.

But Ms A's other associations were more unexpected and illuminating. She is a schoolteacher, and she began speaking about a certain child's difficulty learning any grammar, particularly foreign grammar. Ms A thought that Africa in her dream may represent this student's feeling that grammar is totally exotic and incomprehensible. Ms A said that this child is quite clever, but very disjointed. The student seems unable to make certain connections, and this seems particularly obvious in her total inability to grasp the rules of grammar. After all, Ms A said, grammar, with the patterns it describes, should come more naturally. Then she laughed and said, 'Maybe to my student grammar is so foreign and exotic – just like parents in intercourse must appear to the child – beyond reach, incomprehensible, exotic, foreign'. This patient is often preoccupied and disturbed by very primitive phantasies of the primal scene. In this session, she seems to feel that there are certain natural patterns of interrelationships, as in grammar, and that this includes an intuitive awareness of parental intercourse.

In Ms A's first dream, intercourse is attacked and derided. She has a prejudice against it, like a prejudice against Africans. And her associations to it suggest that she is aware of how her thinking is dislocated by her attack on those natural patterns of relationships. She made an intuitive link between grammar and object relationships. She feels that there is a natural pattern in both.

When I say 'parallel to Chomsky', I do not wish to imply, as the Lacanians do, that the unconscious has the structure of language, but rather that both the object relations structures as studied by us and the structure of language have the same sources in what Chomsky (1968) calls human functions. In fact, I believe that the development of language springs from object relations and therefore has similarities to it, rather than the other way round. I think it is pretty universally accepted now that perception is not passive, not acting on a mind that is a *tabula rasa*; instead, it is an active interaction between the mind and the external world. I have described this interaction (Segal 1964, 1981) as largely an interaction between phantasy and perception. I suggested that the only thing that can be tested in reality-testing is a hypothesis, and that primitive phantasies (which Bion later called preconceptions) are like hypotheses tested in perception.

I believe that this matching of inner phantasies with realities exists from the beginning of life. Freud says, in a famous footnote to his paper on the 'Two principles of mental functioning':

> It will rightly be objected that an object which was a slave to the pleasure principle and neglected the reality of the external world could not maintain itself alive for the shortest time, so that it could not have come into existence at all. The employment of a fiction like this is, however, justified when one considers that the infant – provided one includes with it the care it receives from its mother – does *almost* realize a psychical system of this kind.
>
> (Freud 1911: 220, my emphasis)

To me, the operative word in this footnote is 'almost', because an infant in the care of even the best mother, if totally under the domination of the pleasure–pain principle, would not feed, because he would not know he was hungry. Some anorexic babies bear this out, and in analysing adult anorexic patients, one realizes how they can annihilate the experience of hunger.

The battle between the perception of reality and the omnipotent imposition of phantasy onto reality is, however, a long struggle that proceeds in small steps. Part of this battle is the constant attack on perception by the omnipotent self. This attack is not only on external perception but also on the perception of one's own inner states – and, as I assume, on inborn phantasies (such as those of parental intercourse) which interfere with one's sense of omnipotence, as shown by my patient.

Money-Kyrle (1968) remarks that it is striking how children have every conceivable theory about parental intercourse except the right one, and he considers it an attack on what I would call phantasy or what Bion would call the original preconception of such a happening. Similarly, the wish for narcissistic omnipotence can enviously attack the preconception of a feeding breast. Objects observed clinically are neither pure perception, in the case of external objects, nor pure primary phantasies, if internal, but rather are the result of the interaction between the inborn patterns and experience.

An infant under the sway of omnipotent phantasies creates a world based on his projections; one of the characteristics of this world is rigidity. The objects in the external world are always perceived in the same way, because they reflect and embody the subject's own primitive phantasies and parts of his projected self. They are rigid and repetitive because they are not modulated by interaction with reality.

PATIENT B

A repetitive dream of Patient B, who suffered from a gastric ulcer, illustrates this point. He reported a dream, close to a nightmare, that he had had periodically for as long as he could remember. He recalled that as a very small child, he would awaken from this dream in a panic. In the dream, he was completely tied to a chair in a half-lying position. From all sides, he was threatened by elongated animals with crocodile mouths.

In the course of Mr B's analysis, the dream first occurred in the context of castration fear of having his penis bitten off or chopped off as a punishment for masturbating. In the dream, he was tied to the chair to immobilize his hands. Later, the dream appeared again in the context of Mr B's phantasy of me being pregnant, and of his anxiety about attacking the inside of my body and the babies therein. The unformed, elongated shapes with crocodile mouths represented the dangerous babies inside the mother. The dream kept recurring in various contexts.

In one session, something struck me about Mr B's posture on the couch as he was telling me that the dream had recurred, and I asked him whether he had ever been swaddled as a baby. He said that he had been, for four months. He added that he had been told that during those months, he was always screaming with pain. He had then been diagnosed as having colic. I said that I thought the elongated body and the enormous, dangerous mouth was Mr B's experience of himself at that time projected outside into his object and colouring his perception. After that session, the dream stopped recurring, and eventually the psychosomatic symptom disappeared as well.

At the core of his personality, this patient seems to have had a perception of an object endowed with his own characteristics as a swaddled infant – an immobilized body and a hungry, angry, enormous biting mouth. The perception of this object is deeply repressed and split off from the rest of his personality. At the most primitive level, it is contained in the psychosomatic symptom. But it is also transferred onto other objects: women, children and men. They imbue the perception of those other objects with characteristics that are monotonously the same. Mr B feels very persecuted by his wife, and has a phantasy of a *vagina dentata*. He perceives children as demanding and damaging and is persecuted by men, particularly in his professional life. There is a monotonous rigidity to his object relationships because of the constant projection into them of this basic persecutory object.

PATIENT C

I shall describe a session with another rigid patient, Mr C, which shows a shift – at least temporary and soon attacked again – in the direction of an internal object which includes a correction by reality. This patient swings very monotonously between states of schizoid withdrawal and manic overactivity. Each state is accompanied by feelings of being persecuted, which drives Mr C back into the other state. He is not overtly psychotic; on a superficial level, he functions adequately in reality, but his human relations are superficial and unsatisfactory.

Mr C first entered analysis in late adolescence because of a fear of being schizophrenic. He came to me in middle age because of a general dissatisfaction with himself and his life. In analysis, we could discover basic object relationships underlying these states. In the withdrawn state, he was relating to a breast-womb, inside of which he resides and is free of destructive impulses. In his phantasies and associations following a dream about a pink room, we discovered a phantasy of 'pink brothels'. These were highly erotized phantasies, but girls hardly figured in them. He could withdraw into such states on the couch and feel blissful. In the manic state, in which he could be quite aggressive, he was identified with a phallus, or else he was idealizing his own faeces, which could be seen as food, babies, or a powerful faecal penis. Mr C is a native of Scotland and idealizes the land he owns there. For weeks before and after holidays, he used to withdraw in his mind to Scotland.

The session I report occurred a few weeks before a holiday when he was proposing to go to Scotland. He started the session by telling me three dreams. For some time before this session, Mr C had expressed concern about his memory lapses. He admitted something I had noticed for a long time, but that he denied, namely that if I made a reference to a previous session or past situations, he often had no memory of them at all. The same was true within the session. I could refer to what he had said five or ten minutes before, and he would realize that it was a complete blank in his mind. He would cover up by talking excessively, which he now admitted was often a conscious device to hide his lapses from me. Connected with this excessive talking was Mr C's tendency to dispose of my interpretations with vague associations, abstractions and generalizations – thus stripping the experience of any emotional meaning – and often becoming confused at the end. I sometimes had the experience that listening to the patient was like walking in a mist, unable to find one's way.

Mr C reported that he had been quite moved by the first dream:

> You were in Scotland, and I was thrilled to see you. It was marvellous having you there. But it was not like the last occasion you were in Scotland. I had nothing to do with it. I did not even know what your lecture was to be about. It was a strange experience because I was so pleased to see you, and yet I felt so excluded. It was so awful not even knowing what you planned, what was on your mind.

(I had been in Scotland to lecture a couple of years before during a holiday. The patient, who was there as well, knew about it and came to hear the lecture. He was terribly pleased: he experienced it as though he had arranged the whole thing and could exhibit me, his marvellous analyst, to the Scottish audience.)

In the second dream, the analyst disappears:

> Mr C himself gives the lecture to a very big audience, but he had been given a theme that is much too vague and general, something like 'How to apply analysis to one's work'. He is dissatisfied with it. The lecture itself does not appear in the dream, but afterwards there is a social gathering. A girl, an ex-student of Mr C, shows him a family watch he had given her. It does not work and he promises to fix it. The watch is very big; it is tubular and striped; transparent stripes alternate with black, opaque ones.

Mr C's first associations were to my previous trip to Scotland, and how different it was from the dream. During my actual trip, he had not felt excluded; instead, he had felt enlarged. The painful exclusion in the dream was much more like what he often feels in England. But he found the dream very moving: it was so good to have me in Scotland, even though it was also painful.

In the third dream, the patient 'was trying to mend a crumbling wall'. He thought he had the dream because of the relief he felt after the Friday session, in which we discussed his lapses of memory. He thought that the transparent-and-black stripes of the watch in the second dream were like the memory lapses: 'now I remember; now I don't'. (I also thought that the tubular watch, which was more like a clock, had some link with a black tubular clock I used to have on my desk some years ago. But when I queried whether it might be a clock rather than a watch, Mr C did not have a memory of my clock.) Mr C also connected the watch with feeling shocked when I ended the session on Friday. He usually withdraws and is prepared for the ending, but this time it took him quite unawares. He associated the crumbling wall to a neighbour who had built a wall on a crumbling cliff and had imposed a much-too-heavy superstructure on something that did not have a proper foundation. Mr C said that he had had a very good weekend in Scotland because of the Friday session.

I kept an open mind. Mr C always has a marvellous time in Scotland, and he is invariably manic on holidays. We were a few weeks away from the holiday. I wondered if the good weekend was because of the clear patches (in his head) or because of the black patches, having got rid of the memory of the experience. However, it was significant that he did think a lot about the Friday session, and in contrast to the usual lack of memory, he could immediately connect the dream with it. I took up his associations and linked them also with the generalization and vagueness, which we had also discussed on Friday.

I think the first dream represents a shift. My being in Scotland over the weekend break is myself represented in his mind. He connected it with remembering the previous session and thinking about it. He is delighted, but if he wants to keep me in his mind as I really am, he also has to admit the perception of me as a very separate object. He is not in control, and not only is he not omnipotent (e.g. feeling as he had on a previous occasion that he had made me come to Scotland), he is also not omniscient: he does not know what is on my mind. Hence, when I am this kind of internal object, which includes his reality perceptions, it is a situation for him of both gratification and pain.

The second dream is an attack on this perception. I disappear; Mr C is me; he gives the lecture. In reality he often behaves and feels as though he is me. But the lecture has no substance. The people in the audience are not real perceived objects but instead are projected parts of Mr C's child-self. The tubular watch (and in that, too, a memory of my tubular clock is obliterated) represents very well what he feels about his patchy memory. The too-heavy superstructure, which collapses because it has no foundation, is exactly the case when he gives his empty lecture. Somewhere in the background, the crumbling foundations represent the analyst destroyed in his memory.

This material illustrates the shift in Mr C's perception of the object. The second and third dreams represent his more usual state of mind, with narcissistic object relationships achieved by projective identification, by which the true perception of the object is obliterated. The first dream represents a move to an internal object that is a combination of wishful phantasy – to have me in Scotland, and also to have me as a part of himself in his mind – and a perception – an object experienced as having given gratification, hence desired but not omnipotently possessed.

I want to emphasize that Mr C does not know what is on my mind. I have always been struck by the way some schizophrenic patients have a way of looking into your eyes and saying, 'I know what you're thinking'. Of course, they do. They think they put those thoughts into your mind. Therefore the objects are perceived as being known right through. In schizophrenic patients, this is a core of conscious delusion; in neurotic patients, it is an unconscious phantasy, but it colours the perception of external objects. And the objects are repetitive, always the same, because no new thoughts arise. In contrast, in Mr C's first dream, he does not know what is on my mind. One could say I am not a saturated object, therefore I am open to variation. If Mr C re-projects such an object into the external world, he could recognize what in the object corresponds to his internal phantasies, aspects of his primary objects, or himself – what is known to him – and yet recognize, too, that he does not know everything about his object. It is therefore open to exploration and allows him to differentiate between external objects and their minds, and his internal projected phantasy; and also to differentiate them from one another. In the re-internalization, he also acquires a variety of objects with different characteristics. The move is from rigidity to flexibility in the perception of external and internal objects.

The nature of identifications also changes. In subsequent sessions, Mr C commented on the improvements in his memory. He also told me that in the past he simply did not bother to remember but instead left that to me. It was my job; that is how analysis works. Now he began to feel that he, too, could and should exercise this function. Instead of an empty, narcissistic identification with me, he selectively chose an introjection and identification with a basically necessary function.

In the course of development, the perception of objects normally undergoes an evolution in the direction of a lessening of distorted perceptions. One can see such an evolution in the process of Mr C's analysis, as well as the factors interfering with it and leading to a regression, as shown in the to-and-fro in Mr C's material.

NOTE

1   This paper was presented in 1989 in Vienna at a symposium of the European Psycho-Analytical Federation on the topic, 'What is an Object?' As Professor Joseph Sandler also took part in this symposium, and we shared this experience, I thought it a suitable contribution for this volume. Some of the material presented was subsequently also used in a chapter in *Psychoanalysis, Literature and War* (1997), London: Routledge.

REFERENCES

Bion, W. R. (1963) *Elements of Psycho-analysis* (1984), London: Heinemann.

Chomsky, N. (1968) *Language and Mind*, New York: Harcourt, Brace & World.

Freud, S. (1911) 'Formulations on the two principles of mental functioning', *Standard Edition*, vol. 12 (1958), London: Hogarth Press, 213–26.

Isaacs, S. (1948) 'The nature and function of phantasy', in M. Klein, P. Heimann, S. Isaacs and J. Riviere (eds) *Developments in Psycho-analysis* (1952), London: Hogarth Press.

Klein, M., Heimann, P., Isaacs, S. and Riviere, J. (eds) (1952) *Developments in Psycho-analysis* (1989), London: Karnac Books and the Institute of Psycho-Analysis.

Money-Kyrle, R. E. (1968) 'Cognitive development', *International Journal of Psycho-Analysis*, 49, 691–8.

Segal, H. (1964) *Introduction to the Work of Melanie Klein* (1988), London: Karnac Books and the Institute of Psycho-Analysis.

——(1981) *The Work of Hanna Segal: A Kleinian Approach to Clinical Practice* (1986), London: Karnac Books.

8

THE REPRESENTATIONAL WORLD AND THE LINGUISTIC IDIOM

Theodore Shapiro

Joseph Sandler has contributed immensely to our understanding of the representational world, bringing together the views of the object-relational and ego-psychological viewpoints. In this chapter, I will seek to expand that vision to include what we know about the rules of translation by which we formulate the representational world into language or personal idiom. Since our desired contacts with our patients are through words, we should see how words enable and facilitate movement away from senseless repetitions and enactments of the past, and whether the mental constellations can be translated into meaningful new statements or interpretations. A case example will serve as a vehicle to describe the translation from action to language and the move towards change.

Joseph Sandler's larger contribution to psychoanalysis cannot be summarized in one brief piece, but his specific interest in the representational world has been a persistent theme of his work. In his 1988 plenary address to the American Psychoanalytical Association (Sandler 1990), he distinguished his point of view as following a consistent thread that addresses how patients present themselves and how their inner worlds dictate their behaviour. His unique modification of Kleinian theory, and his adaptation of ego psychology, provide us with an amalgam of the important ways people represent their experiences. This body of work forces us to see the role of memory storage of experience on action and interaction, as well as the effect of significant past interactions on intrapsychic life.

Sandler (1990: 866) writes that there are four areas concerning the relationship of memory and thought to conscious and unconscious fantasies that relate to self- and object representations:

1   the wish for interaction with an object;

2   concern for the way wishes are fulfilled with guiding drives of instinctual wishes, safety, reassurance, affirmation, narcissistic gratification and the wish to do away with pain or anxiety;

3   seeking actualization (i.e. as Freud suggested in 1900, to make perception re-perception);

4   transference as the closest actualization of a wish for a relationship where the analyst will conform to a wish-fulfilling role. Sandler (1990) further writes that the patient tries to actualize while the analyst tries to interpret.

I would like to offer a complementary set of observations derived from my interest in and work with language, regarding the interpretative process that could well be grafted onto Sandler's model. I believe there is intellectual and practical virtue in having a clear description of the process of interpretation from the standpoint of linguistics in order to state better – and thereby understand – the relationship of the verbal process to unconscious fantasy. Before doing this, however, let me note that Sandler indicated that he had been guilty of some misrepresentation 'in not distinguishing between the experiential content of the mental representation – the perceptual and ideational content – and the structural organization behind that content, an organization that lies outside the realm of conscious or unconscious experience' (Sandler 1990: 869).

Sandler and Joffe (1966) did offer an addendum allowing for the sharp distinction between the experiential and the nonexperiential realms. They wrote that the realm of subjective experience (in German *Erlebnis*, but not *Erfahrung*) refers to the experience of the phenomenal content of wishes, impulses, memories, fantasies, sensation, percepts, feelings and the like. All we know, we know only through subjective phenomenal representation. Later on, they commented on the notion that it is not just the child's perception of an interaction that is internalized but rather that these fantasy images are 'unconsciously' manipulated by the ego by means of the ego-function of fantasy, thereby modifying the experience in a highly idiosyncratic manner (Sandler and Nagera 1963). These proposals lay the groundwork for further understanding of how the interpretative process helps bring the patient into relationship with his own fantasies and those fantasies into consciousness under control of the ego, rather than permitting them to dictate the patient's behaviour without conscious appraisal, reappraisal, and judgement about the wisdom of such action and interaction.

The linguistic frame of reference to which I refer is initially elaborated in my paper, 'Interpretation and naming' (Shapiro 1970):

The interpretation of an unconscious fantasy is an event during the course of an analysis which may be viewed as naming. Varying phenomena, motivational, verbal situational, interpersonal, are synthesized by the analyst into a more or less concise sentence or complex name. This designation can now be considered by patient and analyst as a common lexical property and can be tested for its congruence with the patient's experience in the past, present and future.

(399)

At a later point, I (Shapiro 1988) added:

Insofar as the analytic task and the aim of theory are advanced by the interpretation of unconscious fantasy, we must know how such interpretation is possible, and how it comes about. It is in this light that our interest in symbol formation, the linguistic mode of expression and the mechanisms underlying these processes might be considered.

(82)

In short, I would like to introduce an addendum to Sandler's interest in mental representation in the form of a discussion that taps our understanding of linguistic representation that stands alongside other forms of representation. The patient represents his compromise formations to the analyst around object-relational constellations of wishes in at least two forms: by actualization in words and narratives whose deeper meaning is barely understood by both patient and analyst, or in enactments in the transference. These elements can be viewed from the standpoint of a number of rules of transformation derived from language theory and semiotics (Shapiro 1979). Such a view allows a closer description of the mode of interaction of the interpretative process in words, and better describes the analytic relationship. The analytic situation includes the controlled actualization of object- and subject-related wishes, demonstrates how they are defended and how they become visible in the flow of associations, and provides a choice of stories told, as well as expressed in transference enactments. Knowing these constellations and how the analyst uses words to interpret developing actualizations is central to furthering our aim of comprehending the therapeutic process.

THE MEANING OF INTERPRETATION

To address these issues, let us first ask 'What is an interpretation?' My earlier comments suggest that it is a translation into a verbal medium of what has been represented in another form. In that sense, the vehicle of representation is altered by the analyst in the service of creating a useable verbal statement that can be shared in consciousness and re-referred to repeatedly by both analyst and patient in search of the shortest, most useful description to serve as a mediational paradigm representing the various manifestations and their multiple appearances. Thus a single phrase is used as a cipher representing multiple events, enactments and narratives, as well as serving multiple functions. This cipher or phrase, therefore, can aptly be designated as a polysemantic auditory verbal image that can be explored from the standpoint of how symbols organize experience. I suggest that it may refer to Sandler's nonexperiential realm, insofar as it can be translated into words.

Intralinguistic translation

Mahoney (1987) notes that there are three forms of translation: intralinguistic, interlinguistic and semiotic. In the first form, we describe a word or an event in terms other than in the same code. A dictionary definition is a simple example of intralinguistic translation. When we ask 'What is a bachelor?' the answer might be 'an unmarried male'. Note, however, that the word *spinster*, an unmarried female, has a different array of connotations and a broader array of affective responses, making the translation of particular words particularly eventful and demonstrating that words are not simply labels. Parenthetically, it is similarly not possible to make only one form of an interpretation or to suggest that other forms are equal. Words have affective valence as well as a designative signifying function.

Interlinguistic translation

Interlinguistic translation would simply be the translation from one language to another. However easy this may seem, it, too, is more complex. For example, in translating a noun, there is often a change in nuance and connotation. Words may have a common semantic (e.g. 'moon' in English becomes 'la lune' in French). Nonetheless, each has a different connotative significance. While the English 'moon' has to do with measurement or month, the French word choice reflects a bias towards brightness and light. Both are attributes of the referent but lead to different mental images through awareness of a network of associations. (Similarly, we can well note the intra-psychoanalytic controversy concerning 'cathexis' and 'besetzung' or 'ego' and 'das Ich'.) This problem of connotation has made some, namely Whorf (1962) and Sapir (1921), suggest that there is no possibility of true inter-linguistic translation on a one-to-one basis when connotative factors are taken into account. Indeed, they suggest that each language provides its own world-view of reality. I would add that affective additions derived from group and personal use are also relevant.

Semiotic translation

The third, or semiotic, translation involves a translation from one vehicle of representation to another. The relationship of the sign to the symbol can be looked at as arbitrary in common lexical tokens, such as words, but the relationship of the sign to its referent also may be explained better by contiguity or simile, as in metonymy and metaphor. We speak of 'the Crown' when we mean the agency of the monarch, we speak of 'Number Ten Downing Street', when we mean the office of the Prime Minister. In the metaphor or simile, the sign is chosen by token of a relationship by form. For Homer, 'rosy-fingered dawn' was a clear representation of what a sunrise appeared to be; not surprisingly, it serves us well even now. That we can appreciate this metaphor even today suggests that sunrises have not changed much throughout history.

An interesting variation on this theme comes in the way that references encode different referents. There is some question as to how the letter representing the 'B' sounded in ancient Greek, since there has been some phonic drift from 'B' to 'V' as in other language codes. Fortunately, there is a sequence in one of Aristophanes' plays where the bleat of a sheep is represented – it surely is not 'vaa, vaa' – so the phonic shape had to agree with the sound for 'B' as we use it in modern English. Linguistic drift provides another example of shift in meaning and representation. Shakespearean English approximates modern lexical meanings, but not uniformly.

Psychoanalytic translations correspond most closely to the area of symbolic representation that is semiotic. In the relationship of the patient to the analyst, especially in the transference, we frequently see an enactment of a wished-for relationship to an object. We detect this enactment from redundant descriptions by the patient of relationships with others either in the present (synchronically) or from the past (diachronically). Such redundant and concordant stories expressed in various vehicles aid us in the search for a paradigmatic statement to describe the current interaction.

Indeed, more rigorous empirically defined concepts such as core critical relationship themes (CCRTs) (Luborsky and Luborsky 1993) correspond nicely to Sandler's (1990) clinical concept of role responsiveness. The latter is a more general clinical way of stating the characteristic stance in relation to interactions between patient and analyst. As Sandler (1990) has noted: 'In the analytic situation, the patient unpacks the object aspects of his mental furniture so to speak and tries to position this furniture in ways that make it seem as if it belongs and is appropriate' (878). This metaphor renders what has transpired interpersonally into words, permitting us to grasp the experiential aspects of the patient. It also conveys the experience in the vehicle of language that goes beyond a simple communion attaining the level of communication. Indeed, a carefully crafted relational syntax offers a precise linguistic model of what has occurred that may be accepted or refuted on the basis of any distinctive feature, such as who is the subject or object, or how active or passive the verb is that represents the interaction.

META-STRUCTURES

What are the tacit frames of reference we use, whether we call ourselves object relationists or classical structural ego theorists? What meta-structure accounts for the forms in which we cast interpretations so they achieve status as a communal property in language? Linguistic explanations provide three overlapping ways to analyse the manner in which we represent core stories in language: syntax, semantics and pragmatics (see Shapiro 1979).

Syntax

Syntax refers to the organization of phrases and sentences to express the relational aspects of subject and object, passivity and activity, and their verbal strength and force as imperatives. Insofar as the organization of syntax rests on case grammar, it is a perfect vehicle for representing agent, action, object and indirect object. Insofar as this structure can be pinned down, the self–object oscillations described by Sandler may be seen to have a syntactic format. The forms are then played out with a shift in who is the agent and who is the passive or active object in relation to the action (i.e. the verb). The patient becomes empowered by the language used by knowing that he is unwittingly falling into one or another of these role designators that were beyond conscious grasp before being verbalized (Schafer 1976; Shapiro 1988; Teller and Dahl 1993).

Semantics

Semantics refers to the sign relationship of meaning and signification. What do what you are doing and saying stand for? What is the relationship of the referent to the reference? However, semantics goes beyond the simplest denotative form of a statement. We are more interested in learning how the image the patient presents, or the story the patient tells, refers to an unconscious fantasy or a preconceived standing format not yet articulated. Moreover, how does that format and its representation become a synchronic statement derived from formats of past organizations that remain relatively rigid within the individual's mental life? They may even have been encoded in early procedural memories and unconscious fantasies, remaining inexpressible up to now (Clyman 1992; Shapiro 1991; Shapiro and Emde 1992).

Pragmatics

Finally, pragmatics refers to the sector of linguistics that concerns communication and implied intention that cannot be accounted for solely through semantics and syntax. Such analysis requires observation of language in use and can be done only within the context of a human relationship. It is deciphered in the metalinguistic contextual analysis of a statement, as expressed in the interactions between two people who have additional knowledge of each other, such as role expectations and social conventions and intentions.

An individual entering a room where an elder is seated, on hearing, 'It is warm in here', does not take that as a declarative sentence alone to describe the temperature of the ambient air, but rather as an action request for relief by opening the window or by turning on the air conditioner. In this sense, language is a vehicle for getting things done. The semantics alone or the structure of the sentence betray neither the intended wish nor the unconscious wish.

In psychoanalysis, the prolonged interaction between the patient and the analyst provides numerous opportunities for redundant expression of what is considered a common small set of ideas in varying vehicles and at various times, designed to get something done or to re-create an old pattern. It is through the redundant recognition of these common themes that the analyst is able to interpret, with some certainty, the patient's productions and re-enactments in the analysis that derive from earlier interactions in the family. Sandler's representational world is rendered manageable by the analyst's interpretative words.

A case presentation referred to elsewhere (Shapiro 1977) for different purposes illustrates the varying aspects of the interpretative process from a psychoanalytic linguistic standpoint. The patient's various vehicles of expression were used by the analyst to arrive at a verbal characterization of the patient's behaviour for common scrutiny in the analysis.

CASE EXAMPLE

John, a young professional in his early twenties, entered analysis complaining about his difficulty in functioning well in many areas of life. He was married but avoided intercourse with his wife, masturbating instead to fantasies of oral-genital contact with young girls or dreams of seduction by older women. During his early adolescence, he had been discovered and reprimanded for rubbing his body against the buttocks of a sleeping girl at a party.

The patient would provoke violent arguments with his wife instead of providing her with the solace of a caring or sexually satisfying marriage. Even as he felt righteous about his behaviour, he also felt that he was an impostor, and his self-esteem lagged. To achieve some praise, he frequently and impulsively changed his report of facts to correspond with his fantasy. These mixed motives led him to experience shame and apprehension about discovery.

During the initial phases of analysis, the patient worried greatly about whether his analyst liked him. He continually sought approval while fantasizing, with growing anxiety, that the analyst would take advantage of him and seduce him, that is, that he would be passively victimized much as he had victimized the girl in adolescence. This fantasy was the patient's first representation of his identification with women.

Somewhat later in the analytic work, he began to talk about his wife's older cousin. He spoke of her with great affection, soon revealing that his wife was merely a vehicle by which he could become close to this older woman. After confessing these ideas, he went away on vacation, where he was increasingly sexually active with his wife. This sexual activity stopped, however, once treatment resumed.

During the next phase of treatment, the patient frequently dozed on the couch. His waking comments, however, concerned his sexual exploits and the esteem that they elicited from his friends. Indeed, his wish for admiration for his sexual adventures expanded into increasingly ambitious derivative wishes to be admired for his prowess in many other enterprises. On the other hand, ambition made him feel anxious that his 'avaricious' mother might exact her share of his success. This characterization of his mother stood in sharp contrast to the giving attitude of his wife's cousin.

When the analyst interpreted the patient's passive wishes to be sexually intruded on while sleeping, the patient met those comments with pseudo-stupidity reflected in an apparent lack of understanding and naiveté. Despite such denial, this interpretation led the patient to reveal that during early latency, he had 'manipulated' a girl his own age, as she 'played dumb'. There was growing evidence as well that his passivity was a strong defence against castration anxiety. These interpretations were given further significance by a dream interpretation.

In one dream, the patient described being in a tub with a small frog that grew very large. The animal's skin was associated to a skin condition he suffered that was related to his penis. Indeed, the skin condition was on his groin and genitals, which he believed marked him as a masturbator. As an adolescent, he had, indeed, masturbated in the bathtub. This guilty revelation also changed his aggressive stance into a pitiable one, because it made him appear to be a mere child in a tub with a bath toy. Once these areas were interpreted with respect to their defensive nature, the patient began to expose his sexual wishes towards his wife's cousin more frankly in the analysis. She possessed a series of traits that he contrasted strongly with those of his depriving mother, towards whom he felt only rage and suspicion. The analyst, too, was now viewed as a depriving mother.

The analyst interpreted that the patient had symbolically married his own Oedipal daughter. His wife was his sister and he was the triumphant partner of a mature woman who was exactly the opposite of his biological mother. Subsequently, the patient's psychologically absent father became even more absent from his verbalizations. The interpretation of the patient's symbolic plight was re-represented in a condensed form in a dream: he was behind a woman molesting her. She was wearing 'little girl's pants' that reminded him of his wife's underclothing, but she had the breasts of an older woman. This event was visualized in a large open area where the patient's mother and grandmother were looking down at him while cooking his favourite food. The analyst's interpretation addressed the exhibitionistic elements of this dream, as shown in the wish to be admired and loved. The patient's anxiety about castration, as represented in the preferred approach to the woman from behind, was also aired. In the wake of these presentations, the patient's impulsiveness decreased, he became more attentive to his work, and he ceased to masturbate.

In another dream, the patient was flying about the city as everyone watched. As the analysis proceeded, such phallic-narcissistic-exhibitionistic aims diminished. The patient then focused on his mother's tendency to give him food at her expense (ignoring his adulthood), revealing his wish to take without having to show that he wanted. This theme was also represented in the organizing fantasy and experience of adolescence when he had tried to seduce a sleeping young woman, that is, to take without being noticed and thereby to deny his own need as well as his castration anxiety.

Even as he continued to do well, the patient began to complain to the analyst, accusing him of playing with himself behind the couch. This reversal reinforced the patient's idea that the analyst would become excited by the patient as he slept, giving way to anxiety that he would be forced into fellatio in order to take in the analyst's strength orally.

At one juncture during the analysis, the patient's wish to display inade-quacy and pseudo-stupidity became most prominent in an enactment. The analyst had had a carpet cleaned, and when the patient entered the room he looked at the paper on the floor and asked, as though an innocent child, 'Where shall I walk, on the carpet or the paper?'

DISCUSSION

An analysis unfolds much as a drama does. However, neither analyst nor patient knows the script explicitly. They are more like a new audience than like the author, director or actors. The analyst comes prepared with some predetermined formulae that set the broad outlines of the parameters of the human script, while the patient has a dim awareness of his or her tendency to act repetitively in certain ways. Nonetheless, it takes the development of the unique relationship known as a psychoanalysis to make explicit the script's variations. As the themes become apparent, the analyst gives structure to the shadow narrative (Makari and Shapiro 1993) by verbalizing the interactions and by providing a shorthand description of the significance of the associative links in words in terms of wish and defence. This is an interpretation.

The case presented here provides a variety of verbalizations, story lines, enactments and visualizations in dreams that point to a narrow range of unconscious fantasies, redundantly presented in surface form for those trained to see beyond the obvious. In its briefest verbal form, the case describes a young man who suffered from severe castration anxiety and fear of being overwhelmed by his mother, whom he viewed as controlling and infantilizing. Moreover, he did not have the protection of his father, whom he viewed as weak and irrelevant. Thus he identified with the passive, sleeping young woman and could achieve sexual arousal and satisfaction only by 'stealing' sexual fulfilment from behind. He longingly sought a caring and passionately praising mother who would extol his playing at manhood, but the dangers of such assertiveness forced him to deny his ambition via feigned weakness, pseudo-stupidity, illness and infantilism. His narcissistic fragility is apparent in his repeated need for affirmation to hide his aggression and rage.

This interpretation is too formulaic to help the patient, because it sounds too pat, and yet such description does encapsulate the trends of the case for a most generalized verbal psychoanalytic description. It does not work as a representation for the patient, because he cannot recognize himself in the specifics of the content (the *Erlebnis*), only in the general outlines. So the concise form in words overwhelms the content, which is further confounded by the level of verbal description cast in meta-language. Thus language, when applied to the wrong context, can confound as well as facilitate communication.

Viewed from a linguistic vantage, the language of interpretation must be considered not only as a general message, but also as specific words and grammatical formats appropriate to the interaction between analyst and patient. Do they touch the patient? Are they specific enough? Can they be referred to profitably again? Often, we use the patient's own words and preferred references to designate interaction, or we use repetitive phrases that are familiar or laden with affect, to make our interventions less intellectual and more accessible.

The syntax of the relationship of subject to object is clear but oscillating. The patient initially wants the analyst's praise and affection, but is fearful that it will not be forthcoming if he reveals his secret wishes. He feels like an impostor, even to the point of altering facts enough to become one – perhaps thereby inviting punishment (although he consciously wants praise) but also to protect his narcissistic self-image.

In the case presented here, the first revelation was about an adolescent seduction that occurred while the woman slept. As the analysis proceeded, the syntax of agent–action–object remained the same, but the object and agent changed and had to be interpreted as such. He who seduced from behind now wished to be seduced from behind. These relationships are further explored and expressed later in the analysis in the visual form of dreams. At first, the patient is a child in a bathtub with a skin disease (as represented by a warty frog). Then he is a masterful, exhibitionistic, sexual acrobat admired from the grandstand by his mother – who cooks for him as well.

In the well-known tendency to turn active to passive and vice-versa, these kinds of shifting opposites have been given life by many object relations theorists and ego psychologists (Arlow 1977). The defensiveness of both alternatives is a contribution of psychoanalysis. The minimalist syntactic description describes agency in action, helping us to be alert to hearing who is doing what to whom and to interpreting in words the direction of wishes.

The semantic portion of the equation is most closely related to psychoanalytic symbol formation. Even as Lacan (1956) referred to the play of the signifier, Freud (1900) referred to over-determination, and Waelder (1936) to multiple function. Linguistics refers to polysemy (i.e. many meanings or a rich array of meanings). In this instance, the meaning of the theme of seduction while asleep – and applause for such achievement – apparently went back to latent sexual play as indicated in the case history. If this event is not indeed a historical fact, it is nonetheless a fact of this patient's mental life and therefore meaningful and salient now.

For this patient, generalized Oedipal ambitions were not abandoned, but were instead transformed into more acceptable forms that would permit him to function in some adaptive capacities as a man, a husband and a son. None of these adaptations was accomplished very successfully, because the meanings of the experiences were subject to personal re-interpretation in the form of unconscious fantasies that permitted sexual arousal only if the object was immature or asleep, or could be approached from behind (so he could not see that she was penis-less), and only if he could 'steal' his satisfaction. These conditions are no longer formulaic requirements; they are presented as variations of a specific semantic referent. The vehicles of representation change even as the roles of the patient and the analyst change, but there is a unique referent that takes a number of forms derived from the patient's past memories.

We learn about the patient's adolescent seduction first as the initial revelation that he feared would interfere with the analytic relationship. The latency event is revealed even later, but is juxtaposed with the patient's confession of lust for his wife's older cousin, his impotence and avoidance of coital contact with his wife, and his expressed belief that the analyst was getting sexually excited. All these pronouncements converge on the analyst-listener, eliciting a concise verbal statement that encompasses the varied experiences. The pragmatic language being used links the representations to transference enactments in what Sandler calls role responsiveness.

The analyst's actions or inactions are subjected to personal idiosyncratic interpretations by the patient within the context of his unique idiom. Meanings are no longer simply denotative or connotative, they become personally idiosyncratic or are recast in terms of the patient's irrational need to see things his own way and to influence the analyst to adopt a specific view of him. To the analyst, the pseudo-stupidity, exhibited in the patient's query about whether to walk on a newly shampooed rug, was a reference to a forbidden, sexually aggressive fantasy. The belief that the analyst would act with the patient as he had described himself acting with two young girls, was predetermined by the patient's narrative pull to his own carefully created, albeit unconscious, storyline. Thus when we listen to what our patients say, we must attend simultaneously to what they do and how they assign roles to us derived from their personal history.

This description of the text of an analysis is rather dry and formal, but it does focus on the elements of symbolic play that confront us in an analysis. Such analysis is not only applicable to our work, of course, but to any dialogue. We have not yet taken fullest advantage of this approach to our work.

Joseph Sandler has alerted us and riveted us to the highly significant role of mental representation in psychological life. Yet we need further explication of how we become aware of these unities and how we encode them for verbalization, instruction and dialogue. Until mental representations are verbalized within the context of analysis, they remain entities to be wrestled with within the patient's own mind. When cast in appropriate words, however, they can be communicated and can become a common property to review and argue about, to consider and modify and review yet again to achieve a better fit.

There is no guarantee, however, that the verbal cast will create the desired change. For the patient in the throes of positive transference may accept too readily, just as one in the negative transferential state might develop further negativism. Nonetheless, the feat of stating what had been clothed in polysemantic forms in various vehicles (dream, narrative, enactment) can, once interpreted, be used in the service of understanding and change. The representational world becomes a public issue in concise form, ready for discourse, disagreement and dialogue.

REFERENCES

Arlow, J. (1977) 'Affects and the psychoanalytic situation', *International Journal of Psycho-Analysis*, 58, 157–70.

Clyman, R. B. (1992) 'The procedural organization of emotions: a contribution from cognitive science to the psychoanalytic theory of therapeutic action', in T. Shapiro and R. N. Emde (eds) *Affect: Psychoanalytic Perspectives*, Madison CT: International Universities Press, 349–82.

Freud, S. (1900) 'The interpretation of dreams', *Standard Edition*, vols 4–5 (1953), London: Hogarth Press.

Lacan, J. (1956) *The Language of the Self: The Function of Language in Psychoanalysis*, trans. A. Wilden, Baltimore MD: Johns Hopkins University Press.

Luborsky, L. and Luborsky, E. (1993) 'The era of measures of transference: the CCRT and other measures', *Journal of the American Psychoanalytic Association*, 41 (supplement), 329–51.

Mahoney, P. (1987) *Psychoanalysis and Discourse*, London: Tavistock.

Makari, G. and Shapiro, T. (1993) 'On psychoanalytic listening: language and unconscious', *Journal of the American Psychoanalytic Association*, 41 (4), 991–1020.

Sandler, J. (1990) 'On internal object relations', *Journal of the American Psychoanalytic Association*, 38 (4), 859–80.

Sandler, J. and Joffe, W. G. (1966) 'On sublimation', in J. Sandler (ed.) *From Safety to Superego: Selected Papers of Joseph Sandler* (1987), New York: Guilford Press, 191–207.

Sandler, J. and Nagera, H. (1963) 'The metapsychology of fantasy', in J. Sandler (ed.) *From Safety to Superego: Selected Papers of Joseph Sandler* (1987), New York: Guilford Press, 90–120.

Sapir, E. (1921) *An Introduction to the Study of Speech*, New York: Harcourt, Brace & World.

Schafer, R. (1976) *A New Language for Psychoanalysis*, New Haven CT: Yale University Press.

Shapiro, T. (1970) 'Interpretation and naming', *Journal of the American Psychoanalytic Association*, 18, 399–421.

——(1977) 'Oedipal distortions in severe character pathologies: developmental and theoretical considerations', *Psychoanalytic Quarterly*, 46 (4), 559–79.

——(1979) *Clinical Psycholinguistics*, New York: Plenum Press.

——(1988) 'Language structure and psychoanalysis', *Journal of the American Psychoanalytic Association*, 36 (supplement), 339–58.

——(1991) 'Words and feelings in the psychoanalytic dialogue', *Journal of the American Psychoanalytic Association*, 39 (supplement), 321–48.

Shapiro, T. and Emde, R. N. (eds) (1992) *Affect: Psychoanalytic Perspectives*, Madison CT: International Universities Press.

Teller, V. and Dahl, H. (1993) 'What psychoanalysis needs is more empirical research', *Journal of the American Psychoanalytic Association*, 41 (supplement), 31–49.

Waelder, R. (1936) 'The principle of multiple function: observations on over-dermination', *Psychoanalytic Quarterly*, 5, 45–62.

Whorf, B. L. (1962) *Language, Thought and Reality*, Cambridge MA: MIT Press.

9

INTERNAL OBJECTS

Theoretical perimeter and clinical contour[1]

Max Hernández and Moisés Lemlij

The much-debated notion of internal objects provides the practising analyst with an intuitive picture of important aspects of the mind's inner landscape. In evolving towards its actual definition and usage in the clinical setting, the notion has suffered a radical, creative tension. This presentation will 'shuttle' between its conceptual form and its clinical substance. Thus it fits well in a book dedicated to the work of Joseph Sandler, one of whose main interests has been the evolution of concepts in the interplay between theory and practice.

To explore the notion of internal objects and its heuristic possibilities in clinical work, this presentation will start from those experience-near derivatives of this theoretical construct as they emerge through the discussion of clinical material. The theoretical lines that guide the analysis of this material begin with Freud's early demarcations and definitions of the mechanisms of identification, introjection and incorporation (1914b, 1917, 1921, 1923, 1926), and continue through the ideas developed by Melanie Klein (1946, 1958) on projective identification, which were later expanded by Rosenfeld (1969, 1983) and Bion (1970).

To explore the general usefulness of the concept of internal or internalized objects, whose outline was first drawn by Melanie Klein (1927, 1928, 1929, 1934; see also Baranger 1971), we must take into account the difficulties that derive from the use of the word 'internal' in psychoanalytic theorizing (Strachey 1941). Then we will examine how the notion of internal objects behaves in the clinical setting, using the definition of the internal object as 'a structure in the nonexperiential realm, being built up during development on the basis of the child's subjective perceptual and fantasy experiences' (Sandler 1990: 859). The notion thus defined will be referred to the experiential realm that Winnicott (1953, 1971) defined as the potential space.

Rycroft (1972) has aptly said that 'Freud had provided the verbs for a human psychology, and ego psychology and object [relations] theory, both sensing that the sentence was incomplete, have concentrated on providing the subject and object respectively' (xxv). Nevertheless, one proviso must be kept in mind: the succinctness of Rycroft's metaphor should not overlook the fact that Freud's discoveries 'completely disrupted the old relation between subject and object' (Green 1978: 169). The theory of object relations, as it evolved in the British Psycho-Analytical Society, was constructed to bridge that problematical gap. In more recent years, it has expanded towards areas of experience that seem beyond those signalled by Melanie Klein, Bion, Rosenfeld and Winnicott. But this most interesting field of research, which Ogden (1985, 1989), Bollas (1987) and Tustin (1980) have addressed, is not the topic of this communication. Instead, its focus is on another aspect: how the notion of internal objects can be articulated with concepts belonging to diverse frameworks. This focus requires exploring how a theoretical framework that takes into account issues of psychic structure, object and self-representations, and other classical and mainstream concepts, may accommodate this type of notion.

The fate of the concept under discussion constitutes an interesting example of the significance of the working conditions and circumstances of contemporary psychoanalysis. There is, on the one hand, the expanded system of cross-references that is the hallmark of current editing and publishing. On the other hand, there is an increasing institutional and theoretical openness in the International Psychoanalytic Association. The presidential addresses of Robert Wallerstein (1988, 1990) and Joseph Sandler (1992) have opened the field for a fruitful discussion. The notion of internal objects has suffered a number of modifications when traversing the different 'meaning spaces' (Sandler 1983: 36) provided by the diverse psychoanalytical institutional settings. A number of psychoanalytic clinicians and theoreticians – not necessarily of Kleinian persuasion – have used the concept consistently in their work (Baranger 1971; Baranger et al. 1980; Grinberg 1956, 1963; Jiménez 1992; Kernberg 1979, 1988, 1991a; Ogden 1985, 1989; Sandler 1978, 1988, 1990, 1992). In his 1991 presidential address, Sandler (1992) stressed the positive value of the concept and insisted that it 'can be integrated into psychoanalytic metapsychology which allows for integration' (197). The recent fate of the concept is a clear instance of the growing importance that international cross-fertilization is acquiring in psychoanalytic thinking (Kernberg 1991b).

CASE EXAMPLES

Ms A, a thirty-four-year-old successful professional woman who was married and had three children, came for analysis on account of some distant psychological sequelae of an adolescent bout with anorexia nervosa. During the first year of analysis, she reported the following dream:

> I was happy and calm. Then my mother appeared. She looked angry and asked me to tell her where the loo was. She said she thought she had cancer. I felt indignant and told her to get off my back and leave

me in peace. Besides, she told me she hadn't even gone to the doc-
tor to have a proper diagnosis. The dream flooded me with anxiety
and I woke up. I was lucky to be able to sleep again after an hour.

The morning after this dream, Ms A felt upset, had more problems and
conflicts at work than usual, and could not play golf that afternoon. She
initiated the session that day with a marked feeling of futility and depression.

In terms of the object relations implied, the dream may be understood as
an expression derived from the vicissitudes of an internal object that seems to
be predicated on an archaic image of the mother, a portrayal of the patient's
relationship with a mother who, according to Ms A, rebuffed, disqualified,
and scorned her.

This dream allows the clinician to establish a bridge between its manifest
and latent content. In the former, the mother appears to be telling the patient
about a dangerous illness. Through recourse to intellectualization, the patient
can establish only a minimal line of containment of anxiety. The latent
content may be inferred: an interplay of object relations suffused with
violence and death wishes. In this sense, it is important to see the apparent
relationship between the internal object as the unconscious representation of
an archaic mother and the unconscious self-representation of the patient.
Both types of representation seem intertwined. The concept of internal
object provides an element that fits into a model that appears to understand
and conceptualize satisfactorily the material discussed.

Another brief clinical example illustrates some questions that the concept
of internal objects raises when seen from the point of view of the transference
experience.

Ms B, a social worker, was a single woman in her early forties who
entered analysis because of depressive symptoms that interfered with
her capacity to enjoy life. The analysis, which was in its second year,
seemed to be proceeding quite uneventfully. But during a session
after one weekend, Ms B talked about a feeling of intense excitement and almost instant infatuation with a man she had met at a
party, whom she said was 'a man who can really make me suffer'. A
number of associations related to what was exciting in this man came
about.

From the point of view of this chapter, it is important to stress that the
internal object, which until then had appeared only as an hypothetical
construction on the part of the analyst to explain certain aspects of Ms B's
moral masochistic behaviour, came clearly into focus for the first time in her
associations to an external object. This course of events allowed the analyst to
clarify the active presence of this internal object. It was an exciting yet
rejecting object that Ms B seemed to have internalized in the process of

developing her relationship with her father. This rejecting object had appeared as a way of relating to the analyst that had not been clearly noticeable at the beginning of the analysis.

Another episode in this same analysis shows more clearly and in more detail the effects of the rejecting object in the transference.

> Ms B held strong feminist views, which had surfaced in connection with some critical remarks about the analyst's behaviour. At one point in a particular session, the patient was making some acidic comments about some analysts she thought were closely related to her analyst. She had seen them during a weekend conference. As the session proceeded, the patient began asking herself why she had not chosen a woman analyst. She interspersed some comments addressed to the analyst. Then she realized that it would be 'intolerable' for her to accept 'being under a woman'. At this point, the analyst remembered that the patient could not even tolerate the mention of the word 'homosexuality'.

It is possible to point out here the presence in the transference of a domineering object that was seductive because it was rejecting, which made the patient avoid both a heterosexual and a homosexual object choice. Highlighting this domineering object allows the understanding of the complicated internal object relations that made the patient engage in a number of masochistic moves to assure proximity to this object.

In the first vignette (Ms A), the dream allows a glimpse of the internal object. In the second one (Ms B) there is a progression that begins with the hypothetical construction of an internal object by the analyst, then goes on to establish the correspondence of the internal object to an external object, and finally culminates in the coming of the internal object neatly into the transference. The internal object is an object representation that stands for a significant external object which, in this case material, has been invested with wishes related to the internal object. This rapid shifting of representations has an important effect: the immediate infatuation of the patient. This internal set of circumstances is then deployed into the transference relationship.

To understand the configuration of the internal object, two relevant aspects should be examined: first, the conceptual perimeter of the notion, and second, the contour of a particular internal object in every particular circumstance in the clinical situation. By comparing the two vignettes – submitting the first to the principles of dream analysis and the second to those of the analysis of the transference – we may perceive an initial sketch of the interplay between the conceptual perimeter of the internal object and its practical effects in the clinical setting.

In the first example, the internal object does not appear as the heir to the Oedipus complex, but rather as some sort of internalized structure that came into being before the Oedipal structuralization of the psyche. In a way, this object conforms more strictly to the internalized objects described by Melanie Klein. In the second example, the internal object is defined by the Oedipal aspects of the relationship.

The following material illustrates the existence of a 'benevolent' inner space as a prerequisite for the internalization and maintenance of a good internal object. Unless placed in that space, the good object will be subjected to the patient's violent attacks.

> Mr C, a divorced man in his early forties, was in his first year of analysis. He has serious difficulties establishing a consistent relationship with a woman. He is often infatuated with very beautiful, 'perfect' women, only to find out, as time goes by, that they have some minute defect that grows greater and greater in his mind until he feels that he has to leave them.
>
> The patient had begun analysis just two months after his father died. In an early session, he referred to a dream in which a photograph of his father was lying in the coffin. The photograph was being gnawed by rats and eaten by worms. Mr C was trying to protect the photograph, and he woke up terrified lest the rats and worms would do away with his good memory of his father. At the time, the patient would not accept the analyst's attempts at interpreting this dream. In several previous sessions, he had to go to the toilet to urinate.
>
> In the particular session being discussed, for the first time the patient did not go to the toilet. The issue of going to the toilet had been taken up during the previous two weeks. The patient began the session by saying: 'Doctor, I think there is some dry rot in your waiting room. I have been inspecting it while waiting. You'd better take care, maybe you could find yourself without a consulting room.' From then on, he continued with other associations which he seemed to think were unrelated to this first remark.

One could attempt a 'scenic' comprehension of this session (Lorenzer 1970; Lorenzer and Orban 1978). The patient had displayed in the transference his way of object relating. 'The scenic comprehension is equivalent to the comprehension of the relational situation of the subject with his objects and the interactions between the subjects' (Engelbrecht 1988: 71). Because the main interest of this chapter is to demarcate the clinical and theoretical aspects of the internal object, it is important to emphasize the following points. The patient sought analysis in the midst of a process of mourning. The dream early in his analysis shows the difficulties he was going through because the good, positive memories of his father were being attacked by corroding processes. The patient, who had had enuresis as a child, had a compulsion to urinate at the beginning of every session. In the session when he did not leave to urinate, he substituted a reference to the analyst's waiting room, in which a process of rotting was taking place. The dream shows how the good internal object is endangered by the patient's destructive attacks. The patient resisted the analyst's interpretation for fear it would undermine his own safety.

The need to urinate before starting sessions is a way for Mr C to expel his own destructive wishes via urinary 'attacks'. When he controlled his urge to urinate, his urethral impulses were displaced towards the analyst's waiting room. The urgency and the urinary expulsion prevented him from beginning to understand himself better.

In the case of Mr C's relationships with women, he often ruminated on the particular aspect of a woman's countenance that had attracted him at first. As the rumination proceeded, the object representation became unacceptable. The very preconditions for his falling in love were attacked; hence the idealization of the external object could not prevent the attacks directed against the internal object. Thus the idealization was submitted to the destructive processes that transformed the external object into a denigrated one.

Exactly the same thing happened in the case of Mr C's memory of his father. Mr C's difficulty in maintaining good internalized objects was clearly discernible in the fantasies that followed his abstention from urinating before the session, as well as in his associations to the dream. In the dream's manifest content, the image of his father undergoing the process of putrefaction referred to the idealized father who ends up being destroyed. This process of transforming the good inner object into a damaged one was more clearly displayed in relation to Mr C's comments about the waiting room. Mr C's incapacity to wait corroded the framework in which analysis can happen. The worms, the actual dry rot and the process of putrefaction, which seem to be figurations of Mr C's incessant obsessional rumination, all contributed to the collapse of an inner space where good internal objects are kept alive.

This material certainly evokes Winnicott's (1965) ideas about holding. According to Winnicott, it is not only the complex earliest interactions between the infant and the mother that appear in the transference; the temporo–spatial matrix in which they occur is also communicated in it. Winnicott's clinical research clarifies those aspects of the early holding environment that appear as transference manifestations. It is pertinent to say that this way of interpreting the material is somewhat related to Bion's (1970) ideas about the 'container' as an extension of the good breast functioning as an understanding object.

There is also an important relationship between the internal objects, the self-representation, and aspects of the sense of identity. The following case illustrates this relationship.

Mr D, a married patient, suffered as an adolescent because his cousins laughed at his artistic interests and his delicate, elegant manners. He felt that his male cousins and his peers were trying to deprive him of his most deeply felt form of expression. He married while in college. A 'dedicated' family man, he has three daughters and is a caring husband. Nevertheless, he indulges frequently in homosexual activities, and has had an affair with a woman colleague.

The patient had to stop analysis for a week because of an important business trip on behalf of his father, a well-known businessman. In the first session after his return, he referred to a number of meetings with bankers, which he attended impeccably dressed, feeling in total control of the situation. After the meetings, he changed his clothes, wearing tight jeans, a frilly shirt and a fashionable waistcoat. He was very excited because he had arranged a secret date with his male lover. He related this experience with gusto, and with a note of defiance in his voice. He was pleased that he had used his father's money for this escapade. He also said that he would, of course, pay for the analytic sessions he had been unable to attend while away on business.

While negotiating on behalf of his father with the bankers, Mr D was identifying with his father – or maybe just impersonating him. He felt the enormous satisfaction of being an important man in control of events. Once he finished this activity, he behaved like his immature, delicate and rather hysterical mother, with whom he had developed his earliest sense of identity. In this instance, the identification with his mother had produced a modification of the patient's self-representation. He behaved in a sweet, gentle, feminine fashion. Yet when it came to sexual activity, he played the active part and again felt he had his father's control of the situation. The patient did not appear to perceive this rapid transition from masculine to feminine identifications as a threat to his ego.

This material and the identifications just described raise issues related to the concept of projective identification, which plays a central role in Kleinian object relations theory. As introduced by Melanie Klein, this concept emerged out of 'a rather confused and confusing background of literature on various forms of internalization and externalization – imitation, identification, fantasies of incorporation, and many varieties of projection' (Sandler 1988: 13).[2] This context raises a most important question: does the whole concept of internal objects depend, first, on the acceptance of the crucial importance of projective and identificatory processes in the development of object relationships, and, second, on their pervasive presence in the interplay of transference and countertransference in the here-and-now of the analytic situation?

FROM THEORY TO CLINICAL PRACTICE

A comparison of the four vignettes allows us to examine the match between the theoretical perimeter of the internal object and its clinical contour as it appears in the psychoanalytic setting. The task is to see whether the 'values' in the clinical work correspond to those defined by the theoretical construct. In other words, how can the clinical presentation of an internal object be seen as a derivative shaped by its deep structure? That is, how does the former 'unfold' in the clinical situation, or how does this unconscious structure affect the subjective experience? Once this issue is discussed, one can go on to explore what function the concept of internal object serves, first, in the psychoanalytical-theoretical economy, and second, as an addition to the clinical instrumentarium.

The notion of internal objects is somehow related to that designated by the term 'imago', which – as James Strachey (Freud 1923: 168, n.2) pointed out – first appeared in Freud's (1912a) technical paper on the dynamics of transference and later in connection with the theme of the choice of object: 'These new objects will still be chosen on the model (imago) of the infantile ones but in the course of time they will attract to themselves the affection that was tied to the earlier ones' (Freud 1912b: 181). For some time, the term 'imago' seemed dormant in the psychoanalytic literature, although it appeared as the title of two important psychoanalytic journals. Its clinical use, however, was limited. Freud did not often use the term in his later writings.

It is pertinent in this context to mention an important issue raised by Green (1978) that has to do with Ferenczi's early contribution, 'Introjection and transference'. Ferenczi's paper was written in 1909, before Freud's classical papers on the theme but after his definition of transference in the publication of Dora's case. Its relevance to the issues being raised here comes from the fact that Ferenczi conceptualized the transference as a set of processes based on the mechanisms of introjection and projection. This meaning stands in sharp contrast to that of transference-meaning ('Übertragungsbedeutung'), which Freud included in the editions of his papers on psychoanalytic technique from the year 1924, so as to emphasize a conceptualization based fundamentally on displacement and substitution.

Freud (1914a) also compared the transference to a 'playground' or to 'an intermediate region between illness and real life through which the transition from the one to the other is made' (154). In the field thus created, the Freudian metaphors that compare transference to new editions, facsimiles, new impressions, reprints or revised editions are clearly related to the associative content of the session (Freud 1905). Ferenczi's paper opens the way to metaphors that anticipate some sort of exchange of objects. The former conceptualization corresponded perfectly well with the aim of allowing the patient 'to discover, primarily through his associations and emotional responses, the link between his *present* symptoms and feelings on the one hand and his *past* experiences on the other' (Sandler *et al.* 1992: 38). Ferenczi's paper was a precursor of a different way of looking at the clinical situation and of defining the therapeutic aim: to clear the psychoanalytic encounter of the influence of 'internal presences'.

The term 'imago' was taken up again in connection with clinical work in the British Society. The discussion had arisen in relation to what was then a new concept developed by Melanie Klein. What was questioned was the assumption that the imagos were inside, i.e. were internal imagos. The whole issue has to do with the idea of internal objects. In the long run, regardless of its clinical pertinence, the term 'internal objects' seemed to be a password by which Kleinian analysts recognized each other, or a red light that aroused the suspicion of ego psychologists.

It is interesting to recall that Freud (1940) wrote about the 'internal world' in 1938 and that Hartmann referred to the 'inner world' in his classic 1939 paper, 'Ego psychology and the problem of adaptation'. Both 'internal world' and 'inner world' read 'innere Welt' in the original German (Sandler and Rosenblatt 1962). It is also pertinent to remember the debate on the subject that occurred within the British Society, particularly in the so-called Controversial Discussions. The careful editorial work of Pearl King and Riccardo Steiner (1992) highlights the radical confrontation between two different ways of conceiving of the mind, one represented by Anna Freud and the other by Melanie Klein.

The concept of internal objects played a central role in Fairbairn's theorization. This is particularly evident in his papers, 'Schizoid factors in the personality' (1940) and 'Endopsychic structures considered in terms of object-relations' (1944). Fairbairn developed a very personal way of understanding endopsychic conflict that was related to the later development of Freudian structural theory. He delineated an 'object-relations theory of the personality'. Harry Guntrip (1968) continued Fairbairn's attempts to redefine psychoanalytic theory. Gradually, the concept of internal objects worked its way into mainstream psychoanalysis.

In her 1941 paper devoted to the use of the word 'internal' in psychoanalysis, Alix Strachey referred to a source of difficulty – the word 'internal' is used in several senses in the psychoanalytic literature. Sometimes it 'is equivalent to "mental" or "psychological" or "belonging to the mind"; there are other times when it means "imaginary" or "fictitious". There are also occasions when the word "internal" means "imagined as inside" or "supposedly inside" ' (37). As Strachey says, the use of the word 'internal' in these different senses would not matter much, 'so long as it was always clear in what sense it was being used' (38). Unfortunately, this is not the case. According to Strachey, 'we have managed to confuse a *figment* of the mind with a *function* of the mind' (39). Strachey underlined the hypothesis that the ideas about insideness rest on 'unresolved unconscious phantasies about situations, objects and events inside the subject himself or other people' (41).

Once these difficulties are taken into account, it becomes necessary to return once more to the clinical examples presented here. In the second vignette (Ms B), the notion of an internal object emerged as part of the analyst's free-floating theorizing (Aulagnier 1975). It allowed the clustering of important aspects of the patient's social behaviour so as to relate them to the clinical situation. When the patient referred to the instant fascination she had felt, the analyst perceived that the object of the analysand's ambivalent desire was a sort of external embodiment of an interior 'presence' that fascinated and controlled her. Applying the theoretical construct to the clinical situation illuminated a space of attention in which the contours of the internal presence appeared, first in the patient's associations and then as active transference manifestations.

In the material belonging to the fourth vignette (Mr D) it is possible to observe a constant shuttling between an internal object experienced by the patient as different from himself, and the same internal object standing as the model on which he transiently defined his sexual identity. The alternation of his identifications is so fluid and the changes of his object choices so incessant that the possibility of determining the difference between the theoretical perimeter and the clinical contour seems blurred by the rapidity of unconscious processes. Similarly, the fascination and seduction exercised by the internal object over the ego of Ms B also shaped, though to a lesser extent, her self-representation. The contrasts between these two vignettes permits an understanding of the relationship between the internal object's clinical presentation and its theoretical formulation.

The first two examples (Ms A and Ms B) illustrate how the very notion of internal objects is related, on the one hand, to the superego, and on the other to aspects of the self-representation. The conceptual definition of internal objects depends on whether they are part of the superego structures or are internalizations on which the identifications of the ego are founded. The concepts of superego, self-representation, identification, incorporation, internal world and representational world are more experience–distant and helpful in describing psychic structures. The concept of internal objects has both experience–distant and experience–near aspects that relate to clinical work.

What function does the notion of internal objects serve in the theoretical economy of contemporary psychoanalysis? It is obvious that to answer this question, one must place the idea within the field of experience-distant theorization. Its theoretical perimeter is far removed from experiential boundaries. It is, in fact, a 'structure in the nonexperiential realm' built up through the processes of internalization in the course of the child's development. These processes occur before the advent of the Oedipus complex. When this development occurs, 'the narcissistic and object-related components of the pre-Oedipal internalizations suffer important transformations and their relations acquire new and different meanings' (Hernández 1993: 293).

It is convenient to draw a distinction between objects internalized in the preoedipal period and those modified by the Oedipal conflict or resulting from the internalization of Oedipal objects; their perimeters do differ. Even after the acquisition of language, some of the earliest internal objects remain preverbal. Also, the complex intrapsychic precipitates that are the consequence of the Oedipal situation tend to be more structured and less 'anthropomorphic' than those that belong to the preoedipal period. As growth proceeds, the inner objects may tend to become ego and superego structures that do not behave as internal presences.

But in the analytic situation, the practitioner deals with the clinical contour of the internal object. This notion facilitates the practical understanding of certain clinical interactions. In these examples, it first appeared as an intuition about the first patient's (Ms A's) dream. In the second and fourth vignettes (Mr C and Mr D), the notion of internal objects served as a valuable adjunct to clinical theory in comprehending the object choices and self-representations. But it is clear that within the analytic setting, the concept provides the practitioner with an instrument for grasping some aspects of the transference–countertransference relationship. This is perhaps its most important clinical potentiality and, at the same time, its greatest danger: that of reducing the enormous complexity of the psychoanalytic process to the object-related exchanges of the transference–countertransference interplay.

It is true that finding the proper place for the notion of internal objects within mainstream theory is not easy. The impetus for its development came essentially from the widening of the scope of psychoanalysis, namely the analysis of children and of psychotic and borderline patients. The theories out of which the notion of internal objects emerged fostered an over-inclusive concept of fantasy, which was established without taking much care in determining its semantic and conceptual boundaries or its relationship to classical metapsychology. For the practising analyst, there are many occasions in the clinical situation when contradictory theoretical positions may be present without much disturbance; 'they coexist happily as long as they are unconscious' (Sandler 1983: 38). This coexistence has to do, of course, with the aspect of clinical work that shows the analyst's 'theory in vivo', as Dennis Duncan (1993) has suggested.

In this connection, Winnicott's ideas, particularly those originating in his paper on transitional objects and transitional phenomena (1953), have developed into a valuable, intriguing and elusive concept: that of potential space (1971). The transitional 'nature' of Winnicott's notions has been noted. It also has been emphasized that his ideas 'mirror the very developmental ambiguities he studied' (Ross 1993: 220). The notion of potential space, for example, is a useful clinical tool for understanding the transference, because it defines a metaphoric field for discussing the internal objects and designates an intermediate area of experience. According to Pontalis (1972), Winnicott's work identified 'an area that psychoanalysis had overlooked' because its 'conceptual tools – theoretical or technical – impede its perception and, as a consequence of that, its coming into being' (iv). This third area, which allows for the transition between the me and the not-me, between presence and loss, between child and mother, opens a space between fantasy and reality. There have been some accomplished attempts to discuss the concept, particularly those of Green (1978), Pontalis (1972) and Ogden (1985). The potential space allows room for a 'psychological dialectic of oneness and of separateness in which each creates and informs the other' (Ogden 1985: 132).

Against this background, the case of Mr C seems to be a good example of the clinical relevance of Winnicott's ideas in this context. The transference neither reached the intensity nor developed the sticky and labile quality of those that make the analyst no more than an object of the patient's projective identification. García Badaracco (1992) suggests that in patients who present such a transference, the capacity to create a transitional space is 'severely impaired, thus making it difficult for the transference to become the "playground" to which Freud referred' (214). In the case of Mr D, however, the patient was capable of 'using' the analyst, who was placed beyond the range of his omnipotence (Casement 1985; Winnicott 1971). The vignette illustrates a moment in which the potential space was under siege: the 'playground' was endangered but had not collapsed. There was still room for the mourning process and a space for playing where paradox and contradiction remained available.

THEORETICAL AND CLINICAL DIVERGENCES

The sharpest theoretical and clinical divergences are fuelled by the tension between how the inner and outer worlds are conceptualized. Concepts are more neatly defined if, to begin with, the difference between the worlds of fantasy objects and external objects is taken for granted – in other words, if a clear-cut division between the inner world and the external reality is postulated *a priori*. As a consequence, there are important theoretical, technical and clinical differences. For example, from the point of view of theory, any blurring of the dividing line is tantamount to pathology. In the clinical setting, the exchanges between the patient's inner and outer worlds are conceptualized either as displacements and substitutions, or as expressions of the interplay of projections and introjections, depending on one's perspective; technical considerations vary accordingly (cf. Etchegoyen 1986). The postulation of a third area implies a substantial theoretical and technical shift. The one-to-one relationship between the basic theoretical assumptions and the technical concerns, defined *a priori* as depending on them, suffer an important alteration.[3]

In that which refers to the clinical situation, the technical procedures that aim at creating the conditions for helping the patient may be conceptualized somewhat differently. Transference could be understood both as, first, the influence of the unedited past over the edited present via displacements and substitutions, including the criss-crossing of projections and introjections; and second, as a space or a 'playground' where the role of illusion is fundamental. If this definition is correct, the clinician's task would be to preserve, maintain and repair permanently the space in which analytic work is possible, and to evaluate when and how the patient's potential space is congruent with the space provided by the analyst in the clinical setting. By taking into account the space where the effects of internal objects are expressed and transformed, the analyst could treat the notion of internal objects with greater autonomy. The theoretical dependence of this concept on the mechanisms of projection, identification and projective identification would thus be attenuated.

The principles guiding the theoretical delineation of internal objects belong to different 'geometries' or configurations. There are some differences between the concept of internal objects, as elaborated by the object relations theorists, and its neater theoretical perimeter when it is defined within a theory of unconscious representation following the classical conceptualization. Between the theoretical delineation of the concept and the tangible contour grasped in clinical practice, there is also a space that opens a technical possibility. One can see that the patient's psychical processes are often directed to, or against, the space in which analysis is happening, rather than to, or against, the analytical function itself or the analyst as the object of the transference.

Part of the attraction of the notion of internal objects rests on the fact that it permits the articulation of a genetic-structural model with a model of the internal world, both of which can be applied to the clinical situation. In theory, internal objects, insofar as they are elements pertaining to unconscious fantasy, are in themselves rather simple structures whose effects become manifest in complex forms. But the specific correlation between the underlying structure and its multidimensional manifestations in the clinical setting is difficult to define within the present flux of the psychoanalytic mainstream.

This attempt to understand the concept of internal objects throws a harsh light on some major issues and difficulties faced by the psychoanalytic profession. The possibility of having a unified perspective on the concept of internal objects remains remote.

Long-standing concerns of Joseph Sandler in this area include the exploration of how organized frames of reference have been constructed; the location of the contradictions and inconsistencies that exist in psychoanalytic theory; and the attempts to design a satisfactory theoretical model. His engagement with the complexities of contemporary psychoanalysis, both as a leading theoretician and as a facilitator of psychoanalytic communication, has placed on his agenda the issue of the transformation of mainstream theory as affected by and enriched by such controversial concepts.

SUMMARY

In this paper we have briefly reviewed the evolution and circulation of the theory of internal objects amidst the controversies it elicited, and have included some clinical examples to illustrate the concept. Highlighted by the clinical material, pertinent literature shows how the concept has been modified over time. Distinguishing between the experiential and nonexperiential realms is essential to understanding the relationship between the internal object as grasped in the clinical situation or as formulated metapsychologically.

Also emphasized are some similarities between the transference, the potential space (postulated as a third area of experience between internal and external reality), and the meaning space provided by our scientific institutions and exchanges.

NOTES

1 The authors wish to thank Ms Dana Cáceres for editing assistance.

2 Jones (1948) had a different point of view:

> It is indeed becoming increasingly difficult to distinguish clearly between the processes of introjection, incorporation and identification. The whole theory of 'internal objects', 'good' and 'bad', has thus been enormously extended, with important results both for our understanding of early development and for our daily therapeutic practice.

(11)

3 The significance of illusion in analytic work is at stake. The work of researchers in developmental psychology (cf. Stern 1985, 1992; Emde 1988a, 1988b) shows how an increasingly organized and complex set of representations of the infant's interpersonal world goes along with processes involving the developing senses of agency, affectivity, shame, etc. This research points in two different directions. On the one hand, it goes beyond a merely descriptive differentiation between 'internal' and 'external'. On the other, it brings back once again the controversy between the tradition of illuministic rationalism, as shown most dramatically in 'The future of an illusion', and of a more 'romantic' point of view. Kluzer Usuelli (1992) affirms that Winnicott's arguments legitimize the role of illusion and even tend to make of it the ontological foundation of the subject.

REFERENCES

Aulagnier, P. (1975) *The Violence of Interpretation*, Paris: Presses Universitaires de France.

Baranger, W. (1971) *Positions and Objects in Melanie Klein's Work*, Buenos Aires: Kargieman.

Baranger, W. *et al.* (1980) *About the Concept of Object in Psycho-analysis*, Buenos Aires: Amorrortu Ed.

Bion, W. (1970) *Second Thoughts*, London: Heinemann.

Bollas, C. (1987) *The Shadow of the Object: Psychoanalysis of the Unthought Known*, London: Free Association Books.

Casement, P. (1985) *On Learning from the Patient*, London: Tavistock.

Duncan, D. (1993) 'Theory in vivo', *International Journal of Psycho-Analysis*, 74, 25–32.

Emde, R. M. (1988a) 'Development terminable, interminable: considering theory, therapy', *International Journal of Psycho-Analysis*, 69, 283–96.

——(1988b) 'Development terminable, interminable: innate, motivational factors', *International Journal of Psycho-Analysis*, 69, 23–42.

Engelbrecht, H. (1988). 'The supervision process and the psychoanalytic process', in G. Delgado-Aparicio (ed.) *Psicoanálisis e Identidad*, Lima: Biblioteca Peruana de Psicoanálisis, 69–77.

Etchegoyen, H. (1986) *Foundations of Psychoanalytic Technique*, Buenos Aires: Amorrortu Ed.

Fairbairn, W. R. D. (1940) 'Schizoid factors in the personality', in *Psychoanalytic Studies of the Personality* (1952), London: Routledge & Kegan Paul, 3–27.

——(1944) 'Endopsychic structures considered in terms of object-relations', in *Psychoanalytic Studies of the Personality* (1952), London: Routledge & Kegan Paul, 82–136.

Ferenczi, S. (1909) 'Introjection and transference', in S. Ferenczi (ed.) (1916) *Sex in Psychoanalysis*, Boston MA: Gorham, 30–79.

Freud, S. (1905) 'Fragment of an analysis of a case of hysteria', *Standard Edition*, vol. 7 (1953), London: Hogarth Press, 1–22.

——(1912a) 'The dynamics of transference', *Standard Edition*, vol. 12 (1958), London: Hogarth Press, 97–108.

——(1912b) 'On the universal tendency to debasement in the sphere of love (Contributions to the psychology of love, II)', *Standard Edition*, vol. 11 (1957), London: Hogarth Press, 177–90.

——(1914a) 'Remembering, repeating and working-through (Further recommendations on the technique of psycho-analysis, II)', *Standard Edition*, vol. 12 (1958), London: Hogarth Press, 145–56.

——(1923) 'The economic problem of masochism', *Standard Edition*, vol. 19 (1961), London: Hogarth Press, 159–70.

——(1940) 'An outline of psycho-analysis', *Standard Edition*, vol. 23 (1964), London: Hogarth Press, 139–207.

García Badaracco, J. (1992) 'Psychic change and its clinical evaluation', *International Journal of Psycho-Analysis*, 73, 209–20.

Green, A. (1978) 'Potential space in psychoanalysis: the object in the setting', in S. A. Grolnick and L. Barkin (with W. Muensterberger) (eds) *Between Reality and Fantasy: Transitional Objects and Phenomena*, New York: Jason Aronson, 167–89.

Grinberg, L. (1956) 'On some technical problems derived from projective identification and counter-projective identification', *Revista de Psicoanálisis*, 13, 507–11.

——(1963) 'Psychopathology of projective identification, counter-projective identification and counter-transference', *Revista de Psicoanálisis*, 20, 113–23.

Guntrip, H. (1968) *Schizoid Phenomena, Object Relations and the Self*, London: Hogarth Press.

Hartmann, H. (1939) *Ego Psychology and the Problem of Adaptation* (1958), New York: International Universities Press.

Hernández, M. (1993) 'Playing for time to create a space where change may happen', in M. J. Horowitz, O. F. Kernberg and E. M. Weinshel (eds) *Psychic Structure and Psychic Change*, Madison CT: International Universities Press, 291–310.

Jiménez, J. P. (1992) 'The analyst's contribution to the processes of projective identification', *Revista Chilena de Psicoanálisis*, 9 (2), 54–66.

Jones, E. (1948) 'Introduction', in M. Klein, *Contributions to Psycho-analysis, 1921–1945*, London: Hogarth Press and the Institute of Psycho-Analysis, 9–12.

Kernberg, O. (1979) 'Some implications of object relations theory and technique', *Journal of the American Psychoanalytic Association*, 27, 207–40.

——(1988) 'Object relations theory in clinical practice', *Psychoanalytic Quarterly*, 57, 481–504.

——(1991a) 'Aggression and love in the relationship of the couple', *Journal of the American Psychoanalytic Association*, 39, 45–70.

——(1991b) 'The current status of psychoanalysis', *Journal of the American Psychoanalytic Association*, 41, 45–62.

King, P. and Steiner, R. (1992) (eds) *The Freud–Klein Controversies 1941–1945*, London: Routledge.

Klein, M. (1927) 'Symposium on child-analysis', in *Contributions to Psychoanalysis, 1921–1945* (1948), London: Hogarth Press and the Institute of Psycho-Analysis, 152–84.

——(1928) 'Early stages of the Oedipus conflict', in *Contributions to Psychoanalysis, 1921–1945* (1948), London: Hogarth Press and the Institute of Psycho-Analysis, 202–14.

——(1929) 'Infantile anxiety-situations reflected in a work of art and in the creative impulse', in *Contributions to Psychoanalysis, 1921–1945* (1948), London: Hogarth Press and the Institute of Psycho-Analysis, 227–35.

——(1934) 'A contribution to the psychogenesis of manic-depressive states', in *Contributions to Psychoanalysis, 1921–1945* (1948), London: Hogarth Press, 282–310.

——(1946) 'Notes on some schizoid mechanisms', in *Envy and Gratitude and Other Works* (1975), London: Hogarth Press and the Institute of Psycho-Analysis, 1–24.

——(1948) 'On the theory of anxiety and guilt', in *Envy and Gratitude and Other Works* (1975), London: Hogarth Press and the Institute of Psycho-Analysis, 25–42.

——(1958) 'On the development of mental functioning', *International Journal of Psycho-Analysis*, 39, 84–90.

Kluzer Usuelli, A. (1992). 'The significance of illusion in the work of Freud and Winnicott: a controversial issue', *International Review of Psycho-Analysis*, 19, 179–87.

Lorenzer, A. (1970) *A Critical Revision of the Psychoanalytic Concept of Symbol* (1976), Buenos Aires: Amorrortu Ed.

Lorenzer, A. and Orban, P. (1978) 'Transitional objects and phenomena: socialization and symbolization', in S. A. Grolnick and L. Barkin (with W. Muensterberger) (eds) *Between Reality and Fantasy: Transitional Objects and Phenomena*, New York: Jason Aronson, 469–82.

Ogden, T. H. (1985) 'On potential space', *International Journal of Psycho-Analysis*, 66, 129–41.

——(1989) *The Primitive Edge of Experience*, Hillsdale NJ: Jason Aronson.

Pontalis, J. B. (1972) 'Introduction', in D. W. Winnicott, *Realidad y Juego*, Barcelona: Gedisa.

Rosenfeld, H. (1969) 'Treatment of psychotic states', *International Journal of Psycho-Analysis*, 50, 615–32.

——(1983) 'Primitive object relations and mechanisms', *International Journal of Psycho-Analysis*, 64, 261–8.

Ross, J. M. (reporter) (1993) 'The clinical relevance of the contributions of Winnicott', *Journal of the American Psychoanalytic Association*, 41, 219–35.

Rycroft, C. (1972) *The Critical Dictionary of Psychoanalysis*, London: Penguin.

Sandler, J. (1978) 'On the development of object relationships and affects', *International Journal of Psycho-Analysis*, 59, 285–96.

——(1983) 'Reflections on some relations between psychoanalytic concepts and psychoanalytic practice', *International Journal of Psycho-Analysis*, 64, 35–45.

——(ed.) (1988) *Projection, Identification, Projective Identification*, London: Karnac Books.

——(1990) 'On internal object relations', *Journal of the American Psychoanalytic Association*, 38, 859–80.

——(1992) 'Reflections on developments in the theory on psychoanalytic technique', *International Journal of Psycho-Analysis*, 73, 189–98.

Sandler, J. and Rosenblatt, B. (1962) 'The concept of the representational world', *Psychoanalytic Study of the Child*, 17, 128–48.

Sandler, J., Dare, C. and Holder, A. (1992) *The Patient and the Analyst*, London: Karnac Books.

Stern, D. (1985) *The Interpersonal World of the Infant*, New York: Basic Books.

——(1992) 'The "pre-narrative" envelope: an alternative view of "unconscious phantasy" in infancy', paper presented at the Symposium in Memory of George Moran, London.

Strachey, A. (1941) 'A note on the use of the word "internal" ', *International Review of Psycho-Analysis*, 22, 37–43.

Tustin, F. (1980) 'Autistic objects', *International Review of Psycho-Analysis*, 7, 27–40.

Wallerstein, R. (1988) 'One psychoanalysis or many?', *International Journal of Psycho-Analysis*, 69, 5–21.

——(1990) 'Psychoanalysis: the common ground', *International Journal of Psycho-Analysis*, 71, 3–20.

Winnicott, D. W. (1953) 'Transitional objects and transitional phenomena: a study of the first *not-me* possession', in *Collected Papers: Through Paediatrics to Psychoanalysis* (1958), London: Tavistock, 229–42.

——(1965) *The Maturational Process and the Facilitating Environment*, London: Hogarth Press.

——(1971) *Playing and Reality*, London: Tavistock.

10

UNCONSCIOUS FANTASY AS AN EXPERIENCE OF ACTION

Daniel Widlöcher

Psychoanalysts usually agree about the necessity of using the term 'unconscious' for describing different expressions of mental life. But they disagree about the exact meaning of the term. Two pairs of positions are generally considered: one distinguishes between the unconscious as latent thought and consciousness, and the second distinguishes between what may become conscious and what has no access to becoming conscious. From 'The interpretation of dreams' (1900) to 'An outline of psycho-analysis' (1940), both distinctions have been made by Freud, but not always in precisely the same sense.

One can make clear the distinction in accordance with the descriptive, dynamic, and topical or systematic points of view. From the descriptive point of view, 'virtual' or 'latent' representations that are susceptible to becoming conscious at any moment (the preconscious proper) may be considered unconscious. From the dynamic point of view, 'psychical process', which is temporarily or permanently repressed by the 'second censorship' (Freud 1915: 193), 'however complicated it may be', can, on occasion, 'remain preconscious, even though as a rule it will, as we say, push its way forward into consciousness' (Freud 1940: 160) and may be qualified as 'unconscious'. Finally, from the topical or systematic point of view, 'unconscious proper' may be reserved for material that cannot gain 'easy access to becoming conscious but must be inferred, recognized and translated into conscious form' (Freud 1940: 160).

If the distinction between these three forms of thinking is not so easy to make, it is probably due to some confusion about their differing metapsychological criteria. For many years, Joseph Sandler has pursued a metapsychological reflection on the distinction between the descriptive and the structural unconscious. This distinction has not always been granted the same attention as that paid to it by Sandler, because the unconscious-preconscious has often been considered to be all of the psychic contents that could be accessible to consciousness. So it is necessary to distinguish between 'virtual' representations that are susceptible to becoming conscious at any moment, and representations that are temporarily repressed because of a 'second' censorship, as emphasized by Sandler. Virtual representations are memories or ideas which are implicitly present in the mind and become conscious as far as the present situation calls them up. Repressed memories and ideas are also retained in the same long-term memory system, but are prevented from becoming conscious by forgetting. But the greatest difficulty lies in distinguishing the psychical contents that are radically repressed by the censorship that exists between the preconscious and the unconscious proper, from those that are repressed as a result of the second censorship. A very mundane clinical example illustrates repression due to the 'second' censorship of material previously suppressed by the conflict between the preconscious and the unconscious.

TEMPORARY REPRESSION VIA 'SECOND' CENSORSHIP

Case example

The patient, a thirty-year-old woman who has been in analysis with me for some time, reported in our next session that she had been totally preoccupied over the weekend by the thought of meeting me outside of the office. She had been imagining that she would meet me by attending scientific conferences or art exhibitions, but she eventually realized that she could meet me directly by ringing me up or by staking herself out near my house. She agreed that such behaviour is that of a true lover.

She then tried to remember how the previous session, the last one of the week, had ended; it was on Thursday or Friday, she said. I could not but note her last remark, and the implicit reproach in it, because the session had actually taken place on Thursday (the Friday appointment having been cancelled by me). I was secretly satisfied by the link she was trying to establish between sessions, but I could not see what she was referring to.

Fantasies succeeded one another in this patient, such as the wish to be my daughter. She also brought up various images of fraternal rivalry. A memory came back to her of her mother telling her how happy she was not to have to worry about her or her future.

She then suddenly remembered the end of the previous session. She had been expressing all the interest she now had for her treatment. A little while later, I signalled very abruptly the end of the session by saying the usual 'Bien, bien', in French, an expression which either approves of what has been said (the meaning the patient apparently retained) or marking the end of a sequence of actions or sentences (the meaning I had in mind). Although this coincided with the scheduled time, she could not help but think that I was showing my approval for what she had just said. Obviously, the patient had clearly had an insight into this fantasy after the session but had censored it from her consciousness, while all her conscious fantasies were producing the 'loving' behaviour.

UNCONSCIOUS, PRECONSCIOUS REPRESSION

The other kind of repression is more difficult to illustrate, because the fantasy content cannot be described precisely with the subject's words. Freud gave us a few examples, such as that of 'The Ratman', when he wrote:

> At all the more important moments while he was telling his story his face took on a very strange, composite expression. I could only interpret it as one of *horror at pleasure of his own of which he himself was unaware.*
>
> (Freud 1909: 166–7)

There is also the second phase of 'A child is being beaten'(1919):

> Profound transformations have taken place between this first phase and the next. It is true that the person beating remains the same (that is, the father); but the child who is beaten has been changed into another one and is now invariably the child producing the phantasy. The phantasy is accompanied by a high degree of pleasure, and has now acquired a significant content, with the origin of which we shall be concerned later. Now, therefore, the wording runs: '*I am being beaten by my father*'. It is of an unmistakably masochistic character. This second phase is the most important and the most momentous of all. But we may say of it in a certain sense that it has never had a real existence. It is never remembered, it has never succeeded in becoming conscious. It is a construction of analysis, but it is no less a necessity on that account.
>
> (Freud 1919: 185)

The end of the session whose first part I reported earlier appears to be a good illustration of the structural unconscious. The patient, after remembering the 'conscious' fantasy that had marked the end of the last session, told me she would like me to tell her what I thought of her idea, and how I understood what she wanted to say. She insisted, pressing me, and at the same time felt embarrassed by her own insistence but could not help it. She just could not 'control' herself. I then told her that by pressuring me in such a way, she was behaving just like her sister, who worried her mother by always interrogating her, which in turn made her jealous.

'Oh yes,' she said, 'when I asked you that question, I did not feel that I was myself saying it, I had the feeling of being in a game … that I wanted to play.'

In terms of clinical accessibility, the differences between the two types of repression are obvious. In the first situation, the patient's awareness or attentional investment enabled her to overcome the second censorship and express the fantasy consciously. In the second situation, only construction work permitted her to reconstruct the scenario from several concrete scenes. In one case, the scene was included in the biographic concrete memory, while in the other it was expressed only as an hypothetical construct. In one case, the scene could be represented with words, while in the other, the words were merely used to describe it.

The question therefore is whether the differences observed between these two forms of the unconscious are linked only to the type of censorship and to the modalities of access to consciousness, or if there is a more radical difference in the very nature of such representations. The thesis I would like to defend is that the 'unconscious-preconscious' representation consists of the 'narrative' description of an act, as any representation that may be constructed in the preconscious-conscious system, naming the sources, the actors and the forms of the action represented in a narrative manner, whereas in the 'unconscious proper', the representation is more like an hallucination whereby the action in progress can be represented.

There are two forms of mental representation of action: first, the representation of an action that is not at present realized (past or future action), and second, the representation of the action that is presently realized (the present act). The verbal description of the action is, in the first case, a narrative; in the second case, a statement about what is actually performed. The experience is, in the first case, a memory (or a conscious fantasy or fiction); in the second case, an experience of acting.

There are some particular situations in which the experience of acting does not fit with the real performance of the action. Such is the case in the classical description by William James of a patient with an anaesthetized arm who was ordered to raise it, or in neurosurgical observations. In such cases there is an hallucinatory experience of action. In one sense, as Freud (1900) pointed out, our experience of action in a dream may be said to be hallucinatory. While the preconscious representation keeps the declarative description of the action in memory, the unconscious representation describes the experience of the action itself.

DISTINGUISHING BETWEEN WORD REPRESENTATION AND ACTION REPRESENTATION

I would now like to elaborate on this distinction between the representation and the experience of the action. I propose to replace Freud's opposition of 'word-presentation' ('Wortvorstellung') versus 'thing-presentation' ('Sachevorstellung'), defended in 'The unconscious' (1915) and reused in 'The ego and the id' (1923), with that of 'word presentation *v.* action presentation'.

For defining the presentation of the unconscious proper, the 'action', as an hallucinatory experience, seems more pertinent than the 'thing' concept.

WORD PRESENTATION

Little has been written about the mental operations that enable the agent of an action to describe in words what he is doing or has done. Psychoanalysts have given it little attention; most of what they hear during sessions amounts to action accounts, whether past or future actions, anticipations or fantasies. As the manifest content of dreams, these descriptions encourage patients to seek the underlying content (i.e. precisely the unconscious content being expressed, at least in part, inasmuch as it is directed to the psychoanalyst via transference).

These comments may sound trivial. However, they are contrary to a certain introspective conceptualization of psychoanalytic communication whereby the patient is thought to relate mental states to the psychoanalyst for interpretation. Should that not be the meaning of Freud's (1913) so-called 'blind traveller' metaphor? The analyst, as the traveller, has no access to the scenery unfolding before him outside the train window. He can only ask the patient – the passenger next to the window – to describe what lies beyond the window. What a patient says of his actions or his thoughts is not the exact description of a psychical reality extraneous to the action, but rather is a mere transcription of the experience.

The patient who says 'I just thought that ...' does not describe the internal event that has just happened. He transforms it into an act of speech. He gives a propositional representation, which can be worded in speech, of the action or mental state he has just experienced. Such ability to tell the meaning of an action or to assemble the associative tissue of thought in a propositional form is the very condition of analytic communication, as it is the basis for every human communication, in a more general understanding.

ACTION PRESENTATION

The relationship between the dream model and the concept of hallucinatory representation of action is a good reflection of primary process mental functioning. We shall see later that it matches clinical data, such as during the mourning process and during psychoanalytic treatment. Indeed, it appears to clarify the distinctions between the descriptive and the structural unconscious.

DREAMS

There is an ambiguity in Freudian theory about the relationship between dreams and wishes. It was established in 'The interpretation of dreams' (Freud 1900) that the representations ('scenes') that make up a dream represent the realization of a wish. But the question is whether the act of representing a scene (through all the observed distortions, condensing and displacement, in particular) means that the wish, once satisfied, could rest in the illusion of being satisfied. This is the thesis extensively developed by Freud, and it corresponds to the 'hallucinatory satisfaction of our wishes' (Freud 1917a: 230). But, at a very early stage, Freud had to concede that certain dreams contradicted this theory, and the importance granted to repetition compulsion forced him to revise his perspective.

This theoretical wavering seems linked to the ambiguity reflected by the difference between hallucinatory fulfilment of wishes ('Halluzinatorische Wunschbefriedigung') and wish realization ('Wunscherfüllung'). The purpose of representation of wish realization (or, better still, the representation of a wish in the accomplished mode) is not necessarily to make the dreamer consciously believe the wish has been satisfied. One may wonder whether this ability to represent wish satisfaction is perhaps a means to figure thought and not necessarily to ensure satisfaction, functions that may be independent of the dream (i.e. of the scenic dimensions of representations).

Dreams are not thing representations. In spite of the aphorism by which pigs should dream of corn, or of young Anna Freud's dream-speaking aloud of strawberries and porridge (Freud 1900: 130), a dream is never a simple picture. It is an action representation.

The manifest content has always been described as a scene within which an action unfolds, or as a succession of scenes. It is always possible to make an account of it by putting the dreamer in the position of an actor who takes an active or passive part in the dream, or as a spectator of an externally unfolding action. The frame of the dream, the objects and persons present, are there to give a sense to the action. There is no very real context surrounding the scene, but only particular concrete signs that are closely related to the content of the dream action. When they appear incongruous or useless, unrelated to the manifest sense of the dream, it is an indication to look for a scene of which they would be a significant feature, and to suppose that this scene (i.e. its underlying content) is, one way or another, related to the manifest content.

By the associative method, a network of connections is established, but the links then observed always lead to events kept in memory. So a disparate set of events, past or present, long past or recent, constitutes a mosaic of scenes entering the composition of the dream. Objects or persons, their names or any symbolic association, are nothing without the action they contribute. It can be said that the scene signified by the manifest content is the result of a superimposition of scenes imprinted in memory and activated at the time of dream production.

The conditions for representing an action are well defined. Although an object (a landscape, for instance) cannot be comprehensively described in words, an action can be directly expressed by speech. The subject who gives an account of an action in which he is engaged is in a position to describe it with words. The action has a propositional content (its intentionality) and various psychological modalities (to believe and to wish, but also to hope, fear, suppose, imagine, etc.). The propositional content defines the meaning of the action, the state of the world, and the transformation that reflects it.

But the dream follows rules of expression of its own. The manifest content scene is always reflected without any modality of belief or desire. The event is represented in the accomplished mode; it unfolds in the present of the dream. Insofar as the manifest content is taken as a composition gathering the latent content scenes, one can rightly suppose that the latent scenes are also activated into a presentation that depends on the accomplishment modality. One may also think that it is because the activated memory scenes – the scenes of the past – are represented as scenes of the present that their composite expression is also represented in the accomplished mode. The dream therefore contains no belief, no doubt or negation. As to the wishing mode, we now realize that it is absent from the dream proper. Let us be clear: there are wishful expressions (hope, refusal, will) in the dream's content ('I want to get out of this place') but not in the telling of the dream: the scene is there, without any belief or wish mode. The dreamer experiences only that he is performing the action in which he is engaged, whether he is the active agent, the passive subject or the observer.

This reflection, incidentally, helps give a more precise meaning to the word-presentation *v.* thing-presentation dichotomy. No longer referring to a simple object name but rather to the language of action, it can be said that during the conscious day life, the subject, being the agent of his acts or being passively involved in an externally initiated action, is in a position to describe with words what he is doing, without even trying to observe the materialization of his actions. He thus keeps a memory of his actions in the declarative mode. He remains a witness of his own actions. In dreams, conversely, action presentation can only be that of the acting intention being materialized during the current presentation. The dreamer is the actor of his actions. The manifest content is the result of a condensing of presentations, and one is entitled to believe that the desire mode (e.g. wish fulfilment), which characterizes the manifest content, is also that of the underlying content that makes it up.

PRIMARY PROCESS

As the actions described in the account of a dream uncover latent scenes that make up the dream, the scenes that occur in the patient's mind likewise uncover those we usually qualify as derivative of the unconscious. Considering all the properties of a representation that follows the rules of the primary process, one sees that they are identical to those governing the accomplishment of actions. The intent is implemented by the act: to think is to do, to wish is to accomplish (to achieve).

The principle of free energy flow, the absence of a link between unconscious representations, is fully compatible with the concept that the latter, insofar as they are composed of hallucinatory experiences of action, follow the principle that any action is independent of the others. An action can merely follow another, or it can replace it. The displacement specific to this mode of thought results from this property. There cannot be any contradiction, for both actions cannot be incompatible, they can only cancel each other. In contrast, actions can materialize different intentions, thus also reflecting condensation. Lastly, time cannot be represented in a system whereby each thought is expressed by its materialization into an act.

In short, the functioning rules of the primary process are easily explained if one hypothesizes that the primary process governs the production of hallucinatory actions. Anything that the unconscious can figure, the primary process implements in that mode. In this sense, one could say that the unconscious does not wish; it expresses wishes in the mode of accomplishment by simulating their realization.

WORKING THROUGH AND
MOURNING WORK

Another consequence of this way of describing unconscious representations is that it enables us to explain the resistance to change shown by the unconscious during working through in the course of treatment. It has often been observed that the effects of interpretation take time to materialize, whereas interpretation itself has been well heard and understood. The complexity of the processes involved, the multiple determinations of symptoms and symptomatic behaviour, the role of resistances and of repetition compulsion, are all well known. But, independently of these factors, the very phrase 'working through' ('Durcharbeitung') was used by Freud (1914: 155) to express this necessary time. The technical problems raised by this work are well known to practitioners.

The mourning process also requires time. Common-sense psychology has known this for a long time.

Reality-testing has shown that the loved object no longer exists, and it proceeds to demand that all libido shall be withdrawn from its attachments to that object. This demand arouses understandable opposition – it is a matter of general observation that people never willingly abandon a libidinal position, not even, indeed, when a substitute is already beckoning to them.

(Freud 1917b: 244)

It is therefore really a conflict of representations between a reality assessment and previous thought constructs that refer to the same object of love.

What should we think, in clinical terms, of this concept of a leak of libidinal energy, or a wound inflicted by the 'real' loss of the object? Let us suppose that every time a wish recurs, a representation of a link to the object is materialized. The object is really present, by imagination, in the scene that expresses the wish. Therefore, the function of the scene representation ('Vorstellung') is indeed to fill the drive place ('Repräsentanz'). But here the reality testing is incompatible with this representation. Its drive-expressing function can no longer be exerted. The compulsive excitation is 'useless' and progressively loses strength.

DISCUSSION

We must now return to the hypothesis of unconscious presentation as an action presentation. If the libido adhesiveness plays such an efficient role in the resistance of the id, it is because this resistance is going to be expressed in an 'hallucinatory regression' (Freud 1900: 567), the only way to accept turning away from reality and maintaining the illusory presence of the object. The unconscious fantasy maintains the lost object in existence in the inner evidence mode, as the dream represents the wish in the fulfilment mode. It is therefore the topical view that accounts for the resistance of the id. The id is the place for fantasized attachments to the object, which, in their condition of unconscious representations, are figured as hallucinatory experiences.

The originality of the psychoanalytic explanation lies in the proposition that resistance to the actuality of the reality assessment is linked to the unconscious, hence hallucinatory, status of the wish representations. But a question remains: why is mourning not endless? How can reality assessment put an end to the fantasy? If the psychical reality ignores time, how can an end occur? Now we have to explain the 'interminable' and 'terminable'.

It has to be accepted that the conscious evidence of the loss – the reality assessment – gradually transforms the unconscious constructs. At this point, we can risk an analogy: reality in mourning replaces interpretation; reality imposes a new belief, without immediately modifying those that fuel the persistence of the object.

Here is the costly task of counterinvestment: to oppose each memory, each expectation, with reality assessment. Freud repeats (1917b): 'Each single one of the memories and expectations in which the libido is bound to the object is brought up and hypercathected, and detachment of the libido is accomplished in respect of it' (245). He adds, in the case of melancholia:

> The quick and easy answer is that 'the unconscious (thing-) presentation of the object has been abandoned by the libido'. In reality, however, this presentation is made up of innumerable single impressions (or unconscious traces of them), and this withdrawal of libido is not a process that can be accomplished in a moment, but most certainly, as in mourning, be one in which progress is long-drawn-out and gradual.
>
> (Freud 1917b: 256)

Freud thus insistently shows that it takes time to substitute the representation of a new event for all past representations concerned with the same object. In other words, it takes time for present representations to change into past ones. The forgetting that results from mourning therefore is not the forgetting of the past, but rather the forgetting of a 'still present' (Freud 1919: 179): paradoxically, it is the replacement of this present of repetition by a true past that marks the end of mourning (the completion of the mourning process). Mourning takes time because it does not confront the past, but rather is a form of the present; it is not a memory but rather an ongoing action. On the other hand, it leads to an end, when regrets tie up memories.

The memory of the present, contrary to that of the past, gets its actuality from the fact that it is materialized in the form of an action presentation. The mourning time is marked by the repeated actualization of scenes which, issued from the past, are realized in the hallucinatory mode if they fall within the unconscious register.

This unconscious actualization of memories demonstrates the interest of replacing 'thing-presentation' (the term used by Freud to define the nature of the representation exposed to the mourning process) by the concept of 'action presentation'. This unconscious representation is not a description of the past action, nor is it the representation of a goal, but it is indeed the subjective experience of a present action. In the mourning process, the scenes that painfully recur in memory as if taking place in the present constitute actions whose meaning can be worded by the subject.

So the memory of actions is not governed by the same rules as the memory of knowledge. Past actions are not necessarily reduced to a mere description of past events. They can continue to exist as scenarios susceptible to being implemented in the present. As early as 1893, Breuer and Freud

(1893–5) showed that curing hysteric symptoms requires changing the status of a past event through repetition of the traumatic scene, including abreactive repetition (i.e. transference).

What at the beginning could look like a mere analogy between mourning and interpretation work can now be seen as a similarity of mechanisms. The time necessary for reality assessment to act on all the scenes in relation to the lost object is of the same order as that of working through. Interpreting has the same power and limitations as the reality of the loss. The meaning of unconscious derivatives must be interpreted in detail, which presents the patient with the necessity of confronting many particular situations via the interpretations, the meaning of which is nonetheless perceived as well.

However, there is a difference between mourning and treatment. In mourning, past scenes are remembered spontaneously, perhaps slightly bolstered by events in daily life. In treatment, transference ensures the development of repetitions. As rightly emphasized by Aulagnier (1990), the interpretation is meant to make the patient re-live a past experience through a present one: interpretations are made, with 'all the accounts worded by the patient and with their common feature being to update the link that exists between the emotion which expressed his speech ... and the emotion which accompanied an experience lived in the past' (173).

DIFFERENTIATING BETWEEN THE TWO TYPES OF THE UNCONSCIOUS

How can we reconcile this interpretation of the thing-presentation in terms of action presentation and yet still distinguish between the two types of the unconscious? Clearly, we must ascribe this notion of action presentation to the unconscious fantasy as it pertains to the unconscious proper. Or, in other words, we must ascribe it to the unconscious that possesses the structural character of the id.

The clinical example given at the beginning of this chapter helps make that distinction. When the patient forgot what she had thought of at the end of the preceding analytic session, then tried to remember it, the representation that remained unconscious was a memory of a recent past event that had previously been conscious. This event was an action, or a scene, concretely remembered and easily transcribed into words after the repression was lifted. It only took time for the patient to think of her mother, who understood her so well and had so great an esteem for her, for the forgotten scene to be recalled (a scenario where I had signalled, by my session–ending signal, 'Bien, bien', that I approved the fact that she enjoyed coming to the sessions). It could be said that initially, when leaving the session, the patient had been able to keep the scene present in her consciousness in a manner articulated in her own words and by the way I had answered her. Her ability to consciously retain the scene might have occurred because she was able initially to verbalize its meaning when it was consciously experienced and thus fixed in memory.

Forgetting applies to a representation that was fixed from a concrete experience. According to Freud's terminology, the representation that became unconscious retains the characteristic of being both a thing-presentation and a word-presentation. This dual identity might be a property of the fantasies repressed by the second censorship. In contrast, in the unconscious scenario that seemed to come out at the end of the session, we were faced with a situation that was not linked to or related to any special scene; it was expressed instead as a compulsion to speak within the transference, and it was by becoming aware of this compulsory character that the patient benefited from the interpretation.

In terms of action presentation, the difference is just as clear. In the first case, the action took place in the present in the patient's experience, when she perceived my 'bien' as an acquiescence to her satisfaction. Thus our interaction could be considered as a present action experience, of which the patient felt she was the initiator, in which the analyst was taking part. Transference fantasy is, in fact, a scene that unfolds in the present. It is that scene of our interaction which she will keep a memory of by mentioning again after leaving the session. Naturally, the same scene was recalled when her relationship with her mother came up. In the second case, the action was expressed only by acting out; it gathered meaning when the acting out was related to a past scene between her mother and her sister, that she was unaware underlay an unconscious identification with her sibling rival. As in ' "A child is being beaten" ', the scenario reads: 'My sister provokes my mother by continual questioning', but its purpose was to obtain in the transference what she wished for in the past: 'to attract the interest of her mother by continual provocations, as her sister does'. The repetition in transference clearly demonstrates how the unconscious fantasy, which structurally pertains to the id, is not the expression of the wish, but rather is a thought constraint that takes possession of the mind and commands repetition. It does not represent the drive, but is instead the drive itself.

The 'preconscious-unconscious' memory is immediately expressed by recalling the forgotten scene. The 'proper unconscious' presentation is not remembered in a scene, but it is performed in a whole sequence of past and present scenes whose leading thread – the common theme expressed by each scene differently – can be retrieved by gradual construction. These are, in some way, screen memories in action.

The repressed representation was therefore not of the same type in both cases. In the first case, the hallucinatory experience took the form of a forgotten memory, whereas in the second it was formed by rules that produce substitutive formations and acting out.

But is this dichotomy a difference of type, or is it just the difference between two components whose respective weights vary according to the circumstances of repression? On the one hand, scenes help make up the scenario (screen memories or, conversely, an accumulation of scenes, as shown by Anna Freud [1965]); on the other, the scenario, reduced to a few key images, tries to find expression in concrete scenes. It is as if the repression of the preconscious-unconscious was mainly having an effect on the preservation of a scene, but that scene could serve as a screen memory pattern for process in the unconscious proper.

The concept of unconscious representation as an action presentation thus raises several questions, but at least it sheds new light on the issue of the source of impulse, within a perspective that in all points fits object relations theory. Inasmuch as it constitutes an hallucinatory experience of action, the unconscious representation contains its own energy; it is an action trying to be performed, a scene attempting to unfold.

In fact, the distinction here is not so clear, because the scene in the first case, when repressed, was expressed not only by conscious fantasies but also by a compulsion to act. In other words, from the moment when repression forbade the scene to be represented, the scene activated substitutive constructs in the form of conscious fantasies and acting out. What difference is there between the repressed memory and the unconscious fantasy of the id? After all, what is the difference between the experience of an unconscious action (as in the second case) and that of a conscious action (as in the first situation, before the repression)?

Precisely, the question is whether the hallucinatory experience of an unconscious action is identical to the real experience of a conscious action, or is susceptible to becoming conscious. In the latter case, the action has become an event of the past. Indeed, the transferential character of the psychical content makes the repetitive scenario continue into acting out before remembering, and probably into verbal communication later. But the scene itself belongs to the past. On the contrary, the unconscious proper scenario issued from the past is constantly being expressed by the present repetitive behaviour.

Paradoxically, this distinction seems completely opposed to the distinction made by J. and A.-M. Sandler (Sandler 1990; Sandler and Sandler 1984). For them, the unconscious proper is related to past infantile experiences, while the unconscious-preconscious is related to present experiences. They contrast past unconscious with present unconscious.

The difference is perhaps not so clear-cut. Repression by the second censorship transforms the narrative of a recent past event into an unconscious memory. It may be considered a present unconscious. Most debatable is the case of the unconscious proper. Reference to the past seems to be related to the content of the unconscious representation but not to its nature. Internal objects, even those representing early past experiences, are actually taking part in an action scenario or in patterns of action that recur through id derivatives.

According to the most classical model of psychoanalytic technique, present unconscious interpretation tends to lift the defences and to reinforce the associative elements. Interpretation of the past unconscious is more problematic. An interpretative pattern must be elaborated that corresponds to the matrix common to the conscious and preconscious fantasies, so that the scenario can be acted out in the transference. It is not a construct because there is no genetic explanation for this form of interpretation. Instead, it seems closer to dream interpretation work that condenses the underlying content to elicit the unconscious theme that precipitated the latent content within the manifest content. In a way, the action presentation theory would bolster the relationship, underlined by Freud on many occasions, between the psychoanalytical situation and dreams.

REFERENCES

Aulagnier, P. (1990) 'Le temps de l'interprétation' ('Time for interpreting'), *Topique*, 46, 173–85.

Breuer, J. and Freud, S. (1893–5) 'Studies on hysteria', *Standard Edition*, vol. 2, vii–xxxi, 1–311. London: Hogarth Press, 1955.

Freud, A. (1965) *Normality and Pathology in Childhood*, New York: International Universities Press.

Freud, S. (1900) 'The interpretation of dreams', *Standard Edition*, vols 4–5, ix–xxxii, 1–627. London: Hogarth Press, 1953.

——(1909) 'Notes upon a case of obsessional neurosis', *Standard Edition*, vol. 10, 151–318. London: Hogarth Press, 1955.

——(1913) 'On beginning the treatment (further recommendations on the technique of psycho-analysis, I)', *Standard Edition*, vol. 12, 121–44. London: Hogarth Press, 1958.

——(1914) 'Remembering, repeating and working-through (further recommendations on the technique of psycho-analysis, II)', *Standard Edition*, vol. 12, 145–56. London: Hogarth Press, 1958.

——(1915) 'The unconscious', *Standard Edition* , vol. 14, 159–215. London: Hogarth Press, 1963.

——(1917a) 'A metapsychological supplement to the theory of dreams', *Standard Edition*, vol. 14, 217–35. London: Hogarth Press, 1963.

——(1917b) 'Mourning and melancholia', *Standard Edition*, vol. 14, 237–60. London: Hogarth Press, 1963.

——(1919) ' "A child is being beaten": a contribution to the study of the origin of sexual perversions', *Standard Edition*, vol. 17, 175–204. London: Hogarth Press, 1955.

——(1923) 'The ego and the id', *Standard Edition*, vol. 19, 1–66. London: Hogarth Press, 1961.

——(1940) 'An outline of psycho-analysis', *Standard Edition*, vol. 23, 139–207. London: Hogarth Press, 1964.

Sandler, J. (1990) 'On internal object relations', *Journal of the American Psychoanalytic Association*, 38, 859–80.

Sandler, J. and Sandler, A.-M. (1984) 'The past unconscious, the present unconscious and interpretation of the transference', *Psychoanalytic Inquiry*, 4, 367–99.

11

GENDER-DICHOTOMOUS FANTASIES

Their relationships to the inner and outer worlds[1]

Ethel Spector Person

It is old news that a conscious fantasy is itself a compromise formation, incorporating both wish and defence and serving both gratifying and adaptive functions. Still and all, not much theoretical attention is paid to conscious fantasy in the psychoanalytic literature, perhaps out of fear that emphasis will be withdrawn from unconscious fantasy. And what interest there is has generally focused more on connecting the conscious fantasy to unconscious fantasy than on tracing its permutations, enactments, and role in adaptation.[2]

Yet conscious fantasies (or daydreams) are as relevant to the future as they are to the past. Their importance attaches to their fate, not just to their history, and to their role in adaptation, not just to their sources. Clinical observation tells us that while some fantasies are invoked as substitute gratifications to assuage desire, still others describe or delineate desire and point the way to action. Conscious fantasies sometimes serve as dress rehearsals, as guides to behaviour.

Since, by definition, the nature of unconscious fantasy[3] is inferred, we can only gauge its changes through modification in symptoms, dreams or other of its products. But we are privy to observing sequential changes in conscious fantasies. Fantasies, based on desire and imagination, are living things, always changing and moving. That conscious fantasies are malleable and evolve with some regularity Freud had already observed by 1908:

> We must not suppose that ... the various phantasies, castles in the air, and daydreams ... are stereotyped or unalterable. On the contrary, they fit themselves into the subject's shifting impressions of life, change with every change in a situation, and receive from every fresh, active impression what might be called a 'date-mark'. ... Thus past, present and future are strung together, as it were, on the thread of the wish that runs through them.
>
> (Freud 1908: 147–8)

Here Freud clearly indicates that many fantasies are able to undergo change – evolution or adaptation – over time, suggesting that while one's current situation causes an instability or disequilibrium that elicits the memory of an earlier experience (in which a wish was fulfilled), the present and future are implicated as well. So observing, Freud gives us a model whereby a fantasy does not necessarily repeat itself unchanged, but is modified *vis-à-vis* changing psychic configurations and cultural constellations. Modification of fantasy takes place in order to devise a script acceptable to one's conscious and preconscious appraisal and, preferably, one with some potential for being gratified in reality.

A classic case of the evolution of a fantasy in response to internal dynamics is that of a beating fantasy as described by Freud (1919). Freud postulated at least three stages in the fantasy's evolution in girls. In the first stage, the child being beaten is not the female fantasist, but most often her sibling, whereas the identity of the person doing the beating is unclear, only later becoming recognizable as the girl's father. Freud designates this first stage as 'my father is beating the child' (185). The second stage, which is reconstructed, not consciously remembered, takes on a masochistic cast: 'I am being beaten by my father' (185). In the third version, the fantasizer is looking on while another child, or more than one, is being beaten. Generally the children are boys and they are being beaten by a paternal surrogate. The beating fantasy has evolved in response to inner psychic shifts, particularly to the development of the Oedipal phase.

Yet once past the Oedipal phase, many conscious fantasies appear fixed, at least over long stretches of time. However, culture does play an ongoing role in re-scripting some gender fantasies. Put another way, some already formed fantasies remain susceptible to ongoing (or new) influences from the family, the social milieu, and the cultural surround, which may serve to reinforce or, alternatively, to discourage compliance with the norm. The culture provides narrative content that can link up with preconscious wishes and shape new storylines for the underlying lineaments of fantasy, thus promoting new adaptations.

Thus some fantasies undergo evident evolution, while others do not, an issue of some concern not only to patients who are seeking changes in their adaptations (and to their psychoanalysts), but also to reformers interested in social change who correctly intuit that fantasy (along with beliefs and values) may act as a weighty conservative force.

That some 'politically incorrect' fantasy themes, particularly sexual ones, remain essentially unchanged, despite changing social mores, came as an unhappy surprise to many feminists. (Take, for example, the persistence of rape fantasies in men and in women.) So-called 'retrograde' fantasies have persisted, even in circumstances in which the fantasizer himself or herself wanted to relinquish the fantasy. Many women and men continue to be aroused by sexual fantasies, some of which they consciously disapprove of.[4]

This chapter addresses the topic of the malleability of some gender fantasies, and the imperviousness of others, in response to internal (psychic) reconfigurations and external (social) changes. I will not focus on the modification of fantasy in the therapeutic situation, a topic already familiar to analysts. (Many of the socially induced changes, however, are readily observed in the therapy situation.) What we are able to observe about the construction of gender-dichotomous fantasies and their stability or malleability within one individual over time or in successive generations, may perhaps be teased out to illuminate something about the genesis and fate of fantasy, in particular the question about the degree to which fantasies, once formed, continue to be affected by the external world. The question is, 'Which fantasies are more resistant to change, which more malleable, and why?'

REPEATING FANTASIES AND GENERATIVE FANTASIES

The susceptibility of a conscious fantasy to changes in the social milieu depends on the nature of the fantasy. One way of classifying fantasies has to do with their durability and with the nature of the occasion (or trigger) that prompts them.

Transient daydreams, by definition fleeting in nature, are contingent; they surface in response to a particular external stress, problem or situation. Envious on the occasion of someone else receiving a coveted prize, different fantasizers may conjure up winning the lottery, being offered a prestigious job, or going to bed with the rival's wife. Like dreams, such evanescent mental products may be very hard to remember. But they still serve the immediate function of restoring a lost equilibrium through positing a remedy.

In contrast are those fantasies of a durable, repetitive nature, which may recur unchanged from childhood through adult life or, alternatively, may keep reappearing in re-editions or remakes, sometimes even after long periods of banishment. A daydream that is repeated unchanged or with only slight modification from adolescence or even latency into adulthood becomes a familiar friend, one whose benefits (such as self-soothing or sexual arousal) are cherished. Repeating fantasies include masturbatory fantasies and the erotic fantasies they give rise to: self-soothing fantasies; self-fantasies, including what the Shanes (1990) call the global fantasy; and 'personal myth' fantasies as described by Kris (1956). Repeating fantasies are stimulated not so much by contingent events as by ever-recurring hungers. Many of these enduring fantasies are what are called 'organizing' fantasies – that is, they play an essential role on a day-to-day basis in solving those central unconscious conflicts and problems of early life that continue to exert an influence on the present. Such fantasies are generally not malleable in response to changing social circumstances.

There is a third group, intermediate between the other two, relatively stable over varying periods of time but not so structured or stable as a repeating fantasy. These generative fantasies are future-oriented and are invoked in response to future desire and intentionality. They are very important because they provide the major locus (along with preconscious thinking) for imaginative dress rehearsals and trial actions, thus shaping the fantasizer's hopes, dreams and plans for the future.

Despite major differences, repeating fantasies and generative fantasies also overlap, bleeding into one another. At the extremes of the continuum, the former have a more primitive, dreamlike quality, while the latter are often more practical and realistic, indicating possible future scenarios generally (but not invariably) experienced as desirable. The two kinds of fantasy rest on different primary roots. Repeating fantasy appears closer to primary unconscious fantasy, with relatively little input from the outside world, while reverie or generative fantasy appears closer to more logically articulated thinking. Repeating fantasy, formed early in life, is more drive-instigated and more often uses body metaphors to express itself. Reverie, or generative fantasy, while ultimately shaped by the unconscious (as all fantasy is), is further from it, more responsive to current issues of mastery and narcissistic regulation, and to the lineaments of ambition and future possibility (Person 1995).

Generative fantasies are more susceptible to external influence, that is, more changeable in response to cues from the surrounding culture, and to changes in the culture. Yet repeating fantasies are somewhat responsive; they do not change as much but may be suppressed to a greater or lesser degree, depending on what the culture tolerates.

When generative fantasies cannot be gratified in reality, lacking any direct possibility for enactment or actualization, they are often suppressed (extinguished in terms of manifest content) or at the very least transformed. For example, in adulthood, the writer of novels who daydreams of winning the Nobel Prize for literature shifts his daydreams to winning an Oscar when he abandons writing novels in favour of writing screenplays. The desired narcissistic gratification and the wish for recognition remain the same, but the content shifts so as to bring the daydreams into the realm of possibility, however remote that possibility might seem to an outside observer. Even if a fantasy is not destined to be enacted, it appears to gain credibility and efficacy from the possibility that it *could* be enacted or *might* come true, thereby offering assuagement that the purely fantastical daydream cannot.

The process of sequentially modifying a fantasy to bring it into line with the dictates of reality is a major adaptive strategy in childhood. When it becomes clear that Oedipal wishes cannot be directly gratified, Oedipally tinged wishes and daydreams are relinquished and instead metamorphosed into dreams for the future; in large part, they are reincarnated in a series of crushes, infatuations or love affairs directed towards people who are substitutes for the Oedipal object of desire. Only when Oedipal gratification appears possible does the unmodified wish maintain its full intensity, and even break through into conscious fantasy.

Likewise, the young child's wish to be both sexes is either relinquished or significantly modified in line with the maturing child's growing appreciation of the limits of reality. Suppression or transformation of certain well-nigh universal fantasies takes place as the growing child or adolescent discovers that his or her fantasy is dissonant with the appropriate gender prescription. In general, fantasies that chronicle desire (rather than assuaging it) seek some available route for direct gratification, often requiring modification of the fantasy, for example, by shifting onto a substitute object, or by trying (out of awareness) to have a surrogate enact the fantasy (as when a parent influences a child to enact a fantasy in his or her place).

THE GENDER DIFFERENCE

Many fantasies are found as frequently in one sex as in the other, for example, fantasies of affectionate bonding (Person *et al.* 1989, 1992). Yet some fantasies are more frequently reported by one sex, while others are almost entirely gender-dichotomous (peculiar to one sex only).

Repeating fantasies are by definition resistant to change, and relatively nonresponsive to cultural impact. Their immutability has to do with the fact that they do not draw their content primarily from cultural scripts, but instead from individual conflict resolution. Consequently some gender-dichotomous fantasies are immutable because they are the end product of distinct patterns of male or female development. Women and men experience different childhood conflicts, rivalries and longings, with resulting differences in conscious and unconscious fantasies. There are additional root causes of these differences, too, including different body experiences and physical capacities, which are recruited to express various impulses, feelings and wishes.

Consider the following fantasy, culled from a novel, which shows how body functions can provide gender-distinct envelopes for expressing universal impulses, feelings and wishes. No man could fantasize as did this fictional female character, who, on getting her menstrual period during a service in an orthodox synagogue, where she hated being, mused as follows:

> I was directed to a bathroom with a bare light-bulb, slung on a chain above a green toilet. I looked down at the dark blood gathering in heavy drops at the vaginal opening. As these drops splashed into the bowl below, the water streaked pink like a sunset, then darkened further into a deep maroon. Dark red like my mother's lipstick and fingernails, like Eve's apple, dangerous but delicious and fascinating. I looked around for toilet paper but there was none. Damn them, all,

I thought. What if I walked calmly upstairs onto the first floor, past the men. … What if I go quickly past them before they can spot me and where the white satin covers the Ark, where the Torah is waiting – what if I climb into the Ark and sit on the Torah and bleed and bleed away, letting my blood seep into the sacred pages, soil away, blot out the letters, left to right, marking the rhythms of the year? I bleed and I bleed and the other women behind the curtains hear the commotion and dare to peek. Then they come, come, all the unclean ones, quickly down the stairs, and sit with me. And the white satin of the Ark turns to red, 'murderers' the man screams and the rabbi faints in his chair.

(Roiphe 1977: 177–8)

What seems to invoke the character's fantasy is her anger, first, at having been sequestered in the synagogue in the balcony with the other women and, second, not finding toilet paper. That is, she was designated as second-class and, furthermore, inadequately provided for. (Were this a real person and not a fictional character, one would look for some earlier experience that primed her towards feeling second-class and uncared for.)

The envelope of this fantasy is quintessentially female, drawn from the memories and images of a cyclical female experience, even though its underlying feelings and impulses – resentment, envy, murderous rage, revenge and restitution – are of course universal, and could be expressed in a variety of alternative ways, some of them sexual. For example, a man feeling slighted or passed over might invoke a rape fantasy (with himself as rapist) as restitution for his deflated narcissism. While culture may play a role in the punishment-through-menstruation fantasy (e.g. drawing on the resentment a woman may feel about purdah), nonetheless its chief determinants have to do with body experiences and interpersonal relationships, not culture.

The fantasy of havoc-through-menstruation is not a common one, however, probably by virtue of the fact that the fantasy is a 'fantastic' fantasy, that is, it has little real possibility for enactment and thereby loses some of its power. And yet, just to establish that no fantasy is entirely unique, I do know of an instance in which a variant of this fantasy was not only entertained but also enacted. A young woman from an orthodox Jewish background visited the Lower East Side of New York every month during her menstruation. Her mission was to touch each shop owner, knowing he would be horrified to be touched by an unclean woman, were he to be aware of it. She felt powerful, and her thirst for revenge was quenched by the knowledge that she, a menstruating woman, considered an untouchable, was 'tainting' extremely religious Jewish men.[5] In contrast, a man's rape fantasy is more potentially realizable, and thereby more widespread. Even if the enactment of such a fantasy were anathema to him, the fantasy would still gain credibility by the knowledge that it might be enacted.

Many gender-specific fantasies, then, are specific primarily by virtue of the fact that they use imagery of female or male genital and reproductive organs and roles, but they express universal affective states or underlying motives. In essence, the individual has 'different modes of mastery' (as Doris Bernstein [1993: 41] puts it) to adjudicate similar underlying disequilibriums, and these modes of mastery are incorporated in fantasy narratives.

CHANGES IN FEMALE FANTASIES

To begin to parse the ongoing contribution of cultural narrative to fantasy, it is useful to watch for any shift in fantasy content that might correspond to a significant shift in the culture. The women's movement, dating from the 1970s, presents us with a natural experiment, so to speak. Using a variety of contemporary sources, it becomes possible to explore the nature and extent of feminism's impact – if any – on the content of gender-related fantasy. Do men and women now entertain fantasies that are different from those of a couple of generations ago?

Although some theorists had anticipated that the women's movement would produce almost global change in the fantasy life of women, others assumed that any change would have to await a radical reconstitution of the family. But such an assumption is based on failure to distinguish among different kinds of fantasy. What appears to be the case is that generative fantasies have undergone evolution more readily than repeating fantasies, which are almost completely resistant to change without benefit of therapeutic intervention.

Gender dichotomies arise in part in response to cultural materials. The culture's mythic materials are expressed in many forms and are conveyed to the child in innumerable verbal and nonverbal communications, not only through their immediate contact with relatives, friends and peers, but also through their exposure to fairy tales, films, popular versions of history and other cultural sources. Bruno Bettelheim (1976) has written an entire book, *The Uses of Enchantment*, on the way in which one kind of cultural product (the fairy tale) speaks to the preconscious and unconscious minds of children. Because fairy tales carry messages from which children can garner solutions to their conflicts and can shape scenarios for the future, they are powerful enough to become culture-wide transcripts for dreams and fantasies. Just as 'Cinderella' and 'Sleeping Beauty' speak to female dreamers about their hopes for the future, so, too, do 'Jack and the Beanstalk' and 'Sinbad the Sailor' speak to male dreamers.

From earliest life, different scripts are provided for girls and boys, for men and women. The two sexes generally grow up dreaming different dreams, incubating different fantasies. Traditionally, women have grown up with one set of romances (dreams, fantasies), men with another. While women have traditionally sought out romantic love, marriage, motherhood and other possibilities for bonding and for the delivery of tender, nurturant care, men have sought out feats of individual derring-do or exploits on the playing field or battlefield that depend on male bonding, and the sexual conquest of many women as well as the romantic conquest of the heart of one. In general, Ulysses has adventures while Penelope waits.

The fact that some kinds of fantasies are entertained more frequently by women, while others are entertained by men, has long been reported by both psychologists and psychoanalysts. By 1904 Theodate Smith had already published work on the psychology of daydreams that noted the sex differences that occur at different ages. He observed that young children often use fairy stories as the narrative spine of their fantasies, but that even when both sexes use the same stories to frame their fantasies, girls and boys differ in their use of the original material. Responding to the story of Aladdin, for example, nearly all the girls retained the original materials in their fantasies, preserving the magic carpet *qua* carpet, whereas boys transformed the carpet into flying machines or balloons. According to Smith, as children grow older and begin to develop their own independent interests, boys' fantasies revolve around their exploits as athletes, explorers or cowboys. Girls might fantasize travel, but only if it were comfortable and deluxe, not adventurous and exploratory. In essence, girls are less adventuresome.

In adolescence, future-oriented daydreams (generative fantasies) reveal comparable gender differences. Boys dream of achieving honours in military or naval service, law, medicine, politics, music, acting, and so on. Girls, on the other hand, dream of 'useful womanhood', a term that encompasses their duties as wives and mothers or their roles in other nurturant endeavours, such as nursing. And just as fairy tales provide raw material for the child fantasist, so, too, are teenage books frequent sources of plot material for the adolescent fantasizer. Implicitly if not explicitly, Smith's work presents us with a model for the incorporation of cultural narratives into daydreams.

Smith's observations about gender differences presage Freud's observations of 1908. In a passage that telescopes a great deal of information about daydreaming, Freud commented on the sex difference:

> The motivating wishes vary according to the sex, character and cir-
> cumstances of the person who is having the phantasies; but they fall
> naturally into two main groups. They are either ambitious wishes,
> which serve to elevate the subject's personality; or they are erotic
> ones. In young women erotic wishes dominate the phantasies, almost
> exclusively, for their ambition is generally comprised in their erotic
> longings; in young men egoistic and ambitious wishes assert them-
> selves plainly enough alongside their erotic desires.

> (146–7)

Freud believed these differences to be innate, not cultural. Nonetheless, as already noted, Freud did appreciate that fantasies were malleable, responding to the subject's shifting impressions of life and changes in situation. And this has proved to be the case. As cultural scripts change, so, too, do many of our fantasies.

Not too surprisingly, generative fantasies relating to work, career and levels of ambition have changed in response to economic reality (the fact that more women are in the workplace) and to the newly emerging values and beliefs of feminism. Thus no-one today would support Freud's contention that women's ambitions are generally expressed through erotic longings. Freud's (1908) observation that women fail to generate ambitious fantasies had relevance to his culture, but not to ours.

This ought not be too surprising. Egoistic and ambitious wishes provide narcissistic gratification insofar as they are capable of being fulfilled. For a woman to hold onto ambitious wishes in Freud's day would have been counterproductive – such wishes could only end in humiliation and despair. But with real opportunities, women have expressed the universal (Western) need to assert and assuage narcissistic longings. This may account for the fact that perhaps the greatest change in women's lives and expectations has taken place in the area of escalating work aspirations and ambitions, revealed not only in new kinds of behaviour, but also in the appearance of daydreams and reveries that centre on professional accolades, achievements and struggles.

It is not so much that these fantasies represent totally new aspirations. They flickered through the consciousness of many women in previous generations. But they were quickly suppressed out of fear of ridicule or out of an inner sense of violating the dictates of femininity. For example, one woman, now in her late forties, remembers that as a prepubescent girl, she fantasized equally frequently about being a heroic soldier and a sought-after sweetheart. As she entered her teen years, she gave up the soldiering fantasy and condensed it with the sweetheart fantasy to originate a femme fatale fantasy, one in which she wielded power vicariously through her seduction of a ruler or magnate. By creating a femme fatale fantasy, she managed to incorporate the wishes that underlay her heroic soldier fantasy – wishes for narcissistic aggrandizement, power and aggression – but expressed them in a way more consonant with prevailing feminine gender stereotypes, insofar as those longings were fulfilled through her sexual and romantic control over a powerful man. The remnants of the original soldier fantasy are perhaps to be found in the martial music that always plays in her mind (unaccompanied by any narrative) at moments of decision making. Today, many more women would be able to float the heroic soldier fantasy or a derivative (e.g. an astronaut fantasy) without the necessity of disguising the heroic motive in an erotic jacket.

In response to changes in cultural mores, many women now in their fifties or older first formulated work aspirations relatively late in life, thereby modifying or revivifying old and often buried fantasies. In the younger generation, the gender difference in achievement fantasies has diminished dramatically. Now that a critical mass of working women has come into existence, even more conformist women are able to incorporate explicitly ambitious and competitive wishes into their dream scenarios. In fact, if one were to examine the achievement fantasies of a typical group of contemporary men and women, it would be hard to differentiate them by sex.

Women are now being drawn not just to scripts of hard work and advancement but also to more adventurous storylines. Witness the popularity of such books as Beryl Markham's *West with the Night* (1983), which poetically describes her life as a pioneer aviator. (Accounts of such lives are the best evidence that change does not occur all at once, but rather that certain free and rebellious spirits lead the way – and some go in new directions not out of a contrary spirit but out of necessity.)

Fantasies pertaining to procreation, both to the raising of children and to the acts of begetting and birthing them, usually evolve over an individual's lifetime, with the fantasy of being pregnant or having children receding or coming to the fore depending on life stage and circumstances. Changes in cultural mores and expectations have resulted in widespread change in these fantasies, too, for men as well as for women. Given a wider range of options, women (and men, too) are now freer to fantasize a life without children. Moreover, one may now fantasize (and have) a spouse with no children, or children with no spouse. And lesbian and homosexual couples fantasize more about having children together, now that many states are recognizing their right to be parents.

The wider range of procreation fantasies (and the freedom to forgo them) draws on the new reproductive technologies (and birth control) as well as on cultural change. The long-existing 'Adam' fantasy of being the last man in the world who has viable sperm and who *de facto* is the one man who can repopulate the earth draws on a man's potential to produce large numbers of sperm. (This is a cosmogonic fantasy, a godlike fantasy of begetting a new world.) Now that it is possible to produce multiple eggs in one menstrual cycle and to have them harvested for future use, some women are entertaining comparable fantasies – 'Eve' fantasies – that express the same kind of narcissistic wish. One woman fantasizes donating ten eggs to be fertilized by ten different men of different racial and ethnic backgrounds, the fertilized eggs all to be carried to term by surrogates.

Generative fantasies and some repeating fantasies remain susceptible throughout our lifetimes to ongoing or new influences from the family, the social milieu and the cultural surround, and to technological innovations, and these factors may serve to reinforce or, sometimes, to discourage compliance with the norm. Throughout life, preconscious and conscious fantasies can change through exposure to new life narratives that one sees being lived out, and through access to film and fiction, much as the children Theodate Smith observed fashioned their daydreams out of fairy tales.

Movies in particular, because of their visual larger-than-life quality, offer us a scaffolding on which to mould our amorphous preconscious fantasies and yearnings into daydreams and life dreams. But it is often a question of the preconscious responding to something indirectly perceived in the film. As the film critic Molly Haskell (1994) puts it,

> movies, being basically conservative, generally hold up traditional and officially sanctioned notions of maleness and femaleness, but if that was all there was to it, i.e. if these models were mutually exclusive and rigidly defined, movies would soon lose their audiences. The ones that have held up are precisely those in which there is an inner tension between surface acceptability and subversive challenge ... those which challenge the gender conventions of their time.
>
> (405)

In *Gone with the Wind*, for example, Scarlett O'Hara is not just a Southern belle.

Some literary critics believe that changes in fantasies ride to some degree on what has been rendered in fiction. Change may be achieved through the reader's preconscious perception of subversive themes embedded within superficially conventional scripts. Looking at the power the novel *Jane Eyre* exerts on many readers, Jean Wyatt (1990) observes that

> Charlotte Brontë's *Jane Eyre* is in fact rich in fantasies that address the pleasures and frustrations of growing up in a patriarchal nuclear family structure: Fantasies of heroic rebellion against tyrannical parents, fantasies based on a split between good mother (Miss Temple) and bad mother (Mrs. Reed), and fantasies of revenge on more powerful brothers and prettier sisters (John and Georgiana Reed). Perhaps most appealing, Rochester offers Jane the excitement combined with frustration and enigma that characterize father–daughter interactions in a traditionally structured nuclear family. Against the pull of its Oedipal love fantasy, *Jane Eyre* presents an equally passionate protest against patriarchal authority.
>
> (23)

The fantasies embedded in the novel are divided, perhaps even polarized.

Wyatt offers different explanations for the reasons so many women have found this novel to be revolutionary in their lives. On the one hand, *Jane Eyre* offers the gratification of a father–daughter relationship with Jane's romantic attachment to Rochester, a man twice her age who is powerful, authoritative and distant. Their union after he has been blinded is ambiguous;

even though she now takes care of him, he is still the strong oak. Wyatt believes that the popularity of the book rests on the female reader's ambivalence towards her own father. But to the degree that this is a radical novel, or one that predisposes the reader to change, it may have to do with the way Jane defines herself. As Adrienne Rich (1979) put it, 'As a child, she [Jane] rejects the sacredness of adult authority; as a woman, she insists on regulating her conduct by the pulse of her own integrity' (106).

In art, there is a conduit through which the preconscious of the creative writer or artist in all its ambivalence and ambiguity speaks to the same qualities in the preconscious of the consumer. That is why books and movies can simultaneously gratify contradictory fantasies. The unconventional, often subliminal fantasy opens up possibilities for new ways of being in the world. While fantasy is often conformist, it also has an important potential for being the instrument of radical change.

Although repeating fantasies are relatively impervious to social change, some sexual fantasies have shown considerable modification, with specific fantasies achieving expression within the changing cultural climate of the past thirty years.[6] The major change is that many more women are in touch with their sexual fantasies. This is the result not so much of newly minted fantasies, but rather of greater access to the preconscious, courtesy of the women's movement, sexual liberation, and more written depictions of female sexual fantasy, including books like *My Secret Garden* (Friday 1974), a write-in collection of female sexual fantasies. Fantasies have also proliferated, because along with changes in sexual rhetoric, actual sexual practices have changed and offered new material – and pleasures – about which to fantasize.

The sea-change in the manifest content of women's fantasies includes more focus on seducing rather than on being seduced, and on forcing rather than being forced. This may be the result of greater access to the preconscious or to reversals of pre-existing fantasies rather than to new fantasies. Not many fantasies are created *de novo*, unless they have had an already existing anlage in the preconscious. But once a fantasy is formed, the fantasizer may rotate roles (e.g. the well-known example of someone who alternates masochistic and sadistic roles in a relationship).[7]

FANTASIES IN MEN

Because men and women live in the same society, it would be short-sighted to postulate radical changes in women with no comparable changes taking place in the fantasy life of men. But, by and large, there has been less written on changes in male fantasy, perhaps because less scholarly and practical attention has been paid to male psychology, compared to the vast outpouring of material about women. Perhaps, too, it is because the changes in men's lives and in the fantasies that encode them are not as expansive as is the case with women.

In fact, some have argued that the increasing opportunities for women have posed a challenge to the traditional sphere of men, both at home and in the workplace. Men's prerogatives have been eroded not only through the increasing power of women and of teenage children, but also in recent decades through the overall diminution in opportunities for upward mobility. It was much easier for men to meet the culturally set stereotypes for performance in the booming economy of the 1950s. Some have argued that male hegemony has also been negatively affected in the United States by the loss of the war in Vietnam, resulting in damage to the American collective mythology of the invincible hero–warrior (Gibson 1981).

The traditional male prerogative of being an absolute patriarch and ruler of his own family in his own household has undergone considerable erosion.

> In fact, what outlets are there for the achievement of the masculine prowess depicted in fairy tale, myth, and fiction? Although he may have been raised to be a giant killer, a hero, 'What does a boy do in his adult years?'

This is the question posed by the authors of a recent book, *The Courage to Raise Good Men* (Silverstein and Rashbaum 1994: 184). They make use of John Updike's *Rabbit* series to depict the plight of the modern male:

> What Updike is telling us is that there is no suitable arena in which a grown–Rabbit can continue to prove himself a hero. Once off the basketball courts of youth, he's lost, always planning for the place 'where they remembered him when,' the crowds, the glory, the adulation.
>
> (184)

So what the adult American male does is 'at night he lights up a good cigar … and shoots out home. He mows the lawn, or sneaks in some practice putting, and then he's ready for dinner' (Updike, quoted in Silverstein and Rashbaum 1994: 183).

Such dislocation as many modern American males are experiencing has inspired a small rash of books and groups, purporting to bring enrichment to men, including Bly's *Iron John* (1990), and weekend retreats devoted to the search for male bonding and the exorcism of the female presence. It also appears to have caused a shift to more intensely aggressive fantasies of sexual mastery, and perhaps to vigilante and paramilitary fantasies as well.

Observers from diverse disciplines have suggested that macho sexuality has come to be sanctioned as the cultural ideal or, conversely, that it accurately portrays male sexuality. Robert May (1980) suggests that in addition to the cultural directive for males to be assertive in general,

> the popular prescription for male sexuality is also heavily invested with assertion and activity. The man is supposed to be constantly on the move and on the make. The image of the tireless seducer differs only in style and degree from that of the rapist.
>
> (131)

The only question is whether the male attracts and seduces the female or instead overpowers and forces her. Yet whether the fantasy itself has changed or is merely more culturally sanctioned remains an open question. According to Kate Millett (1970),

> as one recalls both the euphemism and the idealism of descriptions of coitus of the romantic poets … or the Victorian novelists … and contrasts it with Miller or William Burroughs, one has an idea of how contemporary literature has absorbed not only the truthful explicitness of pornography, but its anti-social character as well. Since this tendency to hurt or insult has been given free expression, it has become far easier to assess sexual antagonism in the male.
>
> (46)

Although there are many developmental reasons why male sexuality is so often infused with hostility towards the female (Horney 1932; Person 1986a, 1986b), at the very least its explicit rendition in fiction and film allows the repeating fantasy of aggressive sexuality greater conscious expression. (In my own questionnaire study of a nonpatient population, 44 per cent of the men entertained fantasies of sexual domination [Person et al. 1989].)

Short of violent sexuality, many men embrace some version of macho sexuality and the belief that other men are truly in possession of it. On one level, macho fantasies are adaptive and counteract underlying fears. But at the same time they may also serve to aggravate a pre-existing sexual anxiety, because many men literally believe other men are doing better.

Aggression is also manifested in the non-sexual arena. Jay William Gibson (1981) traces an escalation in the United States of vigilante fantasies and of what he calls paramilitary fantasy culture, beginning in the 1970s after the Americans were defeated in Vietnam. This cultural development is exemplified in a number of ways, for example, through a new kind of movie: *Death Wish*, *Death before Dishonor*, *The Terminator* and all the *Rambo* movies. Gibson sees a huge, almost exponential resurgence of war and warrior stories post-Vietnam, including action-adventure films and, perhaps more importantly, the male counterpart to women's romance novels, 'novel series for men featuring commandos, vigilantes and mercenaries who have left normal societies and made battle their way of life' (12). Moreover, as he points out, the magazine *Soldiers of Fortune: The Journal of Professional Adventurers*, first published in 1975, was printing up to a quarter of a million copies by 1986 and has acquired several competitors. Clearly, there is an expanding audience for paramilitary fantasy material.

Tellingly enough, the rising interest in paramilitary and vigilante fictional material was paralleled by an increase in the number of rifles sold, in the popularity of the annual week-long convention held by *Soldiers of Fortune* magazine in Las Vegas, in war games, in the spread of special combat weapons, and in the proliferation of training schools for self-defence. Among a significant minority of aggressively minded men, the individual fantasy is seeking grounding, rationalization, and organization in culturally mediated fantasy and in group make-believe. For many, paramilitary fantasies serve as a cathartic fantasy function. But at the same time, the boundary between fantasy *qua* fantasy and fantasy as precursor to some form of enactment may be weakening.

My purpose here is not to explicate male psychology other than to indicate that a crisis in the sense of masculinity may have been obscured by the focus on changes in female adaptations. It is worth noting, however, that for all the rhetoric of the move towards more male involvement in nurturance and co-parenting, we have, in fact, spawned a culture with more and more absentee fathers.

MODELS FOR UNDERSTANDING THE TRANSFORMATION OF FANTASY

Creative artists and scientists have provided us with good accounts of how solutions to problems are often worked out and fully elaborated, utilizing a secondary-process mode of thinking, in the preconscious. For example, when the physiologist Walter B. Cannon (1976) had to prepare for a public address, he would garner certain central points and write them down in a rough outline. Over the next several nights, he would have spells of awakening in which he had fresh ideas perfectly worked out that would fit brilliantly into his paper. His ability to delegate a task to his preconscious, and to have it be carried out successfully in almost every instance, led him to believe that this was a universal mode of mental work. Not all of us are so well endowed (although many are) to be able to work out creative solutions to scientific and artistic puzzles, but we each do work out, in the preconscious, ways to achieve our underlying wishes and needs. To this end, we adapt and creatively modify current cultural scripts to form preparatory fantasies. All of us are creative to some extent in spinning and utilizing fantasy as a guide to ensure future gratification.

The formation of preconscious fantasy is triggered by fleeting or chronic instances of disequilibrium (the product of both personal and social events), including narcissistic injuries, competitive ambitions, emotional discomfort, sexual urges, wishes for bonding and wishes to chart the future. The task of the preconscious is to fashion a fantasy that assuages our discomfort, answers our hopes, and, best of all, one that may be realized. To this end, fantasy must both be consonant with unconscious fantasy and acceptable to internalized 'rules', among which are notions of what we believe is gender-consonant. The psychology of gender is, in part, the psychology of conformity.

The Sandlers' (1984, 1987) exegesis of the repression barrier between the preconscious and the conscious mind, a barrier that has close ties to the dictates of family and culture, as perceived through the lens of projective identification and wishful distortion, suggests how the pressure to conform is enacted. The Sandlers draw a distinction between the 'past unconscious' and the 'present unconscious'. Fantasies of the past unconscious are what we generally refer to as unconscious fantasies, that is, fantasies that never become conscious but that are, in a sense, reconstructed in analytic work. Even though the contents of the present unconscious are by definition not conscious, they have a different functional organization from the unconscious, similar to what Freud called the preconscious in his topographical model. The present unconscious is different from the past unconscious in several important ways. The present unconscious is concerned with maintaining equilibrium in the present rather than with reacting to the past, and the present unconscious relies on secondary process functioning. (I would add that the present unconscious also looks to the future.)

The mechanism that leads to repression and conformity can be found in the repression barrier between the system conscious and the system preconscious. The Sandlers (1987) have described this barrier located between the present unconscious and consciousness as having as its fundamental motivation 'the avoidance of conscious feelings of shame, embarrassment and humiliation' (336). From the developmental point of view, one can trace censorship to the point at which the child relinquishes play for conscious fantasizing but has the need to keep some fantasies secret. The Sandlers (1987) describe what happens as follows:

> As the child develops the increasing capacity to anticipate the shaming and humiliating reactions of others (with all the additions he has made to his expectations arising from his own projections), so he will become *his own* disapproving audience and will continually generalize the social situation in the form of the second censorship. Only content that is acceptable will be permitted to consciousness. It must be *plausible* and not ridiculous or 'silly'. In a way the second censorship is much more of a *narcissistic* censorship than the first, the narcissism involved often tends to center around fears about being laughed

at, as being thought to be silly, crazy, ridiculous or childish – essentially fears of being humiliated.

(337)

Fantasies are invoked to secure gratification and maintain equilibrium but, to the extent that the fantasies themselves arouse conflict or fear of humiliation or rejection, they are 'modified, disguised, or defended against in some way' (Sandler and Sandler 1995: 71).

To their present unconscious, which situates conflicts in the present, I would add what I call the cultural unconscious (Person 1991). The term 'cultural unconscious' does not imply any universal cultural content; quite the contrary, it refers to those stories and narratives specific to a particular culture that are internalized in such a way as to shape the individual's preconscious choice of a life path, modes of gratification, and priority of values. The stories give guidelines as to what is culturally acceptable.

Giving due weight both to the present unconscious and to the cultural unconscious, we have a model that can account for a shift or change in the degree to which fantasies can attain or maintain conscious status; in periods of social change, there is a widening, narrowing or modification of acceptable modes of gratification. In other words, the second censorship itself is the locus of impact from the external world insofar as the injunctions of family and society, distorted by projections, are internalized. But it is also the locus that allows for the major re-scripting of generative fantasies that permit cultural evolution (whether positive or negative).

Insofar as unconscious fantasies entail gender markers (for example, as in Oedipal fantasies), this indicates that experience is implicated in the formation of our most basic fantasies. Thus it is not just the content of generative fantasy that is affected by culture; the content of unconscious fantasy is affected as well. However, once formed, unconscious fantasy is relatively impervious to change, whereas generative fantasy is more variable across the life cycle and more easily influenced by changes in circumstances, cultural arrangements and values.

Thus our fantasies are so constructed as to provide us both with continuity and the capacity for change. Constitutional, as well as experiential and conflictual, factors determine whether one greets life with a fistful of commandments or a pocketful of dreams. Our fantasies may reinforce the former, or herald the latter.

NOTES

1 An earlier version of this chapter was first presented as the Doris Bernstein Memorial Lecture at the Institute for Psychoanalytic Training and Research (IPTAR) on 13 January 1993. I am grateful to Norbert Freedman for valuable comments he made in response to its presentation. Some of the material in this chapter appears in a different form in my book *By Force of Fantasy* (1995).

2   Consideration of conscious fantasy does occasionally enter into clinical thinking. We call some men perverse on the basis of their obligatory utilization of the conscious fantasy in order to achieve erotic excitement, and many women have been judged to be masochistic – often incorrectly – because they entertain rape fantasies.

3   In discussing fantasy, the problem is to designate that to which we refer – conscious or unconscious fantasy, manifest or latent content, drive derivative or wish. The ambiguity about the meaning of the word 'fantasy' is comparable to the confusion in the way we use the term 'transference', which is used to describe two different levels of the transference phenomenon – its manifest content and its motivational source. LaPlanche and Pontalis (1968) described the complexity implicit in the term 'fantasy':

> Since we encounter fantasy as given, interpreted, reconstructed or postu-lated, at the most diverse levels of psychoanalytic experience, we have ob-viously to face the difficult problem of its metapsychological status, and first of all, of its topography within the framework of the distinction be-tween the unconscious, preconscious and conscious systems.
>
> (11)

Moreover, theorists disagree as to the nature of fantasy. In the classical Kleinian view, unconscious 'phantasies' are essentially coexistent with drive; in contrast, in the Freudian view, unconscious fantasies relate to drive but as only filtered through ego. In other words, in the Freudian view unconscious fantasies are constructs incorporating aspects of experience.

The Kleinians distinguish between conscious fantasies (with an 'f') and those unconscious phantasies (with a 'ph') that they believe are the primary content of unconscious mental processes. If one were to adhere to the Kleinian distinction, then daydreams, according to LaPlanche and Pontalis (1968),

> would be only a manifest content, like the others, and would have no more privileged relationship to unconscious *Phantasie* than dreams, behav-iour, or whatever is generally described as 'material'. Like all manifest data, it would require interpretations in terms of unconscious fantasy.
>
> (11)

They, however, take the opposite position, suggesting that

> Freud's inspiration is shown by his persistent employment of the term *Phantasie* up to the end, in spite of the very early discovery that these *Phantasien* might be either conscious or unconscious. He [Freud] wishes thereby to assert a profound kinship.
>
> (11)

LaPlanche and Pontalis (1968), Joseph and Anne-Marie Sandler (1984, 1987), and Arlow (1969), too, view conscious and unconscious fantasy on a continuum and, like Freud, argue that conscious fantasy when repressed assumes the status of unconscious fantasy. As Freud (1908) put it: 'Unconscious fantasies have either been unconscious all along or – as is more often the case – they were once conscious fantasies, daydreams, and have since become unconscious through "repression" ' (161).

Because in Freud's formulation, daydreams, preconscious fantasies and uncon-scious fantasies are on a continuum, or in a loop, daydreams ought to take on more theoretical importance than is generally accorded them. Daydreams or conscious fantasies are privileged in relationships to their connection to uncon-scious fantasy not only because they provide content to unconscious fantasy but also because they describe desire. Because fantasy charts desire, fantasy may be predictive of the adaptations people seek, and the sequential changes in patients' fantasies become important data for psychoanalytic practitioners.

4 To some, the persistence of unwanted fantasies appears incompatible with contemporary gender theory, which posits that gender is constructed (the con-structionist view) rather than being inherent in biology (the essentialist view). Because gender is theorized by feminists as the '*construction of* social subjects in sexual difference' (Burgin *et al.* 1986: 3), the implication – and the hope – was that what was constructed could be changed more easily than what was innate. Instead, as it turns out, a construction of gender provides a pattern of develop-ment that 'seems to fix things forever in the given, and oppressive, identities' (Heath 1986: 56). Even though cultural arrangements are critical in initiating the formation of gender identity with its attendant fantasies, revised cultural arrange-ments do not always affect fantasies that have already taken hold.

5 My thanks to Dr Marion Hart for sharing this story with me.

6 Many female sexual fantasies have remained the same. Many female fantasies that do not specifically appear to be sexual – for example, the not-uncommon nurse fantasies (taking care of injured or debilitated men) – may be experienced as erotic. As reported by Barclay (1973),

> caring for someone was probably the most common of all themes. Our original hypothesis was that caring or nurturing fantasies were not sexual, but so many of our female subjects reported them with masturbatory ac-tivity or coupled with intercourse we were compelled to accept them as having the same degree of sexual connotation as the more explicit sexual fantasies reported by men.
>
> (210)

Pregnancy and breast-feeding fantasies are other examples of sexually tinged fantasies. The fantasy of nursing a man back to health is related both to longing for the father and to the fear of rejection. The fantasy allows a recapitulation of the closeness of the mother–daughter interaction (the experience of intense nurturance), except now the woman is herself in the nurturant role and therefore in the position of power. Moreover, to the degree that women are fearful of men and of their phallic aggression, the fact of the male partner's illness or incapacity defangs him and disarms him. In a culture where men are deemed the powerful ones, the nursing fantasy restores egalitarianism and a sense of safety. (In some fantasies, the male may even be symbolically castrated.)

7 We generally think of fantasy as built around a kind of narrative, with a subject, an action, an object and sometimes a context or a scene. In these narratives it is usually easy to identify the fantasizer. But some theorists envision fantasy as providing a setting for desire. As LaPlanche and Pontalis (1968) put it:

> Fantasy is not the object of desire, but its setting. In fantasy the subject does not pursue the object or its sign: he appears caught up himself in the sequence of images. He forms no representation of the desired object, but

is himself represented as participating in the scene although, in the earliest forms of fantasy, he cannot be assigned any fixed place in it.

(17)

The conscious and preconscious fantasies with which we deal in everyday life and clinical practice are by and large fixed in terms of the subject and structured narrative, but this is not necessarily true of unconscious or even preconscious fantasy. From this perspective, it is much less startling to see reversals of plot, seducing rather than being seduced, than to see whole new inventions of narrative.

REFERENCES

Arlow, J. (1969) 'Unconscious fantasy and disturbances of conscious experience', *Psychoanalytic Quarterly*, 38, 1–17.

Barclay, A. M. (1973) 'Sexual fantasies in men and women', *Medical Aspects of Human Sexuality*, 7, 205–16.

Bernstein, D. (1993) 'Female identity anxieties, conflicts, and typical mastery modes', in D. Bernstein, N. Freedman and B. Distler (eds) *Female Identity Conflict in Clinical Practice*, New York: Jason Aronson, 39–68.

Bettelheim, B. (1976) *The Uses of Enchantment: The Meaning and Importance of Fairy Tales*, New York: Knopf.

Bly, R. (1990) *Iron John*, Reading MA: Addison-Wesley.

Burgin, V. D. J., Donald, J. and Kaplan, C. (eds) (1986) *Formations of Fantasy*, London: Methuen.

Cannon, W. B. (1976) 'The role of hunches', in A. Rothenberg and C. R. Hausman (eds) *The Creativity Question*, Durham NC: Duke University Press, 57–67.

Freud, S. (1908) 'Creative writers and day-dreaming', *Standard Edition*, vol. 5, 141–53. London: Hogarth Press, 1959.

——(1919) ' "A child is being beaten": a contribution to the origin of sexual perversions', *Standard Edition*, vol. 17, 175–204. London: Hogarth Press, 1955.

Friday, N. (1974) *My Secret Garden*, New York: Pocket Books.

Gibson, J. W. (1981) 'Paramilitary fantasy culture and the cosmogonic mythology of primeval chaos and order', *Vietnam Generation*, special edn, 'Gender and the war: men, women and Vietnam', ed. Jacqueline Lawson, 1 (3/4), summer/fall, 12–32.

Haskell, M. (1994) 'To have and have not: the paradox of the female star', *Imago*, 50, 401–21.

Heath, S. J. (1986) 'Joan Riviere and the masquerade', in V. D. J. Burgin, J. Donald and C. Kaplan (eds) *Formations of Fantasy*, London: Methuen, 45–61.

Horney, K. (1932) 'The dread of women: observations on a specific difference in the dread felt by men and by women respectively for the opposite sex', *International Journal of Psycho-Analysis*, 13, 348–60.

Kris, E. (1956) 'The personal myth: a problem in psychoanalytic technique', *Journal of the American Psychoanalytic Association*, 4, 653–81.

Laplanche, J. and Pontalis, J.-B. (1968) 'Fantasy and the origins of sexuality', *International Journal of Psycho-Analysis*, 49, 1–18.

Markham, B. (1983) *West with the Night*, New York: North Point Press.

May, R. (1980) *Sex and Fantasy: Patterns of Male and Female Development*, New York: Norton.

Millett, K. (1970) *Sexual Politics*, Garden City NY: Doubleday.

Person, E. S. (1986a) 'Male sexuality and power', *Psychoanalytic Inquiry*, 6, 3–25.

——(1986b) 'The omni-available woman and lesbian sex: two fantasy themes and their relationship to the male developmental experience', in G. Fogel, F. M. Lane and R. S. Liebert (eds) *The Psychology of Men: New Psychoanalytic Perspectives*, New York: Basic Books, 236–59.

——(1991) 'Romantic love: at the intersection of the psyche and the cultural unconscious', *Journal of the American Psychoanalytic Association*, 39, 383–411.

——(1995) *By Force of Fantasy: How We Make Our Lives*, New York: Basic Books.

Person, E. S., Terestman, N., Myers, W. A. Goldberg, E. and Borenstein, M. (1989) 'Gender differences in sexual behaviors and fantasies in a college population', *Journal of Sex and Marital Therapy*, 15, 187–98.

——(1992) 'Associations between sexual experiences and fantasies in a nonpatient population: a preliminary study', *Journal of the American Academy of Psychoanalysis*, 20, 75–90.

Rich, A. (1979) 'Jane Eyre: the temptations of a motherless woman', in *Our Lives, Secrets and Silences*, New York: Norton, 89–106.

Roiphe, A. (1977) *Torch Song*, New York: Farrar, Strauss & Giroux.

Sandler, J. and Sandler, A.-M. (1984) 'The past unconscious, the present unconscious and interpretation of the transference', *Psychoanalytic Inquiry*, 4, 367–99.

——(1987) 'The past unconscious, the present unconscious and the vicissitudes of guilt', *International Journal of Psycho-Analysis*, 68, 331–41.

——(1995) 'Unconscious phantasy, identification, and projection in the creative writer', in E. S. Person, P. Fonagy and S. A. Figeura (eds) *On Freud's Creative Writers and Day-dreaming*, New Haven CT and London: Yale University Press, 65–81.

Shane, M. and Shane, E. (1990) 'Unconscious fantasy: developmental and self-psychological considerations', *Journal of the American Psychoanalytic Association*, 38 (1), 75–92.

Silverstein, O. and Rashbaum, B. (1994) *The Courage to Raise Good Men*, New York: Viking.

Smith, T. (1904) 'The psychology of daydreams', *American Journal of Psychology*, 15, 465–88.

Updike, J. (1981) *Rabbit is Rich*, New York: Knopf.

Wyatt, J. (1990) *Reconstructing Desire: The Role of the Unconscious in Women's Reading and Writing*, Chapel Hill NC: University of North Carolina Press.

12

ACUTE AND CHRONIC COUNTERTRANSFERENCE REACTIONS

Otto F. Kernberg[1,2]

THE ASCENDANCE OF COUNTERTRANSFERENCE ANALYSIS

The early concept of countertransference defined it as the analyst's unconscious reaction to the patient or to the transference derived from the analyst's own transference potential. Such countertransference was to be overcome by the analyst's self-analysis so that the analyst could return to a position of technical neutrality (Little 1951; Reich 1951). This concept of countertransference and our view of its importance in the psychoanalytic situation have since undergone significant changes. Under the influence of psychoanalytic contributions in the 1950s, particularly those of Paula Heimann (1950) and Heinrich Racker (1957), a global or totalistic view of countertransference, defined as the analyst's total emotional reaction to the patient, emerged and gradually prevailed. Now the task became the analysis of the various components included in the analyst's global countertransference, including

1   unresolved or reactivated unconscious conflicts,
2   the analyst's external reality and reactions towards third parties,
3   the contributions of the patient's transference, and
4   the reality of the patient's life.

(Kernberg 1965)

Particularly under the influence of Racker's concepts of concordant and complementary identification in the countertransference (emphasizing the contribution of the transference), the analyst's exploration of countertransference now permitted a sharper diagnosis of the patient's activated internalized object relations. Countertransference analysis became an important tool in the analysis of the transference.

More recently, in technical contributions of the 1980s and early 1990s (Alexandris and Vaslamatzis 1993; Carpy 1989; Grinberg 1993; Hamilton 1990; Kernberg *et al.* 1989; Loewald 1986; McDougall 1993; Ogden 1993; Pick 1985; Segal 1981; Spillius 1988; Volkan 1993), countertransference analysis has emerged as a crucial aspect of psychoanalytic technique, because it provides fundamental information about the nature of the dominant transference at any particular time. Insofar as some authors (e.g. Mitchell 1988) view transference developments as importantly influenced by the analyst's unconscious contributions to the analyst–patient interaction, the pendulum may have swung in an opposite direction from what we can see, in retrospect, as an early phobic attitude towards countertransference.

In my view, countertransference provides a significant source of information about the analytic situation. In fact, it is one of three such sources: the patient's subjective experience, communicated by means of free association; his nonverbal behavioural manifestations during the hour; and the analyst's emotional response to these behaviours. These sources of information are unavoidably influenced, at any particular moment, by the extent to which the analyst preserves an internal freedom to explore his own reaction to the patient, and, last but not least, by the analyst's theoretical organizing frame and clinical experience.

The importance of countertransference as a source of information varies with the severity of the patient's illness. The more severe the patient's character pathology, and the more intense, regressive and primitive the transference, the more countertransference reactions will come into the foreground. Particularly with severe character pathology, powerful negative countertransference reactions may dominate the analyst's observational field, at least temporarily. The most important primitive defensive operation and means of communication of the transference under such conditions – projective identification – explains the activation of such intense counter-transferences. Generally speaking, one might say that the less the patient is able to contain a primitive experience in subjective awareness, the more this experience is expressed in behaviour and in the analyst's countertransference.

Thus, by means of projective identification, the patient's threatening and intolerable self- or object representations, charged with primitive, aggressive affect, are projected onto the therapist while the patient unconsciously attempts to induce in the analyst a corresponding role response (Sandler 1976). Yet, at the same time, the patient attempts to control the analyst under the impact of this projected self- or object representation and its threatening affect. Typically, it is a complementary identification in the countertransference that creates the risk of flooding the analyst's psychic experience at such moments.

In addition, the persistence of the patient's unconscious effort to maintain or repeatedly reproduce the same primitive transference reaction in severe psychopathology (as is also true of some better functioning narcissistic patients with enormous resistance against establishing a dependent relationship in the transference) may reinforce the countertransference by means of activating chronic (in contrast to acute) countertransference reactions. In other words, there may be chronic distortion or stagnation in the analyst's emotional disposition toward, or capacity to work with, the patient, rather than sudden and transitory countertransference developments (such as forgetting an appointment, a momentary irritation with the patient, or *lapsus linguae* in an interpretive comment).

Because of my experience treating patients with severe character pathology with psychoanalysis as well as with psychoanalytic psychotherapy, my attention has been drawn to the technical implications of the activation of intense countertransference reactions when faced with severe regression in the transference, and to the particular distortions and technical difficulties derived from chronic countertransference reactions. The following cases illustrate these clinical situations.

ACUTE COUNTERTRANSFERENCE REACTION

Mr A suffered from an obsessive-compulsive personality disorder. His obsessive doubts intruded into the successful business he headed, paralysing his ability to make decisions. In addition, he was aware of a growing irritability with the younger men in his firm, protégés he himself had brought into the business. Arguments with them, as well as his obsessive doubts, resulted in significant secondary anxiety and depression and motivated him to enter psychoanalysis.

In the course of three years of analysis, it had become clear that Mr A's obsessive doubts reflected an internalized submission to, and rebellion against, a powerful father, who had been very successful in the same field as the patient. Mr A's unconscious guilt feelings over successfully competing with his father, as well as his obsessive doubts, were activated in the transference. At times he desperately tried to guess what I might counsel him to do, in an effort to make decisions on the basis of what he thought I would suggest. At other times he resented what he experienced as my efforts to control him and subject him to my strict rules of behaviour.

When Mr A was a child, his mother had treated him as her preferred son, only to 'betray' him to his father by passively acquiescing in the father's authoritarian behaviour towards Mr A. As a result, the patient's wish to depend on a good mother was displaced from her to his father, and repressed homosexual impulses towards his father were split off from a romantic attachment to women who represented aspects of his mother. The patient was married, but seldom approached his wife sexually, which reflected his unconscious Oedipal guilt, his deep-seated suspicion and resentment of women, and his difficulty in expressing dependency needs *vis-à-vis* women.

The following situation illustrates a typical acute countertransference reaction with Mr A and its management. In the last session before a week-long separation, during which the patient had a commitment out of town that coincided with my own absence, Mr A began to obsessively discuss whether he should give in to the financial demands of an artist whose work he wanted to acquire, or whether he should stand firm on his counterproposal. His anger at the artist gradually became stronger. He complained bitterly about the lack of gratitude of this young man, whom the patient had helped in the past. Mr A also expressed indignation at the defiant and inconsiderate way the man was treating him. I raised the question of whether, in the middle of this disappointment, Mr A might also be disappointed with me for not helping him make a decision. He responded with irritation that I was wrong; he was not expecting anything from me, and this analysis was proving completely useless.

I wondered aloud whether Mr A's disappointment with me might have something to do with the forthcoming week-long separation. I reminded him that I had wondered whether he had set up a business trip at the time of my absence to avoid feeling left behind and alone. Mr A responded that, on the contrary, he would have to cancel an additional hour at the time of his return because of flight complications. At that moment, I remembered that I had a similar flight problem, and I told the patient that I had planned to suggest to him a session at a later time on the day of our first appointment.

Mr A then became really enraged at me. He wanted to know why I was bringing up a change in his schedule in the middle of a session, when my usual practice was to convey new information of any kind to him only at the beginning of a session. He went on to say that I was disrupting his flow of free association, showing how distracted I was by raising issues that concerned only me and being totally neglectful of his needs; this was the last thing he would have expected at the final session before our separation.

As the patient's anger increased, over the next few minutes, I experienced a series of rapidly changing feelings. First, I felt guilty for not having remembered to make my suggestion at the beginning of the session, feeling that I had indeed been neglectful, and I wondered what might have influenced me in this regard. I remembered that I had experienced a fleeting sense of guilt before the session for having to make a last-minute change in Mr A's schedule, and I wondered to myself whether I was acting like Mr A's mother; that is, pretending to be interested and concerned for him. Then, as his attacks on me intensified, I became irritated, feeling that he was making a mountain out of a relatively minor molehill. I thought that I had fairly acknowledged my mistake. Finally, while the patient continued to express his rage over my unreliability, I thought that I was now in a relationship to him similar to the one he had experienced when confronted with his father's dissatisfaction with his performance. Mr A was now enacting the role of his father and projecting his 'unreliable self' onto me, replicating, at the same time, his problematic relationship to the young artist.

I commented on his disappointment and its transformation into rage at me, and on his sense that I was unreliable because I was not helping him with his problem with the young artist and was neglecting the particular intensity of his need to be understood and cared for when a separation brought about feelings of abandonment. I interpreted that I was like an unreliable mother who only pretended to care for him. This was a most painful experience for Mr A. He could protect himself by changing the experience, by making me an unreliable son and enacting his father's demands in relation to me. To be an angry father scolding an unreliable son was preferable to feeling like an abandoned son relating to an unreliable mother.

Mr A said that he had felt that the artist was like an unreliable, unloving son, and that it was true that he had been treating both the artist and me in ways that reminded him of what he hated in his father. He added that he did not feel as fearful as he had in the past about some forthcoming important meetings; he felt more like an equal with his colleagues. He then remained silent. After a while, I commented that I sensed a change in his emotional disposition. He said he was no longer angry and actually felt sad thinking of our separation for a week. I said that insofar as it was less frightening to him to identify himself with his father (in spite of traits in his father that he was critical of), he was also more able to acknowledge his wish for my concern and dedication to him without experiencing it as a sexual threat. The patient then remembered that he had felt less inhibited about having sex with his wife the previous night. The session ended shortly afterwards.

This illustration of an acute countertransference reaction, with its immediate internal exploration by the analyst and its utilization as part of the material to be incorporated into transference interpretation, is in contrast to the next example.

CHRONIC COUNTERTRANSFERENCE REACTION

Mr B suffered from a severe narcissistic personality. His three marriages had all ended in divorce because of his sexual promiscuity and his inability to feel emotionally invested in the same woman with whom he had a sexual relationship.

For many months in the early part of treatment, Mr B's intense defence against deepening the transference relationship was quite noticeable. Gradually, it was understood as a defence against unconscious envy of the analyst, whom Mr B saw as a married man able to enjoy a relationship with his wife that was both emotionally and sexually satisfying. After triumphantly regaling me with his sexual exploits, he fell back into despair because of his incapacity to maintain a sexual relationship with a woman who mattered to him emotionally. He gradually became aware that the idea that I might have a good marital relationship filled him with a sense of inferiority and humiliation. He then began to be able to tolerate conscious feelings of envy of me.

Mr B's childhood had not been cheerful. He described his father as a complaining, distrustful, eternally dissatisfied man who attacked his wife, both in public and in private, for all her shortcomings. According to Mr B, his mother herself was a domineering, combative woman. On the basis of his childhood experiences, Mr B was convinced that all expressions of concern for another person were completely phoney.

He experienced his mother as being chronically and totally unreasonable, filled with strange ideas about people, often affected by illness, and possessing a strong-willed nature that could not be challenged. During early childhood, the patient and his older brothers had accepted her ideas as fact, only to gradually resent them bitterly as they became aware of a different reality during their school years. Although Mr B's mother had never seen a psychiatrist, the impression I developed of her from Mr B's description was that she must have been nearly psychotic. The struggle between the parents and their now-successful son continued to this day, marked by a series of break-ups, followed by reconciliations.

In the third year of Mr B's analysis, he acquired a new mistress, Miss C, who was an aggressive and domineering woman quite unlike the previous subservient women with whom he had been involved. Mr B stressed that his sexual relationship with Miss C was very satisfactory; he insisted he did not love her, but was strangely attracted to her precisely because she did not defer to him as his previous lovers had done. His relationship with her deepened over a period of time, acquiring characteristics of sadomasochistic interactions that often made me wonder whether Miss C was exploiting this wealthy man financially, or was herself very masochistic in tolerating his reiterations that he did not love her.

Clearly, for the first time in his life, Mr B had replicated his sadomasochistic relationship with his mother. At the same time, a subtle change occurred in the transference in the direction of its 'emptying out'. That is, I sensed that the patient was so totally absorbed in the reality of his daily life with Miss C that it was largely replacing his world of fantasy. I also felt that the patient seemed increasingly 'unreal' in his behaviour towards me. He became more and more 'shadowy' and made me think of an 'as if' personality at the same time as his conflicts with Miss C became clearer.

Over a period of months, the content of the sessions became increasingly invaded by Mr B's references to all the struggles he was having with this girlfriend, the complicated involvement in these struggles of members of both their families, and the increasing chaos in Mr B's life that appeared simultaneous to the development of what seemed to be his robot-like behaviour in the analytic sessions. For example, in reaction to an interpretation, the patient would move backward on the couch into a half-sitting position, supporting his chin in his hand as if reflecting on what I had said. He brought typewritten pages with descriptions of dreams that he wanted to read to me. When I asked why he felt the need to bring these typewritten summaries of his dreams rather than to talk freely about them in the hour, he offered the chagrined statement that he was only interested in accelerating the analytic work. Then, with a resigned gesture, he would proceed to relate the dreams from memory.

The interpretation of Mr B's behaviour was made more difficult by the subtlety of all these developments, which may here appear clearer than they did in the actual sessions. Over a period of months, I had the feeling of carrying out an 'as if' analysis, in the sense that my interpretations would become so cleverly integrated into the patient's associative material that I could no longer assess their effect. When I communicated to him that I was experiencing an enormous distance in our relationship, he freely acknowledged that he felt independent of me, which must indicate that he was now much healthier than before.

Mr B's ongoing friendliness, his apparent attention to everything I said, and his apparently uninhibited flow of free associations only punctuated my feeling that our relationship was completely phoney, but I felt strangely reluctant to confront him with my feeling, as it would be hopeless even to try. I sensed that either he would not understand what I was saying and would think I was being paranoid, or else that he would react in a helpless way, as if I were making impossible demands on him – an obviously 'good' patient, who was improving in his understanding and in his life.

In some sessions, Mr B made me feel that the only thing he needed to get better was for me to inculcate in him the capacity for tender love towards Miss C. In short, I felt paralysed in an emotional experience of 'phoniness', because of the sense of enormous emotional distance in our relationship. The alternatives were either to have him experience me as 'crazy' if I persisted in confronting him with the robot-like aspects of his behaviour, or to overwhelm him with demands for authenticity that he would not be able to comprehend.

Only gradually did I realize that my sense of impotence resulted from identifying with the patient in his relationship to his 'crazy' mother: I was submitting to the patient (mother) like a submissive son who was carrying out a pseudoanalysis as prescribed by his mother. I thought that the patient was unconsciously identifying with his mother, pretending to be caring and treating me as a son who had to be manipulated into obedience. In my efforts to break out of this situation, I was tempted to act like an impatient, controlling mother who would pretend that she knew exactly what was going on in her child without listening to him, overpowering him and forcing him either to protest in rage or to obligingly submit.

In this context, the patient gradually became aware of his incapacity to understand women and of the relief he experienced with his girlfriend because her aggressive behaviour was so obvious (unconsciously, he projected his own identification with his mother onto her). He also recognized that, in the context of ordinary social friendliness, he could not tell what kind of personality any of the women had with whom he became involved. Moreover, he discovered, in the middle of his violent interactions with his parents, that they still had an active sexual life – apparently the only interaction that had functioned satisfactorily over the years. He reacted with shock to the sudden awareness that his relationship with Miss C resembled that between his parents even more than he had thought. And I suddenly understood that what had been missing throughout these months was any significant reference to his father, in contrast to the total invasion of the transference by the relationship with his mother that I have outlined.

I suddenly also realized that I had been absorbed by the patient's descriptions of his difficulties with women. With some frequency, I noticed myself being distracted in the hours with this patient, thinking of other aspects of my work, and it seemed to me that I had been evading him, just as a frightened boy would not dare enter a collision course with an overpowering mother. And I remembered a childhood memory of my own father's avoidance of a conflict with my mother at home by escaping into his work. In immediate continuity, I then remembered how at high school I had led a rebellion against a tyrannical teacher, followed by intense fear of his retaliation.

Reflecting on and elaborating those fantasies over several weeks, I thought I was identifying with the patient as an impotent child, denying my own identity as an autonomous yet concerned fatherly image for him; I was implicitly colluding with the patient's fantasy that a self-castrating submissiveness was the only alternative to a violent father in dealing with a 'crazy' mother. This violent father image, in turn, represented the patient's projection of his own Oedipal protest onto the 'reasonable father' who might be able to bring order, and rescue mother from her own primitive entanglements. Remnants of my own Oedipal disposition had become activated in the process, contributing to my experience of paralysis in the treatment of Mr B. Then, a few weeks later, the following session occurred.

Mr B started by saying that he had had an uncanny experience of proposing a major business deal to a firm connected with a foreign country, and that he had become afraid that this business deal would be resented by a competitor attempting to do a similar deal with still another country. The patient suddenly became afraid that agents working for his competitor and the other country might try to steal information from him about the specific technology involved. While telling me that he knew this was a paranoid reaction, he was still afraid after leaving the office of the representatives of the foreign firm, and he thought that two men were following him that afternoon and late into the evening. He said he had become very anxious and was oscillating between a sense that this was exaggerated and a feeling that it might be true and he should watch out. The patient felt genuinely anxious in conveying this information to me.

At the same time, and frequently in recent months, the patient would turn towards me from time to time and smile, as if to say, 'I know this is crazy, and I know you understand that I understand'. I said that I realized he was oscillating between fear and a sense that the fear was absurd. I also acknowledged that he was looking at me as if to reassure me he was aware of this tension, and perhaps also to reassure himself that I was still on his side rather than silently concluding he was crazy. The patient immediately said that he did not think I would think he was crazy, and he smiled at me with a reassuring expression in his face.

I told Mr B that I felt he was giving me a reassuring smile as if some danger had to be avoided in this situation. The patient replied jokingly that the only danger was that I might be aligned with the foreign country with whom his competitor was colluding. I now realized that the patient had not told me which country it was, and I mentioned this to him as a further indication of his fearfulness of me. My fantasy was that the foreign competitor was my country of origin, but I did not communicate this to the patient. He then became clearly uneasy; he reluctantly commented that the thought had crossed his mind that my office was wired, and that it would be easy for me to obtain confidential information from him that I could use for my own purposes. He went on to associate about the possibility of break-ins into psychiatrists' offices, linked it with the Watergate affair and several films in which psychiatrists had been involved in shady, even dangerous, deals. I pointed to his effort to defend himself against a vision of me as spying on him by projecting the enemies as foreign agents rather than I myself being a foreign agent operating dangerously against him.

Again smiling, Mr B somewhat ironically said that he thought that I, rather than being dangerous, might need protection. He remembered an incident in which a woman he (correctly) considered psychotic had appeared in my waiting room and attempted to enter my office before he did. On that occasion, he had become intensely fearful that she might reappear later in the session with a gun, and in attempting to shoot me would shoot him. He said, half-jokingly, 'That woman might reappear any day and stab you in the back'. I said that I wondered whether he was trying to make a joke out of a fantasy that otherwise might be very frightening to him, namely, that I might stab him in the back by betraying his technical innovations to a competitor.

As I was saying this, I had two contradictory feelings: that I was on the right path in interpreting Mr B's 'phoney' friendliness as a defence against an underlying paranoid relationship in the transference, and, at the same time, that I was forcefully invading the patient with interpretations beyond his capacity for immediate awareness, 'brainwashing' him, as it were, enacting the role of a paranoid mother. For some fleeting moments, I felt really 'paranoid' in interpreting a primitive persecutory fantasy to this smiling, relaxed patient. But then I felt that my fantasy reflected my fear of asserting myself as a father who could transcend this madness and transform what seemed a 'violent' interpretation into a 'reasonable' one.

Mr B remained silent and suddenly appeared very tense. I told him that he looked very tense all of a sudden. He said he had just had the image of himself stabbing his mother. He fell silent but continued to look extremely tense. Then he said that he was very upset, and that he would never do such a thing. I told him that I thought he was trying to reassure both me and himself that he would never stab his mother, afraid that his wishes to stab her might be the same thing as actually stabbing her. I also wondered whether his fear and his wish to stab his mother might be connected with his fear of my stabbing him in the back: I interpreted his projecting his own rage into me. I also felt that such murderous rage contained the disqualification of the reasonable father, and I had the fantasy that I was in this role of a 'reasonable third person'. But then I thought I might be too far beyond the patient's present experience, so I said I would not be surprised if his immediate response included some effort to transform our discussion into a humorous situation in order to take the edge off the frightening feeling that we were exploring.

The patient then said that he was not surprised I would say this, but that he had been thinking very seriously of how enraged he had become at his mother in their last extended telephone conversation. He then proceeded to talk with great emotion about an aspect of her discourse that seemed to him totally crazy and that he felt impotent to puncture. I said that I wondered whether he had been putting his sense of impotence in dealing with a crazy mother into me, while he enacted the role of the crazy mother himself in the session. He did this by conveying to me his crazy behaviour, telling me that he knew it was crazy, and yet enacting it in his watchful turning around to observe me. I added that, in attempting to show him the serious aspects of what was going on beyond the nicety of his friendly smile and his comments, I might have been easily derailed by these very niceties, or I might have appeared to be crazy by pointing to the madness going on in fantasy in this room, namely the danger that I might stab him like an impotent, enraged boy would stab a crazy, dominant mother. A lengthy silence followed. The patient said that it was true that he always tried to keep things on an even keel with me, and, in fact, that had been his usual behaviour with all women except Miss C. He now realized how enraged he was at all women. The session then ended.

What I did not bring up with Mr B was his identification with mother in the absence of the Oedipal father. My countertransference reaction – my enactment of an identification with a weak father, and my awareness of a dissociated image of a violent father – was still too strong to permit me, at that point, to introduce this new perspective. Yet my thinking had become freer, and I was no longer enmeshed in a pseudo-friendly, robot-like relationship in the transference.

Now a new theme emerged in the treatment and began to pervade the sessions: a condensation of Mr B's fear of aggressive, frustrating, dominating and manipulative women, on the one hand, and, on the other, his desire to do better than his henpecked, distant and aloof father. Mr B also experienced a related despair over ever being able to compete with me as an idealized version of an unavailable father model.

COUNTERTRANSFERENCE DIAGNOSIS AND MANAGEMENT

A comparison of the cases of Mr A and Mr B illustrates the changing role of countertransference analysis in dealing with the shift from less to more severe psychopathology. Although with Mr A I did not refer to my own countertransference disposition (in the sense of what might have motivated my neglecting to tell the patient about the suggested change in our first session after being apart), there was an aspect of my own transference disposition towards the patient that influenced my failure to mention this scheduling change at the beginning of the session, as well as the intensity of my momentary countertransference reaction after the patient scolded me for interrupting his train of thought.

In the case of Mr B, I believe that his contribution to my chronic countertransference disposition towards him over several months was of overriding importance. Rather than reflecting any specific aspect of my own past, my countertransference pointed to my general concern over the 'as if' quality of the relationship. I believe that I experienced the combination of a general narcissistic response – a relatively normal one, I would assume – to long-standing failure in the task, and a superego-determined guilt reaction over not helping him, all of which fed into the sense of frustration, impotence and confusion the patient had experienced in the relationship with his mother that he was projecting onto me.

Similarly, Mr A's communication by means of the content of his free associations was clearly dominant in the sessions. The nonverbal aspects of his behaviour and my countertransference disposition were less important than in the case of Mr B in determining the overall integration of my understanding, and my interpretation of the transference. In the case of Mr B, the patient's nonverbal behaviour and my countertransference illustrated the need to integrate into one formulation the patient's communication of his subjective experience, my observation of his behaviour in the therapeutic interaction, and the countertransference.

I see my countertransference with Mr B as illustrating, first, the chronicity of countertransference reactions with some patients presenting severe character pathology. The robot-like quality of his behaviour in the hour, my sense of unreality and impotence, and the underlying projective identification in the transference – the enactment of the relationship between a crazy mother and a pseudo-submissive son – represented the patient's contribution to my countertransference. My identification with one aspect of my father reflected my contribution, although the patient's own incapacity to identify with a strong and generous father also played a part. The patient's verbal communication centred on his relationship with women in the present reality; his nonverbal communication and my emotional reaction centred on his maternal transference. My sense of impotence, of being caught between phoney friendliness and violence, went beyond the effect of his projective identification. Leon Grinberg's (1993) concept of projective counteridenti-fication has a place here, as well as the complementarity between the deeper layer of the patient's Oedipal problems and what the chronic challenge in the transference evoked in my own countertransference potential.

The problem, in the case of chronic countertransference reactions towards patients presenting with severe psychopathology, is that the very slowly developing, diffuse, 'invasive' nature of these reactions may infiltrate the entire psychoanalytic process to such an extent that they interfere with immediate analysis of them. Thus the analyst may be required to engage in consistent work outside, as well as during, the sessions in order to understand and transform them into an interpretation.

Lucia Tower (1956) has suggested that some chronic countertransference reactions can be understood only retrospectively, that is, after the analyst has shifted to a different emotional position. From this viewpoint, the older assumption, that to be too preoccupied with a patient outside the sessions indicates some problem in the analyst, needs to be modified. The extraordi-nary preoccupation with a particular patient outside the sessions may sometimes derive simply from a lack of understanding due to inexperience or the unusual difficulty of the case. More frequently, however, such preoccu-pation arises from the development of chronic countertransference reactions in cases of severe psychopathology.

I have found chronic countertransference reactions to be particularly frequent in the treatment of patients with a severe narcissistic personality, patients with a regressive sadomasochistic transference, patients who express a very primitive type of hatred in unconscious efforts to destroy the very communication with the analyst (the syndrome that Bion [1958] described as including pseudostupidity, curiosity and arrogance) and patients with 'as if' characteristics and a psychopathic transference. In addition, patients with severe paranoid regression and transference psychosis also may bring about chronic countertransference reactions, as well as patients whose acting out may take objectively dangerous forms, such as being suicidal, being homicidal or actively persecuting the analyst (e.g. threatening a lawsuit). In all these cases, very primitive internalized object relations, and sometimes truly psychotic nuclei, become dominant in the transference and apparently defy ordinary efforts to resolve these regressions interpretively.

Here I would like to point to some particular aspects of countertransference management that are helpful under conditions of chronic countertransference development. First, I have found it very helpful to try to imagine how a 'normal' patient would react towards a 'normal' analyst, under the condition in which an interpretation has been given that the patient has been unable to accept or to understand, or that is immediately incorporated into a psychotic system or distorted in ways that interfere with further work. Or else, what would a normal interaction be like between a patient daring to depend on the psychoanalyst as a trustworthy person who attempts to help without being omniscient or omnipotent? Such an internal confrontation between an imagined potentially normal interaction with a patient and the present transference–countertransference bind will help to clarify what is abnormal or strange in the content of the patient's subjective experience and behaviour, and in the countertransference itself, and how these three elements might be understood in their mutual relationships.

From a purely cognitive viewpoint, what I have just outlined may appear almost obvious or trivial. In practice, however, under the impact of chronic countertransference developments, it is much more difficult to reconstitute that theoretical frame of normality, and it may be much easier for an 'outsider' than for the analyst caught up in the situation. Collegial consultation may therefore be helpful at any point during an analyst's career.

Some emotional attitudes of the analyst may become important in the treatment of patients with severe psychopathology, because they provide an important counterbalance to the risk of developing chronic countertransference reactions. It is, of course, crucial for the analyst to tolerate the conscious experience of powerful countertransference reactions, to contain them, and to use them for self-exploration, as well as for diagnosing the total transference situation (Winnicott 1949). Another attitude is to be courageous enough to interpret a situation when a chronic stalemate tends to induce a sense of futility and hopelessness in the analyst (an attitude of passivity that can easily be rationalized as patiently waiting for the situation to resolve itself). Obviously, I am not talking about the analyst's 'bombarding' of the patient with interpretations, but rather about a psychological attitude of 'vehemence' when the analyst sees a situation clearly and yet feels afraid to share this understanding with the patient. It is an attitude involving cognitive clarity and contained emotional concern and courage.

Usually, an as-yet-not-fully-diagnosed expression of omnipotence or omnipotent control dominates the patient's transference at such times. The probing of unconscious transference meanings in the 'here and now' may require fearlessness over the possibility that the patient may experience the interpretation as a 'violent' invasion, as Piera Aulagnier (1981) has described in psychotic patients. The mechanism involved may be the projective identification of the patient's omnipotence, while the consequence may be the paralysis of the analyst as the patient experiences every intervention as an attack.

The analyst's interventions under such conditions may fall along a broad spectrum, ranging from tentative suggestions and hesitant questions to direct statements, to the extreme of expressing a strong conviction. With the safeguards mentioned, this interpretive variance may reflect both a therapeutic 'impatience' in every session, and a willingness and disposition to work, matched with as much patience as necessary over an extended period of time. This combination of analytic 'impatience' in the short run and 'patience' in the long run is the opposite of an unconscious effort by the analyst to avoid a particularly difficult or painful transference–countertransference bind by withdrawing from the transference situation and maintaining a level of friendliness and relaxation that avoids facing the aggression in primitive transferences and in the enactment of omnipotent control. There are times when relaxed friendliness becomes indifference, and when a 'vehement' statement is an expression of concern. The analyst's capacity to shift from one to the other is an indicator of internal freedom to interpret. An analyst's strong conviction is compatible both with technical neutrality and with an objective, concerned relationship with the patient.

In treating patients with regressive transferences, the analyst must learn to tolerate the development of 'scenarios' in which a countertransference is fully explored by letting it resolve into a narrative, that is, a temporal sequence of events that transform the 'scenario' of an enacted object relationship into a story that illuminates the meaning of the scenario. For example, the analyst's sexual fantasies about a patient may develop into a countertransference narrative of a sexual relationship with the patient, its presumed beginning, and final destruction in light of what the analyst knows about the patient and himself. The tolerance of such scenarios – which evolve naturally out of chronic countertransference dispositions – may facilitate the analysis of subtle aspects of the transference linked to these countertransference developments, and it may highlight aspects of the transference to which the analyst was previously blind. Such tolerance may also open the road to the self-analytic function of the analyst that may recover unconscious aspects of his own countertransference predisposition.

NOTES

1   Director, Personality Disorders Institute, New York Hospital–Cornell Medical Center, Westchester Division; Professor of Psychiatry, Cornell University Medical College; Training and Supervising Analyst, Columbia University Center for Psychoanalytic Training and Research.

2   First presented at a 'Dialogue on countertransference' with Dr Hanna Segal, at the 38th Congress of the International Psychoanalytic Association, Amsterdam, July 1993.

REFERENCES

Alexandris, A. and Vaslamatzis, G. (eds) (1993) *Countertransference: Theory, Technique, Teaching*, London: Karnac Books.

Aulagnier, P. (1981) *La Violence de l'Interprétation*, Paris: Presses Universitaires de France.

Bion, W. R. (1958) 'On arrogance', *International Journal of Psycho-Analysis*, 39, 144–6.

Carpy, D. (1989) 'Tolerating the countertransference: a mutative process', *International Journal of Psycho-Analysis*, 70, 287–94.

Grinberg, L. (1993) 'Countertransference and the concept of projective counteridentification', in A. Alexandris and G. Vaslamatzis (eds) *Countertransference: Theory, Technique, Teaching*, London: Karnac Books, 47–65.

Hamilton, N. G. (1990) 'The containing function and the analyst's projective identification', *International Journal of Psycho-Analysis*, 71, 445–53.

Heimann, P. (1950) 'On countertransference', *International Journal of Psycho-Analysis*, 31, 81–4.

Kernberg, O. F. (1965) 'Notes on countertransference', *Journal of the American Psychoanalytic Association*, 13, 38–56.

Kernberg, O. F. Selzer, M. A., Koenigsberg, H. W., Carr, A. C. and Appelbaum, A. H. (1989) *Psychodynamic Psychotherapy of Borderline Patients*, New York: Basic Books.

Little, M. (1951) 'Countertransference and the patient's response to it', *International Journal of Psycho-Analysis*, 32, 32–40.

Loewald, H. W. (1986) 'Transference–countertransference', *Journal of the American Psychoanalytic Association*, 34, 275–87.

McDougall, J. (1993) 'Countertransference and primitive communication', in A. Alexandris and G. Vaslamatzis (eds) *Countertransference: Theory, Technique, Teaching*, London: Karnac Books, 95–133.

Mitchell, S. A. (1988) *Relational Concepts in Psychoanalysis*, Cambridge MA: Harvard University Press.

Ogden, T. H. (1993) 'The analytic management and interpretation of projective identification', in A. Alexandris and G. Vaslamatzis (eds) *Countertransference: Theory, Technique, Teaching*, London: Karnac Books, 21–46.

Pick, I. B. (1985) 'Working through in the countertransference', *International Journal of Psycho-Analysis*, 66, 157–66.

Racker, H. (1957) 'The meanings and uses of countertransference', *Psychoanalytic Quarterly*, 26, 303–57.

Reich, A. (1951) 'On countertransference', *International Journal of Psycho-Analysis*, 32, 25–31.

Sandler, J. (1976) 'Countertransference and role responsiveness', *International Review of Psycho-Analysis*, 3, 43–7.

Segal, H. (1981) 'Countertransference', in *The Work of Hanna Segal*, Northvale NJ: Jason Aronson, 81–7.

Spillius, E. B. (1988) *Melanie Klein Today*, vol. 2, New York: Routledge, Chapman & Hall.

Tower, L. E. (1956) 'Countertransference', *Journal of the American Psychoanalytic Association*, 4, 224–55.

Volkan, V. D. (1993) 'Countertransference reactions commonly present in the treatment of patients with borderline personality', in A. Alexandris and G.

Vaslamatzis (eds) *Countertransference: Theory, Technique, Teaching*, London: Karnac Books, 147–63.

Winnicott, D. W. (1949) 'Hate in the countertransference', *International Journal of Psycho-Analysis*, 30, 69–75.

13

PSYCHOANALYSTS'
THEORIES

Robert Michels

INTRODUCTION

The title of this contribution, 'Psychoanalysts' theories', rather than the more familiar 'Psychoanalytic theories', is deliberate. Psychoanalytic theories are found in books, journals and libraries, and as part of the scholarly dialogue of that small group of psychoanalysts who generate formal theories and speak and write about them. These theories are complicated, confusing and abstract. They are also represented, although not always with great precision or accuracy, in the minds of all working psychoanalysts, including that majority who would never consider writing a paper on psychoanalytic theory, where they contribute to what I am calling 'psychoanalysts' theories'. My focus is on these latter theories, which are situated in the minds of practising psychoanalysts rather than in books or journal articles, and which therefore make a difference to patients. I will discuss their history, their subject matter and their several functions. As psychoanalysts, we should anticipate that these latent or implicit theories might be quite different from the manifest public ones; that elegance, logic or consistency might turn out to be only minor virtues in this kind of theory; and that psychoanalysts not only might not know what their implicit theories are, but also might argue vehemently that they are actually something quite different.

I believe that Joseph Sandler (1983) was addressing this same subject, although reaching a different conclusion, when he wrote:

> The fledgling psychoanalyst will bring with him into his consulting room what he has learned from his own analyst, from his supervisors and other teachers, and from his reading. He will carry in his head the theoretical and clinical propositions that he has gathered from these various sources, and these propositions will be, for the most part, the official, standard or public ones. The human mind being what it is, he will continue to underestimate the discrepancies and

incongruities in the public theories and will learn to move from one part of his theory to another without being aware that he has stepped over a number of spots in this theory that are conceptually weak.

With increasing clinical experience the analyst, as he grows more competent, will preconsciously (descriptively speaking, unconsciously) construct a whole variety of theoretical segments which relate directly to his clinical work. They are the products of unconscious thinking, are very much partial theories, models or schemata, which have the quality of being available in reserve, so to speak, to be called upon whenever necessary. That they may contradict one another is no problem. They coexist happily as long as they are unconscious. They do not appear in consciousness unless they are consonant with what I have called official or public theory, and can be described in suitable words. Such partial structures may in fact represent better (i.e. more useful and appropriate) theories than the official ones, and it is likely that many valuable additions to psychoanalytic theory have come about because conditions have arisen that have allowed preconscious part-theories to come together and emerge in a plausible and psychoanalytically socially acceptable way.

(Sandler 1983: 37–8)

In contrast to Professor Sandler, I suggest that we recognize the role and importance of these part-theories. Therefore we can change our rules for psychoanalytic acceptability, rather than wait for part-theories to become acceptable.

HISTORY

At one time, psychoanalysts believed that they should construct scientific theories about the workings of the human mind, particularly the influence of biological factors (i.e. the body, the brain, or the inherited constitutional endowment) on the mind. Their view was that these theories could then be applied to a variety of problems, including the treatment of patients. Freud's earliest explication of psychoanalytic theory fits this mould. However, a number of observers have pointed out that the theories of the mind developed by psychoanalysts were actually by-products of the clinical situation, abstracted from rather than applied to it. Psychoanalytic theorists, starting with Freud himself, did not study biological data – brains, bodies or evolution. Rather, they collected experiences in their clinical work and then speculated about biological models that might be consistent with those experiences. Furthermore, critics added that the biological theories that were developed did not serve some of the functions desirable for a good scientific theory; specifically, they did not generate strategies for testing or for possible invalidation and, more generally, they were not very helpful in furthering scientific inquiry. At the same time, although psychoanalysts had developed a rather credible psychological science in their clinical work, they were much less interested in developing it systematically than in elaborating their speculative biological hypotheses.

A first step towards developing theories based on psychoanalytic data was to bring psychoanalysts' speculations closer to their clinical experience. Theorizing shifted from neurobiology and evolution to psychology. Psychoanalytic models of perception, cognition, learning, memory and personality were developed. The results, however, were only mixed. The new theories were closer to the data generated by the psychoanalytic method, but they often seemed to offer little more than the existing models of academic psychology. They seemed less exciting and less evocative of new clinical insights than were the earlier speculations, and served as perhaps little more than formalizations or tautological restatements of clinical observations. A common complaint was that psychoanalysis had become a complex and dull general psychology rather than an exciting, if unscientific, speculative biology.

The next step involved redefining the subject matter of psychoanalytic theory so that it focused on the events occurring in clinical psychoanalysis that can be studied by the psychoanalytic method, rather than either on biological speculations stemming from those events or on subsequent psychological reformulations of them. However, this change of focus raised new problems. The original biological theories suggested the causes or underlying meanings of the patient's mental experiences and, therefore, the kinds of interpretations an analyst might want to make. The psychological theories that followed attempted to describe and formulate what might be happening in the patient's mind, and although they might not lead to interpretations, they did help to organize and integrate clinical data. The new clinical theories studied the therapeutic process – what transpired in the consultation room between analyst and patient – but did not tell the analyst what to say. Analysts could continue to make the same interpretations that analysts have always made, but if they could no longer be grounded in biology and could not yet be grounded in clinical theory, the only justification that remained was professional tradition. This led to the danger that there would be no way of deciding whether a given interpretation was correct or, perhaps better, whether it was truly psychoanalytic, and – because different analysts interpreted the tradition differently – the field threatened to become chaotic.

Several theories emerged, however, as possible replacements for the original biological theories and as sources of interpretative inspiration. These emerging theories drew on extra-analytic bodies of knowledge, as well as on clinical psychoanalytic data – knowledge that many believed to be useful in suggesting interpretations in the analytic situation. The most well-known theories were about child development, based in part on the direct observation of children. Others included social or group psychology, anthropology, linguistics, and, more recently, neurobiology.

SUBJECT MATTER

The same issues may be considered from the perspective of the several types of theory rather than from the viewpoint of the history of the development of theory. Such a perspective would recognize that each type of theory can be traced back to the beginnings of psychoanalysis, although from time to time the dominant mode of theorizing may have shifted in the evolution of the discipline. It would also underline the different epistemological status of the various types of theories, rather than their developmental continuity.

There have been at least three distinct types of theories in psychoanalysis: bridging theories, psychological theories and clinical theories. Because of the recurrent failure to clarify which type is being discussed, there has been considerable confusion about these theories. Both the scientific status and the clinical implications of each type are quite different.

Bridging theories

Bridging theories attempt to explain mental phenomena by tracing them across some boundary to a domain outside of mental life. There are a variety of different bridging theories, depending on the boundary that is crossed and the subject matter that lies beyond it. Mental life can thus be traced to the brain and its somatic origins, as in Freud's 'Project for a scientific psychology' (1950), his drive theory, Karl Pribram's writings (1989) or Morton Reiser's monograph (1984). It can be traced to its phylogenetic and evolutionary origins, as in Freud's 'Totem and taboo' (1913), John Bowlby's work (1969) or contemporary ethology. Mental life can also be traced to its developmental protomental origins, as in Freud's 'Three essays on the theory of sexuality' (1905) or in the work of Anna Freud, Margaret Mahler, Rene Spitz, David Levy, Robert Emde, Daniel Stern, or any of those who study babies and children to learn about the origins of mental life. It can be traced to its social origins in studies of parent–child, family and group relations, as Freud did in his papers on the Oedipus complex and group psychology, and as the Sullivanian and object relations theorists have done.

Common to all these bridging theories is that they draw on knowledge from other fields of observation and other disciplines in order to speculate about mental life. There are two corollaries to this fact. First, bridging theories often provide rich images or metaphors and evocative formulations that can translate mental experience and generate valuable clinical interpretations. Second, these theories themselves cannot possibly be tested in the psychoanalytic situation, because they are based on hypotheses and observations from non-analytic settings. The clinical interpretations they inspire can be tested and can be shown to be valuable or useless, but such findings neither support nor refute the theories that generated them. Clinical psychoanalysts like these theories; philosophers of science disdain them, viewing them as systems of interpretative metaphor that can neither be validated in the psychoanalytic situation nor lead to a science of psychoanalysis.

It is interesting to note the similarity between psychoanalytic theories that come from other areas – biology, developmental psychology, linguistics, anthropology – and those that are brought to psychoanalysts by their patients. Both of these theories serve to limit the domain in which analytic exploration is appropriate. Both our scientific theories and our patients warn us not to go beyond some boundary; that some phenomena cannot be understood simply in terms of the inner world but are determined instead by forces – biological or social or developmental – that are constraints on that inner world. When a patient presents such a theory, it is always possible that it is 'true' (and perhaps it is always a little true). However, any experienced analyst also explores its role as a resistance and, in the process, expects to find not the limits of analysability but rather the area of most fruitful inquiry. No doubt this experience in the clinical setting is one reason why analysts are often mistrustful of any theory that seems to provide extra-analytic justification for limiting the boundaries of analytic inquiry.

Psychological theories

The second type of theory is psychological theory. It involves models of mental functioning, rather than suggestions about the origins of mental life. Chapter 7 of 'The interpretation of dreams' (Freud 1900), parts of 'The ego and the id' (Freud 1923) and many of Heinz Hartmann's writings exemplify psychological theories. Unlike biological or social or anthropological theories, psychological theories represent what psychoanalysis should be about for those who believe it should be a general psychology. These theories are less likely to suggest metaphors or meanings or to inspire creative clinical interpretations, whereas they are more likely to offer systems for organizing and integrating clinical data. Rather than trying to explain why things happen, they provide guidelines for describing, classifying and discussing what is happening. They are useful to some clinicians, while others associate them with the dangers of an overly mechanistic and sterile technique. They tend to be far more prominent in the didactic curricula of institutes than in the mental life of analysts at work.

Clinical theories

The third type, clinical theories, are rooted in the clinical situation. These theories are also psychological, but they are about a very special and restricted area of psychology: what happens in the consultation room. They also can be traced back to Freud's earliest papers, such as 'Studies on hysteria' (Breuer and Freud 1893–5), but are most prominent in his papers on technique, such as 'Analysis terminable and interminable' (1937) or in more recent works by Otto Fenichel, Ralph Greenson and others. Clinical theories do not provide a general psychology, but rather are about the specific psychology of transference, resistance, alliance, working through and acting out, as well as similar concepts. They are directly concerned with the analytic situation and often suggest general clinical strategies and hypotheses that can be tested there. However, they seldom suggest the content of specific interpretations or interventions, although they may suggest formal principles for conducting an analysis. They are like the theories of harmony, rhythm and musicology – vital for dissecting, understanding and discussing music, but insufficient for composing a symphony.

In recent years, interest in psychoanalytic thinking has shifted from the first extra-analytic type and even the second, general psychological type to this third, clinical type of theory. This shift has made it more likely that theory and practice can be mutually enriching, and has invited ideas such as those discussed here.

FUNCTION: RELATION OF THEORY TO PRACTICE

Let us shift from an overview of the history of psychoanalytic theory and a consideration of the different types of theories to a discussion of the functions of theories, how they are used and the roles they play. Although theories are important in teaching, supervision and research, the place to start is with what interests psychoanalysts most – the role of theory in practice.

Scientific basis of practice

Most professions based on scientific knowledge and theory expect the practitioner to learn and master the theory and then apply it to individual problems or cases. Some view psychoanalysis in these terms. For example, Ralph Greenson (1968) said that the analyst 'must listen to the material of his patient, permitting his own associative fantasies and memories to have free play as he does so; yet he must scrutinize and expose to his intellectual capacities the insights so obtained' (16). Greenson echoes Fenichel in presenting the image of an analyst oscillating 'between the use of empathy and intuition on the one hand and ... theoretical knowledge on the other' (16).

Generation of interpretations

There is a problem, however, when this somewhat restricted version of the traditional view of the role of theory in the science-based professions is applied to psychoanalysis. This problem generates a different view of the relationship between theory and practice. Our instructions to practising analysts suggest a state of mind that is 'free floating' or 'evenly hovering', that is open to empathic perception, trial identification and adaptive regression. But this state of mind is not that of someone applying a complex scientific theory to a body of data. Rather, it is the state of mind of someone using theory as a source of inspiration to extend and enrich a network of associations. The psychoanalyst who knows and uses psychoanalytic theories this way listens to the patient, enriched by an associative context that includes the shared experiences of the entire community of psychoanalysts, past and present, as well as the psychoanalyst's own clinical and personal experience.

Viewed from this perspective, there is little difference between psychoanalytic case histories and psychoanalytic theories, or between psychoanalytic theories and other theories. The only question is: does the theory enrich the experience of the analyst with the patient? Furthermore, there is little concern about compatibility or contradiction among theories. Finally, within this perspective, we do not ask whether psychoanalytic theories are true or false, just as critics do not ask whether works of art are true or false, philosophers of science do not ask whether scientific theories are true or false, and psychoanalysts do not ask whether interpretations are true or false. The critic wants to know what impact a work of art has on the audience and the culture. The philosopher of science wants to know whether a theory fosters scientific inquiry, generates hypotheses and suggests experiments. The psychoanalyst wants to know whether an interpretation stimulates new material and leads to therapeutic progress. We want to know whether a psychoanalytic theory helps psychoanalysts to analyse, or whether it guides them to new insights and understandings. In each case, the test is not one of truth or falsity, but rather one of assessing the impact of an intervention on an ongoing process (Michels 1983).

However, even this view of theory as a source of inspiration or metaphor rather than as a systematic scientific structure to be applied to the data of specific clinical situations, may overemphasize the cognitive aspects of psychoanalysis and the primacy of insight. It seems to imply that the most important role of the analyst is to make interpretations. In fact, theory has an additional and often more powerful impact on clinical work, one that generates a third view of the impact of theory on psychoanalytic practice.

Influence on the analyst's role

Theories influence the analyst's stance, manner, attitude and approach to the patient, the analyst's role, and particularly the analyst's perception of that role. The following examples illustrate such influence.

Listening

The first example goes back to the very beginning of psychoanalysis and to the core of its meaning. One of the essential aspects of psychoanalysis is that the analyst listen to the patient. One of Freud's first major theoretical formulations was that the patient's words, no matter how fragmented, incoherent or irrelevant they might seem on the surface, conceal a hidden but important meaning, and, furthermore, that meaning can be deciphered by paying close attention to what is said and how it is said. Whether this theory is 'right' or 'wrong', whether the analyst ever understands the patient's real meaning, whether the uncoding is correct or fanciful, indeed whether it even makes sense to speak of a 'real' meaning, this theory helps to sustain the analyst's attentive and patient listening and thus supports a central feature of the psychoanalytic stance. (The special importance of being listened to by someone who is trying to make sense out of what one is saying may stem from the universal experience of having a parent try to make sense out of the infant's meaningless babbling and, in the process, to transform a psychologically prestructural organism into a communicating social being.) The meanings discovered by psychoanalytic inquiry may be therapeutic, but the experience of being listened to by an attentive, concerned guide in the search for meaning may well be even more therapeutic.

Nonjudgemental interest

A second essential of psychoanalysis is that, in addition to listening attentively and patiently, the analyst must be interested and curious without being critical or judgemental. Developing nonjudgemental interest may be even more difficult than listening attentively, because we are all socialized to make judgements about behaviour (our own and that of others) and to hold people responsible for what they do. We make exceptions only when we believe persons to be so infantile or helpless or disorganized that they are not in charge of their lives. We know, however, that such an attitude towards a patient, except in psychiatric crises, seriously compromises psychoanalysis. Here again, we have a theory that is helpful. The concept of a dynamic unconscious – of powerful forces that shape behaviour and that are at the same time both within the patient and yet outside awareness – supports the paradoxical but crucial belief that the patient should not be judged or held morally culpable, despite being the master of his or her own fate. Once again, the issue is not whether this concept is 'true' or 'false'. (Indeed, the Anglo-

American debate on criminal responsibility and the insanity defence has foundered on this essentially meaningless question.) However, regardless of its epistemological status, or whether it ever generates a specific clinical interpretation, this theory comes to our aid by maintaining an essential component of the analytic attitude.

Libido theory

For a third example, I will consider a more complex theory, one of the oldest, most powerful and most criticized theories in psychoanalysis: libido theory. Again, my interest is not in whether the theory is true or false, or even in whether it can be tested or falsified, but rather in what difference it makes to a practising analyst. Libido theory suggests that the analyst should search for patterns based on infantile bodily experiences. Rather than accept the patient's conscious level of discourse as the most critical or significant one, the analyst should constantly attempt to translate or reformulate, to find forbidden, primitive, exciting and, particularly, naughty meanings in the most mundane statements. This process of reformulation is what makes psychoanalysis seem to outsiders interesting, ridiculous and disturbing, all at the same time. Analysis requires not only that analysts listen and avoid moral disapproval, but also that they translate and elaborate on their patients' themes. It is not enough for analysts to be friendly, supportive and receptive; they must also be interesting. True or false, libido theory generates some of the most interesting statements made by psychoanalysts.

Psychic conflict

A fourth and final example of the theories that guide psychoanalysis is the concept of psychic conflict. Once again, regardless of the scientific status of this concept, it leads the analyst to accept and tolerate – and perhaps even to search for – paradox, ambiguity and contradiction. Particularly in its more comprehensive formulation as the principle of multiple function, the concept of psychic conflict encourages a continuing openness to new or additional meanings and understandings rather than a search for closure and correct or final answers. This theoretical concept encourages the continuing exploration that is central to the analytic process.

Effects of alternative theories

If theories function in part by shaping therapeutic attitudes, then alternative theories may have different impacts. This is true not only because of their differential validity or scientific status, or even the different interpretations they suggest, but also because they encourage different stances.

For example, structural theory focuses on divisions within the patient's mind and encourages the analyst to maintain an active interest in what is being excluded or omitted. Its proponents believe that this examination of what is not said is central to psychoanalysis, in that it sheds light on psychic conflict, repression and the dynamic unconscious. Its critics fear, however, that structural theory places the analyst in a constantly adversarial or, at best, in a neutral, uninvolved or unempathic posture *vis-à-vis* the patient, thus encouraging detached observation rather than emotional participation.

Object relations theory emphasizes the internal world, a derivative of the social field, the mental representations of the relationships between the patient and significant others. Just as structural theory reduces mental life to conflicts among components of the mind, object relations theory reduces it to interactions among images of self and others. The critics of object relations theory are concerned that it overemphasizes social and environmental determinants of behaviour at the expense of intrapersonal and, particularly, biological ones, and furthermore that it encourages the analyst to be excessively preoccupied with what is going on between patient and analyst rather than within the patient's mind. Its proponents believe that it re-humanizes a psychoanalytic model that had begun to consider people as though they were machines instead of social beings.

Self psychology emphasizes the inherent growth potential of the individual and suggests that other people in the patient's life, including the analyst, are either incorporated as vital substrates for this growth programme, helping to nurture and promote it, or that they become irrelevant and even destructive to it. Proponents of the model emphasize the positive, affirmative orientation it encourages, often seeing alternative theories as encouraging an inappropriate focus on problems that are but symptoms of arrested psychic development. Critics are concerned that self psychology achieves this affirmative stance by colluding with the patient in denying the darker aspects of mental life (e.g. hostility and negative feelings that are more than reactive responses to environmental precipitants), along with disavowed aspects of mental conflict.

Support for the analyst

Finally, theories operate, quite simply, by comforting the psychoanalyst. This function is in addition to that of organizing knowledge that can be applied to clinical data, their interpretation-generating or metaphoric function of suggesting meanings and relationships, and their impact on the general stance, manner, attitude and approach of the analyst. Psychoanalysis is a difficult profession, and psychoanalysts spend much of their time uncertain – perhaps even confused or bewildered – as they attempt to comprehend amorphous or chaotic experiences that do not always fit into place. The work is lonely, and psychoanalysts crave reassurance, support and company. Theory can provide that support.

A theory can be seen as a kind of transitional object: it links the psycho-analyst to a teacher or mentor; it provides a sense of security, a reassurance that someone knows and understands; and it gives refuge when the going is difficult. Moreover, as with some other transitional objects, analysts may cling to a particular theory all the more when others ridicule it or try to take it away and replace it with a cleaner, more modern substitute. Old theories, like old teddy bears, are not less beloved because they are torn or perhaps a little smelly.

This comforting function of theory is especially important for students or novices. It provides a partially illusory safety and reassurance that continues until accumulating personal clinical experience diminishes both its power and the need for its supportive function. When this process goes smoothly, all is well. However, at times the de-idealization of theory precedes the develop-ment of personal experience, and the student is prematurely left without adequate support. Many such students become critical of psychoanalysis and turn against it. Other students may elevate theory above clinical experience and never de-idealize it. Such students become followers of psychoanalysis, rather than independent professionals, and they tend to become the favourite targets of attacks by those who do not place theory above clinical experience.

This nonspecific function of theory for psychoanalysts is reminiscent of one of the functions that interpretations play for psychoanalytic patients. Interpretations both comfort and reassure, whether or not the patient understands and uses them. Interpretations, like theories, are evaluated in terms of their impact on the process, and, as with theory, it is of little interest to question whether they are true or false. Both interpretations and theories serve to clarify what is confusing and to provide links between easily observable surface phenomena and deeper structures hidden from direct view. By doing so, both help to bring into awareness those deeper structures (Michels 1983).

In summary, theories are important to analysts' analysing. They generate rules and guidelines, suggest meanings and interpretations, inform the basic stance and posture of the analyst, and provide comfort and security. The first of these functions, the traditional role of scientific theory in professional practice, may well be the least important.

FUNCTION: RELATION OF THEORY TO TEACHING AND RESEARCH

Psychoanalysts teach, and theories are educational aids. Clinical maxims, such as 'analyse the resistance before the content' or 'focus on the material associated with the patient's strongest affect', are condensed theories that are frequently used in supervision. However, rather than focusing on theories, good supervision focuses on clinical material: on the patient, the analyst and the events that transpire between them, or, from time to time, on the reflections of those events in the supervisory process. In general, the supervising psychoanalyst uses theory in much the same ways as does the analysing psychoanalyst, although the relative emphasis of its several functions differs. The supervisor is far more likely to function in a cognitive mode and to apply theory in a truly scientific way. The supervisor may draw on theory for metaphor and inspiration, although good supervision is more concerned with enhancing the supervisee's sensitivity to meaning and ability to construct metaphors. One's supervisory stance, like one's analytic stance, may be coloured by a favourite psychoanalytic theory, but supervision is education, not treatment, so the supervisor's attitude should be informed more by educational than by psychoanalytic theory. Finally, supervisors are further along in their own developmental course and less likely than analysts to need the emotional support provided by theory.

Although theories have a place in the consultation room and the supervisory office, they are most usually found in the curriculum and the classroom. As part of the curriculum, theories play a central role in pedagogy. In fact, they are more central to the classroom teaching of psychoanalysis than most other disciplines because the primary data are hard to come by, and the history of the field is as much a history of theoretical reformulation as it is one of new primary observations. One corollary of this central role is our concern that candidates should begin their clinical work before they have had too much classroom instruction, lest their premature and excessive exposure to theory lead to notions or styles inappropriate to the conduct of analysis. There are few other fields that raise such concerns about too much education interfering with practice. Bertram Lewin (1965) has even suggested that theories originate as derivatives of teaching, that they grow out of the teacher's attempt to explain to a student, or, in his words, that 'teaching and theorizing coincide and that the business of teaching leads to the production of theories' (138).

Professions based on scientific knowledge involve both teaching and research. To an astonishing extent, psychoanalysis has focused its academic activities on teaching, with the role of research largely replaced by theoretically informed discourse. However, in recent years, there has been some interest in activities that are more similar to the scientific research associated with other professions, particularly in the areas of child development and clinical process. Theories are essential for such research: they define problems and make the difference between simply collecting data and developing new knowledge that can have a cumulative impact on the field. Psychoanalytic theories have been productive in stimulating research in other fields, such as developmental psychology, and there is even some suggestion that psychoanalytic theory has, in turn, been enriched by new knowledge from developmental psychology. The more critical question is whether theories have fostered research in psychoanalysis itself. Here the answer is less clear. Systematic research is rare, and the questions it addresses often seem minor. One result is that serious and talented clinicians often have little interest in research. Another is that some of the most creative and original thinkers in the field are sceptical about the future of psychoanalytic research. A major challenge is whether psychoanalysts can develop theories that will stimulate research that might lead to new knowledge in psychoanalysis.

CONCLUSION

Freud (1933: 81) said that the 'right abstract ideas' produce order and clarity when applied to the raw material of observation. Interpretations in clinical analysis also do this; theories do the same in the scientific study of psychoanalysis. They also enrich the clinical work and codify and crystallize what has been learned. Without theories, the field cannot progress. However, a question that has long troubled psychoanalysis is how to decide which theories are the 'right' ones. Validation by some objective test, the strategy in most sciences, has largely eluded psychoanalytic inquiry. The sanction of authority, never very attractive, is no longer even possible, since there is no agreement on the appropriate authority. Theories borrowed from other disciplines are increasingly unsatisfactory, while those stemming from the study of analysis itself are more productive of formal principles than of suggestions for content.

Our best current guide to the content of clinical interpretations is a tradition that was originally developed on the basis of extra-analytic theorizing but has now largely fallen out of favour. Perhaps our clinical theory again has a guideline to offer, that the right theories are right for the same reasons that right interpretations are right – not because they are true or validated outside the psychoanalytic process, but because they lead to progress, new material or new ideas, rather than to stasis and stagnation. Good theories generate problems that lead to better theories, and therefore any theory that remains unchanged fails the test.

REFERENCES

Bowlby, J. (1969) *Attachment and Loss*, New York: Basic Books.

Breuer, J. and Freud, S. (1893–95), 'Studies on hysteria', *Standard Edition*, vol. 2, vii–xxxi, 1–311. London: Hogarth Press, 1955.

Freud, S. (1900) 'The interpretation of dreams', *Standard Edition*, vols 4–5, ix–xxxii, 1–627. London: Hogarth Press, 1953.

——(1905) 'Three essays on the theory of sexuality', *Standard Edition*, vol. 7, 123–45. London: Hogarth Press, 1953.

——(1913) 'Totem and taboo: some points of agreement between the mental lives of savages and neurotics', *Standard Edition*, vol. 13, vii–xv, 1–162. London: Hogarth Press, 1953.

——(1923) 'The ego and the id', *Standard Edition*, vol. 19, 1–66. London: Hogarth Press, 1961.

——(1933) 'New introductory lectures on psycho-analysis', *Standard Edition*, vol. 22, 1–182. London: Hogarth Press, 1964.

——(1937) 'Analysis terminable and interminable', *Standard Edition*, vol. 23, 209–53. London: Hogarth Press, 1964.

——(1950) 'Project for a scientific psychology', *Standard Edition*, vol. 1, 281–397. London: Hogarth Press, 1966.

Greenson, R. (1968) *The Technique and Practice of Psychoanalysis*, New York: International Universities Press.

Lewin, B. D. (1965) 'Teaching and the beginnings of theory', *International Journal of Psycho-Analysis*, 46, 137–9.

Michels, R. (1983) 'The scientific and clinical functions of psychoanalytic theory', in A. Goldberg (ed.) *The Future of Psychoanalysis: Essays in Honor of Heinz Kohut*, New York: International Universities Press, 125–35.

Pribram, K. (1989) 'Psychoanalysis and the natural sciences: the brain–behaviour connection from Freud to the present', in J. Sandler (ed.) *Dimensions of Psychoanalysis*, Madison CT: International Universities Press, 139–63.

Reiser, M. (1984) *Mind, Brain, Body: Towards a Convergence of Psychoanalysis and Neurobiology*, New York: Basic Books.

Sandler, J. (1983) 'Reflections on some relations between psychoanalytic concepts and psychoanalytic practice', *International Journal of Psycho-Analysis*, 64, 35–45.

14

PSYCHOANALYTIC
HEURISTICS

Jorge Canestri

This contribution is based on two works by Joseph Sandler (the second written in collaboration with Anne-Marie Sandler) published in 1983 in the *International Journal of Psycho-Analysis*: 'Reflections on some relations between psychoanalytic concepts and psychoanalytic practice', and 'The "second censorship", the "three box model" and some technical implications'. These two works develop concepts that are closely linked to each other; in fact, it could be said that the first work finds its 'stimulus' in, and is theoretically dependent on, the second.

The purpose of the second paper was to formulate certain theoretical proposals that link the topographical and the structural concepts of Freud's thinking on the constitution of the psychic apparatus. The authors translate these proposals into a theoretical scheme – the 'three box model'. When considered in close connection with clinical practice, the Sandlers' text has theoretical implications – finding a bridge between the two conceptual frameworks – that consequently have a bearing on the theory of technique. There is, moreover, an epistemological aspect to it regarding the construction of psychoanalytic theory and the production of new theories, models and heuristic schemes.

This epistemological aspect is explicitly dealt with in the first work, and it will be the object of my comments, which focus on an idea that I share with J. Sandler (1983): 'What is critical is not what psychoanalytic theory should be but what should be emphasized within the whole compass of psychoanalytic thinking. And what should be emphasized is that which relates to the work we have to do' (37). I wish to point out here that these epistemological comments do not make general reference to the validity or the scientific standing of psychoanalytic theories, which have already been presented often enough, but to the practical use of analytic theories – to what 'we have to do'.

The 'three box model' described by the Sandlers derives from the well-known statements by Freud, which they examine very accurately, about the existence of several censorship systems. Here I will refer to the following extract from Freud (1915b):

The *Ucs.* is turned back on the frontier of the *Pcs.* by the censorship, but derivatives of the *Ucs.* can circumvent this censorship, achieve a high degree of organization and reach a certain intensity of cathexis in the *Pcs.* When, however, this intensity is exceeded and they try to force themselves into consciousness, they are recognized as derivatives of the *Ucs.* and are repressed afresh at the new frontier of censorship, between the *Pcs.* and the *Cs.* Thus the first of these censorships is exercised against the *Ucs.* itself, and the second against its *Pcs.* derivatives. One might suppose that in the course of individual development the censorship had taken a step forward.

In psycho-analytic treatment the existence of the second censorship, located between the systems *Pcs.* and *Cs.*, is proved beyond question.

(193)

It is possible to hypothesize, as Freud does, the presence of several censorship systems. It is also important to remember the role played by attention in providing the conscious with access to derivatives of the unconscious.

The model created by the Sandlers integrates the propositions of structural theory, and so the second system, which is the one that will be worked on here, includes 'parts of the unconscious (structural) ego ... as well as unconscious parts of the superego; and it embraces the Preconscious system of the topographical model' (Sandler and Sandler 1983: 420). This second system continually elaborates the derivatives of the unconsious. It is oriented towards the present in its search for adaptive solutions, and it is the creative centre of 'current unconscious fantasies and thoughts' (Sandler and Sandler 1983: 421).

This theory of thinking adheres faithfully to the Freudian idea that the thought processes are produced by simple 'relations between presentations of objects (Sachvorstellungen)' (Freud 1915b: 202), and that they acquire complexity and intelligibility by becoming linked to the word-presentations ('Wortvorstellungen') and by obeying the rules of the secondary process. The creative activity of the second system, directed towards the production of 'current unconscious fantasies and thoughts', and bringing about changes in self- and object representations, is characterized as: 'the gyroscopic function of fantasy' (Sandler and Sandler 1983: 421).

We must remember, however, that these are 'fantasies of the second kind', or 'here-and-now adaptive solutions' (421) that differ considerably from the fantasies of the first system. The difference must be emphasized so that the model does not become concealed through an underestimation of the complexity of the psychic apparatus as described by Freud. In fact, certain post-Freudian psychoanalytic models tend to reason almost exclusively in terms of the unconscious system.

A final characteristic of the second system (or 'second box') – which is fundamental in this work – is that although it makes use 'of the most complicated secondary processes ... [it] has a high tolerance for contradictions' (Sandler and Sandler 1983: 421). This fact explains how essentially contradictory theories and thoughts can coexist without disturbing each other as long as they remain outside consciousness:

> This phenomenon has been described in relation to the creation of unconscious (preconscious) theories which may be contradictory but are tolerated outside consciousness. It was noted that the absence of contradiction was not that which is ascribed to the contents of the system Unconscious or to the id (J. Sandler 1983).
>
> (Sandler and Sandler 1983: 421)

This comment refers to the hypotheses set out in Joseph Sandler's 1983 paper. As he said, it is a known fact that psychoanalytic concepts have multiple meanings whose dimensions vary according to the context, use and extent of knowledge. Sandler believes it is possible to carry out fruitful research into these 'dimensions of meaning' in the mind of every psychoanalyst. In a 1982 paper, Peter Fonagy indicates two research strategies to solve or at least to clarify some of the conceptual ambiguities of psychoanalytic theory: experimental studies of psychoanalytic conceptualization and laboratory experimentation.

RECOGNIZING PRECONSCIOUS THEORIES

Another well-known fact, as Sandler rightly pointed out, is that there exist 'official theories' and 'private theories'. Official theories are the offspring of the psychoanalyst's academic training, while private theories have a more complex and varied origin. Sandler (1983) discussed the clinical experience of the psychoanalyst who, coming into contact with a great variety of problems and with the reactions they produce in him,

> will preconsciously (descriptively speaking, unconsciously) construct a whole variety of theoretical segments which relate directly to his clinical work. They are the products of unconscious thinking, are very much partial theories, models or schemata, which have the quality of being available in reserve, so to speak, to be called upon whenever necessary.
>
> (38)

When and why these preconscious theories come to light – if they do – is another fascinating psychoanalytic as well as an epistemological problem (heuristics and sociology of knowledge). The fact that preconscious theories are not usually valued very highly in scientific circles does not mean that psychoanalysts do not use them in daily practice. Taking into account the data that each one of us gathers from clinical practice, and especially from supervisions, it could be said that in most interventions we use private schemata rather than official theories. As Sandler (1983) has noted, these schemata are internally contradictory, if only for the reason that they are made up of pieces of models that are incompatible or only partially compatible with each other, or of other material not necessarily tied to the psychoanalytic theory *sensu stricto*. This other material comes from at least two sources: the 'Weltanschauung' (concept of the world) of each analyst and the 'spontaneous philosophy of scientists' (Althusser 1967). In a paper entitled 'Il existe une philosophie spontanée des savants', the French philosopher L. Althusser (1967) hypothesized that a certain type of relationship between philosophy and science can be observed; it should be analysed in the scientists themselves, because they are 'carriers' of a spontaneous philosophy, the so-called spontaneous philosophy of scientists. This philosophy should be distinct from the concept of the world, the whole set of ideas that human beings have about the world and about themselves. On the contrary, the spontaneous philosophy comprises the ideas (conscious or not) that the individual scientist has regarding his or her scientific work and science.

Althusser does not deny that these two realities are profoundly linked, but he also believes that it is necessary to distinguish between them in order to analyse them. The spontaneous philosophy of the scientist usually reveals contradictory content, essentially manifested between two elements: one of internal origin (intrascientific); the other of external origin (extrascientific). The first is made up of convictions or beliefs gained through everyday scientific practice itself (Althusser 1967). If this element is elaborated conscientiously and theoretically, it is possible to obtain theses from it. The second element is made up of convictions or beliefs that do not derive from scientific *practice*, but instead are reflections on scientific practice of philosophical theses generally belonging to the philosophies of science.

EXPLORING PRECONSCIOUS THEORIES

The first element (intrascientific) of the spontaneous philosophy of the scientist closely corresponds to Sandler's (1983) formulations about the preconscious construction of a whole variety of 'theoretic segments' (38). I believe that Sandler is right to stress the importance, from the point of view of psychoanalytic research, of considering the analyst himself as an instrument for making inquiries. Not being able to participate in any other way in the scientific work, the philosopher (e.g. Althusser) has to sound out the scientist's texts to find the contradictions expressed in the construction of the theory. The analyst, on the other hand, can examine the theories as they result from his or her experience (where they are, in fact, used) in a variety of ways; some of them almost certainly form part of the practice itself. In addition to Fonagy's (1982) two proposals about exploring this preconscious knowledge of the analyst, I should like to add another two: supervision and psychoanalytic concepts.

Supervision

The first proposal about exploring the analyst's preconscious knowledge involves supervision. If, as Sandler (1983) affirms, the psychoanalyst's private preconscious theories are more consonant with the patient's material than are officially acknowledged theories, and if these preconscious theories are open-ended and in transformation, then it is reasonable to suppose that they will better manifest themselves in the specific ambiance of his or her work, that is, in the analytic situation itself.

Therefore, besides implementing specific research projects like those Sandler mentioned (1983, Sigmund Freud Institute, Frankfurt), we also have to use the setting of actual supervision to carry out research. Supervision is an ambiance that comes as near as is possible to the private reality of the analytic situation. In it, the supervisor has an advantage over the therapist, not so much by virtue of greater experience and competence, but above all because of the position the supervisor occupies in respect to the 'object' in clinical psychoanalysis, which is formed not only by the patient's material but also by the situation and the analytic relationship. In this case, when I speak of position, I have in mind the phenomena and the laws of perspective: if the centre changes, the representation changes.

If my definition of the object in supervision is correct, then the preconscious theories that guide the analyst's intervention in the analytic situation and that contribute considerably to its constitution cannot but be the object of the process of supervision. The setting of supervision, because of its nearness to the original object (the analytic situation), and because of the privileged position of the supervisor – who is the only one able to see the object in its entirety from a different perspective – therefore appears to be an excellent setting for inquiry into the specific area of the analytic experience.

Because it is not only analysts in training but also experienced analysts who are subject to supervision, the quantity and the quality of material available is quite rich and varied. A supervisor who is aware of these phenomena will be able to transmit to the supervisee information about the preconscious theories that influence his or her work and contribute to the formation of working methods, both with a particular patient and in terms of more general tendencies.

Obviously the supervisor, in turn, works during supervision with his or her own preconscious theories, which may become clearer to the extent that he or she is prepared to examine them. Careful attention to the supervisory work thus constitutes another setting for inquiry.

Psychoanalytic concepts

The second proposal about exploring the analyst's preconscious knowledge involves that of examining the learning of psychoanalytic concepts during analytic training. The Argentinian psychoanalyst E. Pichon Rivière perfected a teaching technique that took into account group dynamics (Pichon Rivière 1970). He gave the name 'operative group' to a particular type of group engaged in the task of elaborating and learning a concept previously developed during a short lesson. The group had a coordinator whose aim was to discover the dynamics that prevailed while the group members worked on the concept and on the learning situation. The coordinator interpreted the group's dynamics as it learned and discussed theories and models. The coordinator had to be especially careful that the group did not transform itself into a therapeutic group (Pichon Rivière called them 'groups of the therapy of learning'). These operative groups can be an excellent method for studying the actual 'doing' of theories and models in the mind of the psychoanalyst.

It would be desirable for psychoanalytic institutes to include a seminar based on these ideas during the final year of training. This would allow teachers to test the mental ability of the candidates and to reflect on the candidates' learning methods, on how they relate to their teachers' theories, and on the metacognitive ideas with which they undertake their training.

In Althusser's description, the second element that makes up the 'spontaneous philosophy of the scientist' corresponds to those convictions that do not derive *from* scientific practice but rather are the reflection *on* the practice of formulations from the philosophy of science. In their day-to-day work, scientists may be more or less aware of being influenced by certain philosophical orientations, in the same way that they may be more or less proficient in epistemology, methodology, and so forth. Nevertheless, they cannot avoid responding in a generally incoherent manner to this influence, especially when they are unaware of it.

Moreover, if the external influence is received unknowingly and without the necessary instruments for querying it, it is often in contradiction to the internal element. In the specific case of the psychoanalyst, therefore, there would be a triple contradiction: between the analyst's preconscious theories, models or schemata (corresponding more or less to the internal element of the spontaneous philosophy of the scientist); the official public theories of the psychoanalytic discipline; and finally, the theses or indications coming from the philosophy of science (the external element of the spontaneous philosophy of the scientist).

The internal and the external elements can be unconscious (descriptively speaking). As far as the private theories are concerned, I favour the use of supervision – on account of its intimate relationship to analytic experience itself – as a suitable setting for revealing and taking advantage of the contradiction. But for the external element, the solution must be sought elsewhere.

In general, the analyst has little knowledge of the philosophy of science and the methodology of research. Psychoanalytic institutes, even though they may not provide complete training, should at least ensure that analysts are not wholly unprepared on this subject. Theoretical and clinical seminars on a detailed comparison between various psychoanalytical theories and models would certainly help, although this would still not be enough. Having an epistemologist discuss with the candidates in an ad hoc seminar the alternatives proposed by contemporary epistemology could perhaps help to remedy this type of contradiction which, unlike the former, does not appear to be advantageous.

CORRELATING THEORY AND FANTASY

The attentive reader of Sandler's work will have noticed that the preconscious, private theories formed in the analyst's mind are closely connected with the 'fantasies of the second kind' of the 'second box' of the model – theories, therefore, that are like fantasies. I do not mean that theories must be tested and submitted to the criticism of reality, for this is obvious. It is rather a question of verifying the fact that, at least as far as the construction of theories in psychoanalysis is concerned, the logic of discovery (heuristics) cannot be separated from the logic of justification.

Before developing this idea further, I should like to emphasize that Freud himself on several occasions pointed out the close identity between fantasy and theory, describing the mechanism of scientific creativity as a 'succession of audacious fantasy and ruthless criticism carried out by reality' (Freud 1915a: 94).

Since 1985, when the careful and patient research of I. Grubrich-Simitis brought to light Freud's (1915a) work, *Übersicht der Übertragungsneurosen*, as well as some items of his correspondence with S. Ferenczi (today complete), we have come to possess precious instruments for better understanding how Freud conceived of the processes that govern scientific creativity. In Freud's (1933) obituary of Ferenczi, he says in reference to the 'Thalassa' of the Hungarian analyst: 'It is a vain task to attempt already today to distinguish what can be accepted as an authentic discovery from what seeks, in the fashion of a scientific phantasy, to guess at future knowledge' (228). To find out to which order of concepts scientific fantasy ('wissenschaftlichen Phantasie') belongs in the Freudian *épistéme*, it will be helpful to go back in time and refer to Freud's letter to Ferenczi of July 1915, in which we read at the beginning: 'Dear friend, in the preparation of "Übersicht der Übertragungsneurosen" I find myself dealing with fantasies that disturb me and it will be difficult for them to have any result for the public' (Freud 1915a: 89). In a later letter, we find this phrase:

> I must state that one must not make theories; they must turn up like an unexpected guest in the house, while one is busy enquiring into details.
>
> [Ich halte darauf, dass man Theorien nicht machen soll – sie müssen einem als ungebetene Gäste ins Haus fallen, während man mit Detailuntersuchungen beschäftig ist.]
>
> (Freud 1915a: 94)

The sense of duty ('müssen' – 'they must turn up') can be conveyed thus: they must impose themselves – like an uninvited guest who has not been asked to visit us – in the same way, therefore, as the fantasies that Freud said he was dealing with in his letter of 12 July.

I am inclined to think that these are some of the numerous indications provided by Freud about the theory of a research method announcing that theories, like fantasies, impose themselves on us like uninvited guests. Here it is changed into the imperative: it must be so. In this sense, it could be thought that the hybridization between scientific and literary elaboration, proclaimed by Grubrich-Simitis (1985) as a stylistic peculiarity pertaining to a certain age and common to the speculative works of Freud and Ferenczi, should instead be conceived of as a necessary 'participation' between science and literature, between the construction of knowledge and speculation, between reasoning and imagination.

Freud was always conscious of following a certain type of idea and a certain line of research 'by repeatedly combining factual material with what is purely speculative and thus diverging widely from empirical observation' (Freud 1920: 59); he was acutely aware that he was moulding 'scientific myths' or modelling 'visions' regarding, for example, the primitive horde or the killing of the primordial father (Freud 1925). This suggests that we should be careful when criticizing metapsychology, confusing the literary with the metaphorical or fictional level. Moreover, considering the method of hybridization between scientific and literary elaboration as necessary, and the participation of scientific fantasy in scientific reason, means accepting the impossibility of simply doing without metapsychology.

Obviously, this does not mean that the anachronisms of Freudian construction must not be discussed and eliminated, that the imported theories bearing the signs of time that has passed cannot be substituted, that scientific fantasy must not be controlled. This kind of orientation would be contrary to the deepest meaning of the whole Freudian discourse. In his prose, the scientific fantasies in 'Syntheses' are given other names: fictions, auxiliary or intermediate representations, strategies, conventions. The methodological requirement for anyone who is going to use fantasy or fiction in the method is that of justifying them, that is, of demonstrating that they are advantageous. However, the methodological requirements must not be confused with the theory of the causes that produce scientific fantasies or fictions, as is well illustrated by Sandler's hypotheses on preconscious theories.

To illustrate what I mean by justifying scientific fantasy or fiction, I will quote from one of my previous works (Canestri 1986):

> At the end of the last century and the beginning of this one, ethnology was very much influenced by the concept of development of a biological stamp. Assimilating the history of institutions to biological development presupposed the 'archaic states' of the institutions (for example, primitive promiscuity), and eventually, as the result of a concatenation of progressive complexity and perfection arrived at the institution of the conjugal family. This fiction corresponded to an ideological prejudice and forced ethnological thought to introduce stages that were undemonstrable and non-existent. In its conceptual apparatus, psychoanalysis retains a fiction that bears a certain superficial similarity to this: the Freudian fiction of the primitive horde in 'Totem and Taboo'. The phenomena described are non-existent in both cases. Nevertheless, the fundamental difference is that while psychoanalytic fiction finds correspondence in the logical necessity to include in the theory the value and the symbolic significance of the dead father, the ethnological fiction is gratuitous and even harmful. It did not function as an intermediate representation nor did it prove to be an element capable of enhancing the progress of thought; on the contrary, it was a hindrance.
>
> (600–1)

In her 1993 book analysing the genesis of poetry, particularly that of Dante (to whom she has dedicated years of research), Maria Corti, an historian of the Italian language, mentions a quotation of Novalis: 'If we had a Fantastic, as we have a Logic, then we would have found the art of invention' ('Hätten wir auch eine Phantastik, wie eine Logik, so wäre die Erfindungskunst erfunden') (3).[1] I cannot say that psychoanalysts have found the Fantastic ironically invoked by Novalis, because that would be presumptive as well as mistaken; but I do believe that, in the specific field of the construction of psychoanalytic theory, psychoanalysts are able to catch a glimpse of what contributes to their invention. As Freud said, scientific fantasies – the preconscious theories enumerated by Sandler – are halfbreeds whose roots are embedded in the unconscious (although not in a descriptive sense) and spread into the preconscious where they sometimes come to light. The theories Sandler speaks of belong to the 'second box'. Nevertheless, we also know that infantile fantasies, which are linked to the most archaic and intimate

209

nucleus of the self, can find a place in theory. It is possible to find examples, and I have attempted to analyse one in 'Moses and monotheism' (Canestri 1993), so I shall not elaborate on it here.

SYNTHESIZING THE LOGIC OF DISCOVERY AND THE LOGIC OF JUSTIFICATION

We should now return to the statement about the inadequacy of the separation between the logic of discovery and the logic of demonstration. We know that it was the epistemologist Karl Popper (1934) who took up and presented Reichenbach's (1934) distinction between the 'logic of discovery' and the 'logic of justification'. Popper (1934) said: 'If we make a distinction, as Reichenbach does, between a "procedure for finding" and a "procedure for justifying" (a hypothesis), then we have to say it is not possible to reconstruct the former rationally' (Erkenntniss 5: 170). It is not a question of creating confusion again by taking psychologism into the field of the logic of justification, but rather of inquiring into the validity of Popper's statement on the radical impossibility of rationally reconstructing the logic of discovery. I quote from a paper of mine (1993) on the subject:

> More than 40 years ago, Imre Lakatos, although acting within the enlarged framework of the falsifying Popperian conception, was to contest the division made by the great master. In analysing the logic of mathematical discovery, Lakatos (1976) reveals a certain short-sightedness in Popper's approach. Lakatos says that when Popper (in 1934, in fact) divided the aspects of discovery into psychological and logical aspects, in such a way as not to leave any room at all for heuristics as an independent field of enquiry, he obviously did not notice then that his 'logic of discovery' was more than a mere *strictly* logical reconstruction of scientific progress. But Popper, who laid the foundation of this (fallible) logic of discovery, did not deal with the meta-question of what the nature of his enquiry was and did not notice that this is neither psychology nor logic, but an independent discipline, the logic of discovery, heuristic. Lakatos' recognition of the existence of an 'intrinsic unit of logic of discovery and logic of justification' is, in the words of G. Giorello, 'an attempt to understand *those problems, those procedures by trial and error, those tactics and strategies of research* that make scientific practice as fascinating an activity as any creative activity' (1976, italics added). ... Lakatos' proposal states the need for the improvement of proof control procedures (logic of justification), which does not, however, exclude their being part of the same logic presiding over the discovery itself. This unity is given the

name of heuristics, which has the task of comprehending the 'becoming' of science.

(Canestri 1993: 118–19)

I am convinced that the logic of Freudian research and of psychoanalysis are contrary to the radical division between the logic of discovery and the logic of justification, a division that would go against the very nature of psychoanalytic theory and, above all, of psychoanalytic experience. Works like those of Sandler that analyse the 'doing' of the theories, models and schemata in the analyst's mind as he works with his patient, and in the multifocal complexity of the construction of the theory as it develops in practice, tend towards a synthesis between the logic of discovery and the logic of justification, and contribute to the study of heuristics in the field of psychoanalysis.

ADDRESSING THEORETICAL PLURALISM

Moving in the right direction to make the implicit theories known, however, means an inevitable increase in theoretical pluralism and in the babelization of the language of psychoanalysis. As the language of theory has to take increasing account of the 'idiolect' (idiosyncratic or private language) of models and private schemata, so it becomes more polysemic and open to interpretation. Each theoretical language thus becomes a 'linguistic game' (in the Wittgensteinian sense) with its own idiosyncrasies that in many ways are difficult to agree on.

It is a known fact that psychoanalysis is faced with a phenomenon of theoretical pluralism – expressed by R. Wallerstein (1988) as 'one psycho-analysis or many?' The problem is how this fact is conceptualized. Briefly, two interpretative tendencies can be proposed. One is that psychoanalysis has 'an indispensable core' composed of a few propositions (Cooper 1985), to which are related various 'puzzle solutions' dealing with partial problems. The other posits that we are faced with actual divergent theories about the functioning of the mind that are complete in themselves. Both Cooper and Sandler have made comments aimed at avoiding the traps that are so frequent in work on psychoanalytic theories. Cooper (1985) has pointed out that many theories or models originally conceived to resolve specific local and clinical problems (e.g. the theories on narcissistic personalities) – that is, 'puzzle solutions' – end up expanding until they include the whole range of all the possible problems posed by clinical work and by the theory itself, and thus become transformed into a system of their own. Similarly, Sandler (1985) emphasizes that the real problem is not deciding in certain cases which theory is right and which is wrong, but rather up to what point (by what extension of facts) a theory is right or appropriate.

These considerations are undoubtedly useful but do not solve the problem. Having accepted the pluralism of psychoanalysis, we are left with the question of how to interpret it. In the works just mentioned (Cooper 1985; Sandler 1985) which formed part of the 1984 workshop on 'Models of the mind' organized by the American Psychoanalytic Association, Sandler's main proposal on this question was to substitute with an historical-developmental criterion an essentially intrinsic criterion (i.e. of coherence, quantity of data explained, consistency) when evaluating a theory. Cooper voiced a similar perspective in his introduction to the workshop.

To my mind, the idea of applying an historical-developmental criterion to psychoanalytic theory is certainly convincing and absolutely necessary in the teaching of psychoanalysis. It remains to be seen whether this criterion, as Sandler hypothesized, can enable us to find a way of conceiving the existence of *one* theory capable of integrating several models. According to Sandler (1985), 'If we take a historical-developmental viewpoint we can escape quarrels about which theory is right and which is wrong. We are then in the position of being able to ask why this, that, or the other formulation was put forward' (122). It is easy to agree with the second part of this proposal, that such a viewpoint would help us determine the historical-development reasons for privileging one formulation rather than another (reasons that depend on numerous factors, many of which can be clarified by a sociological study of knowledge). However, a historical-developmental viewpoint does not, in fact, eliminate the problem of the greater or lesser value of any theory or model. Even after we have understood why one formulation has been privileged over another, we are no further forward in deciding about the quality of that particular formulation. From this point of view, Popper would appear to have been right (but, then, so was Grünbaum [1984] from the opposite viewpoint) when he stressed the necessity of adequately separating the logic of justification from the logic of discovery.

CONSTRUCTING A MORE COMPLEX HISTORICAL-DEVELOPMENTAL MODEL

In conclusion, I should like to present a slightly more complex historical-developmental model. It is not intended to solve the problem of the validity (or lack thereof) of the various theories, but it could serve to explicate better the present state of the problem of pluralism in psychoanalysis.

In 1983 a book was published in France called *Psychogenèse et Histoire des Sciences* (*Psychogenesis and the History of Sciences*). It was the result of twenty years of work and collaboration between two well-known epistemologists, Jean Piaget and Rolando García, and was finished shortly before Piaget's death in 1980. Piaget's lifework was devoted to the construction of a genetic epistemology using the historical-critical method and the psychogenetic method. On this occasion, it intersected with the studies of Piaget and García (1983), a disciple of Carnap and Reichenbach on the development of scientific thought, in which he took into careful account the genesis of cognition in the child.

The purpose of the two epistemologists was to discover whether, in the words of B. Inhelder, author of the introduction, 'the mechanisms of passing from one historical period to the next in the context of a notional system (algebra, geometry, mechanics) are analogous to those for passing from one genetic stage to the others' (8). Inhelder, therefore, has good reason to emphasize that this work represents the third and most important epistemo-logical synthesis of the Piaget school. I am only going to dwell on one aspect of the model that seems highly pertinent to Sandler's reflections, and of particular use when considering the problem of theoretical pluralism in psychoanalysis.

The model is pertinent for at least two reasons. In the first place, it denies the distinct separation between the logic of discovery and the logic of justification, between the epistemological significance of an instrument of cognition and the modality with which this instrument has been constructed – a problem I mentioned previously. Second, the inevitable consequence of this assumption leads to the adoption of a historical-developmental method for studying cognition and theories. How could the model be useful from the point of view of psychoanalysis? I will try to sum this up through a brief description of one aspect of the model.

From the various fields analysed by Piaget and García, let us consider those aspects relative to the history of geometry because it is the simplest and easiest to deal with. García described three stages in the history of geometry: a first stage from Greek to eighteenth-century geometry that included the brilliant introduction of analytic geometry by Descartes and the equally brilliant invention of differential calculus by Newton and Leibniz; a second stage characterized by the development of projective geometry (Poncelet and Chasles); and a third stage beginning with the Programme of Erlangen by F. Klein (1872) characterized by the 'generalization of geometry', that is, by the subordination of the various forms of geometry into a single group in which the different forms become 'special cases'.

The first stage studies the properties of geometric figures as *internal relations* between the different elements of the figures. This stage is called 'intrafigural' (or intraobjectual) – an expression that, as Piaget and García point out, is also used in genetic psychology to describe the development of geometric ideas in the child.

The second stage relates the figures to each other. Research is aimed at individuating the *transformations* that link the figures through different types of correspondence. This stage corresponds to projective geometry and is called 'interfigural'.

The third or 'transfigural' stage is a result of the Programme of Erlangen. It is brought about by recognition that the transformation system, which leaves certain geometric properties unvarying, forms a group. It is therefore feasible to substitute an analysis of the *internal relations of the group* for analysis of the transformations. The different transformation groups characterizing the different types of geometry (e.g. the various non-Euclidean geometries, such as those of Riemann and Lobatchevsky) become subgroups of a global system containing them all. And these stages 'bear witness to a development in the process of conceptualization of *"geometric notions"* ' (Piaget and García 1983: 128, emphasis added). As a study of the development of theories, this analogy enables me to propose the following analogic exercise relative to psychoanalytic theories.

The first stage corresponds to an internal, intrafigural analysis of a specific psychoanalytic theory or model; it could be the Kleinian model, the model of ego psychology, or another model. This stage requires the model or theory to be *coherent*, with a solid conceptual system; it should not be contradictory but, rather, should be able to take into account a certain number of factors. Every intrafigural analysis can improve the internal consistency of a theory. Sandler (1985) had something similar in mind when he wrote: 'I can think of a dozen ways in which Kleinian theory, for example, might be made more consistent and acceptable, without doing violence to its essence' (127).

The second stage calls for a confrontation between two or more theories by means of an interfigural analysis. In his 1965 book, significantly entitled *Transformations: Change from Learning to Growth*, W. R. Bion made an interesting suggestion for a project of this kind. He proposed a particular form of 'mathematicization' for psychoanalysis that would eliminate the restrictions characterizing the use of associations with space and vision: a 'mathematicization' through which psychoanalysis would take the same steps geometry took when calculus was introduced. Bion favoured the identification of similar configurations between the formulations of psychoanalytic theories by introducing the concept of congruence. Congruence was considered an indication of a problematic and mutual conceptual centre shared by different theories – towards which and away from which they moved. The explicit purpose of the project was to render superfluous the nature (defined by Bion as ad hoc) of many psychoanalytic theories. As things stand at the moment, identification of the points of congruence between theories and the verification of the invariants – that is, interfigural analysis of psychoanalytic theories – is possible. Every analyst who makes a habit of theoretical exercise has ideas on the subject.

The specific difficulty in the present state of our theoretical knowledge appears at the third level of analysis: that of transfigural analysis, which allows for the subordination of transformations into sets, so that the different theories become special cases within a single group. I think we can all agree that Bion's individuation of the points of congruence, the verification of the invariants between theories, and the improvement of the internal coherence of the theories themselves are necessary conditions for aspiring to transfigural analysis. But we also might agree that these steps alone are not sufficient – a point of discussion for later consideration.

Sandler (1985) concluded his presentation at the workshop of the American Psychoanalytic Association by saying: 'It would be useful if a way could be found to follow up the discussion in this book by considering *one* model of the mind, not six' (127). This is no doubt a programme for the future, to which I believe he has already made a significant contribution.

NOTE

1   Novalis, *Fragments, I–II* (1957), Heidelberg: Schneider, I, n.1466: 391. Quoted in Corti 1993.

REFERENCES

Althusser, L. (1967) 'Il existe une philosophie spontanée des savants' ('There exists a spontaneous philosophy of scientists'), in *Philosophie et Philosophie Spontanée des Savants* (1974), Paris: Editions F. Maspero, 98–116.

Bion, W. R. (1965) *Transformations: Change from Learning to Growth*, London: Heinemann.

Canestri, J. (1986) 'La fantasia scientifica: una nota di lettura sulla "Sintesi delle nevrosi di traslazione" di S. Freud' ('The scientific fantasy: a note to the "Übersicht der Übertragungsneurosen" of S. Freud'), *Rivista di Psicoanalisi*, 32, 591–602.

——(1993) 'The logic of Freudian research', in D. Meghnagi (ed.) *Freud and Judaism*, London: Karnac Books, 117–29.

Cooper, A. M. (1985) 'A historical review of psychoanalytic paradigms', in A. Rothstein (ed.) *Models of the Mind: Their Relationship to Clinical Work*, Madison CT: International Universities Press, 5–20.

Corti, M. (1993) *Percorsi dell'Invenzione: Il Linguaggio Poetico e Dante*, Turin: Einaudi.

Fonagy, P. (1982) 'The integration of psychoanalysis and experimental science: a review', *International Review of Psycho-Analysis*, 9, 125–245.

Freud, S. (1915a) [1985] *Übersicht der Übertragungsneurosen*, Frankfurt am Main: S. Fischer Verlag.

——(1915b) 'The unconscious', *Standard Edition*, vol. 14, 159–215. London: Hogarth Press, 1963.

——(1920) 'Beyond the pleasure principle', *Standard Edition*, vol. 18, 1–64. London: Hogarth Press, 1955.

——(1925) 'An autobiographical study', *Standard Edition*, vol. 20, 1–74. London: Hogarth Press, 1959.

——(1933) 'Sándor Ferenczi', *Standard Edition*, vol. 22, 225–9. London: Hogarth Press, 1964.

Giorello, C. (1976) 'Introduzione [Introduction]', in I. Lakatos, *Proofs and Refutations: The Logic of Mathematical Discovery*, Cambridge: Cambridge University Press. Italian edition, Milan: Feltrinelli, 7–34.

Grubrich–Simitis, I. (1985) 'Metapsychologie und Metabiologie', in S. Freud [1915a] *Übersicht der Übertragungsneurosen*, Frankfurt am Main: S. Fischer Verlag, 85–119.

Grünbaum, A. (1984) *The Foundations of Psychoanalysis: A Philosophical Critique*, Berkeley CA: University of California Press.

Klein, F. (1872) *Vergleichende Betrachtungen über Neuere geometrische Forschungen*, Erlangen.

Lakatos, I. (1976) *Proofs and Refutations: The Logic of Mathematical Discovery*, Cambridge: Cambridge University Press.

Piaget, J. and García, R. (1983) *Psychogenèse et Histoire des Sciences*, Paris: Flammarion.

Pichon Rivière, E. (1970) *Del Psicoanalisis a la Psicologia Social* (*From Psychoanalysis to Social Psychology*), Buenos Aires: Calerna.

Popper, K. [1934] (1959) *The Logic of Scientific Discovery*, London: Hutchinson.

Reichenbach, H. (1934) 'Conference published in Erkenntniss', discussed by K. Popper in *The Logic of Scientific Discovery* (1959), London: Hutchinson, appendix 1.

Sandler, J. (1983) 'Reflections on some relations between psychoanalytic concepts and psychoanalytic practice', *International Journal of Psycho-Analysis*, 64, 35–45.

——(1985) 'A discussion of the various theories', in A. Rothstein (ed.) *Models of the Mind: Their Relationships to Clinical Work*, Madison CT: International Universities Press, 119–27.

Sandler, J. and Sandler, A.-M. (1983) 'The "second censorship", the "three box model" and some technical implications', *International Journal of Psycho-Analysis*, 64, 413–25.

Wallerstein, R. S. (1988) 'One psychoanalysis or many?', *International Journal of Psycho-Analysis*, 69, 5–21.

15

THE ANALYST'S
VOCABULARY

Horst Kächele, Erhard Mergenthaler and Michael Hölzer

Time and again it is claimed that formal empirical research in psychoanalysis has no consequence for practice, and vice-versa. This is true as long as clinicians and researchers do not communicate with each other. For more than two decades, a few analysts have been actively involved in the empirical study of their clinical practice based on tape-recorded sessions, which has presented them with both intellectual and emotional challenges. The long struggle to obtain official recognition of tape recording as a valid research tool – initiated many years ago by Shakow, Gill and others – may not yet be over. However, the opportunities offered by the tape recording of psychoanalytic treatments for training and practice were appreciated by James McLaughlin at the International Psychoanalytic Association Congress held in Helsinki in 1982 (see Thomä and Kächele 1992: 24).

One advantage of tape recording is that it makes it feasible to study in great detail the analyst's actual use of psychoanalytic theories. Psychoanalytic technique involves a number of parameters that stress the importance of language as its central tool. Freud's (1916) famous dictum in the 'Introductory lectures' – 'there is only an exchange of words in the analytic situation' (17) – specifies from a didactic perspective the focus of the psychoanalytic method. In general, language consists of rules and symbolic representations that are primarily conceptual tools. This understanding of its symbolic function, which goes back to the work of Cassier (1953), has been brought to the attention of the analytic community in particular by the work of Susanne Langer (1942).

Since Freud developed his own rather idiosyncratic way of understanding symbols, some conceptual work with the different usage of the term 'symbol' had to be done. Victor Rosen, in his paper on 'Sign phenomena and their relationship to unconscious meaning' (1969), demonstrated that the work of the psychoanalyst can be conceptualized as a process of differentiating conventional symbols from sign phenomena. Understanding the common-sense meaning of what is said must be complemented by understanding the additional unconscious meaning any concrete piece of verbal material may carry. The technical rule of using evenly hovering attention is directed to just this process. Listening to his patient's associations, the analyst picks up the conventional meaning of what he listens to. Suspending his reaction to this level of meaning, he then tries to understand potential meaning that goes beyond everyday meaning. By interpreting, the analyst presents a perspective that is not obviously in his or her patient's view.

The distinctive feature of the psychoanalytic technology is interpretation. It is possible to speak of a technological hermeneutics differing in essential features from theological and philological hermeneutics. Psychoanalytic interpretations are made not for texts, but for patients with therapeutic expectations. The attempt to prove the therapeutic effectiveness of psycho-analytic interpretations forces analysts to leave the hermeneutic circle and confront questions regarding the empirical proof of change.

To work on the patient's communications with interpretations requires empathy and introspection. Neither alone would lead analysts to their specific form of understanding. Analysts also need theoretical knowledge obtained by training, be it as part of their own analytic experience or by studying what other psychoanalysts have already described. Yet little is known about how these two domains of knowledge are interwoven within the actual therapeu-tic operation. For many years, we had available only desktop speculation on how the mind of the analyst works (Ramzy 1974). The few empirical studies have cast but a first glance at the immense variability of reasons for actual performance.

One fruitful approach to studying the personal concepts of individual analysts on specific aetiological topics (e.g. psychic trauma) was launched when Joseph Sandler (1983) put into operational terms his own reflections on the relationship of concepts to practice. Subsequently, the study group at the Sigmund Freud Institute developed a way to explore the hitherto unknown realm of what analysts think about their own way of practising (Sandler et al. 1991). Meyer's (1988) experimental approach involved the study of tape-recorded post-session impressions of three German analysts who reviewed a large sample of taped sessions.

Clearly, the relationship between theory and practice is mediated by the analyst's mental operations. Our concepts shape our actual therapeutic practice. However, we know very little about how this process occurs. The very existence of different schools of thought in psychoanalysis raises a question about the extent to which theoretical orientations influence daily practice. One can safely assume that the complexity of the human mind allows for quite a few divergent theoretical constructions that are all viable within the psychoanalytic frame of reference. However, it has not yet been demonstrated that with respect to psychoanalytic results, 'all are equal and all must have prizes' (Luborsky et al. 1975: 995).

The exchange process between the patient's productions, loosely called 'free associations', and the analyst's interventions, loosely called 'interpretations', most fittingly may be classified as a special sort of dialogue.

To provide a setting and an atmosphere that allows the patient to enter the analytic dialogue, the analyst's interventions encompass the whole range of activities. Interventions have to constitute a reasonable answer to the patient's needs, in that they have to follow the basic conversational principle of reciprocity (Grice 1975):

> If any kind of meaningful dialogue is to take place, each partner must be prepared (and must assume that the other is prepared) to recognise the rules of discourse valid for the given social situation and must strive to formulate his contributions accordingly.
>
> (quoted in Thomä and Kächele 1992: 248)

Thus the special rules of analytic discourse must be well understood by the analysand, lest he or she waste time not getting what he or she wants. The analysand has to understand that the general principle of cooperation is supplemented by a specific additional type of metacommunication on the part of the analyst. As noted earlier, the analyst's interventions must add surplus meaning beyond understanding the discourse on a plain everyday level.

In everyday life, surplus meaning is added in various ways. Telling a joke, for example, involves working with a surplus meaning not manifested in the surface material. Jokes have a special linguistic structure and most often work with a combination of unexpected material elements and special tactics of presentation. But not all jokes are funny.

Systematic investigations of the special conversational nature of analytic techniques have been provided by Flader et al. (1982).[1] However, it still remains an open question as to whether conversational analysis is able to differentiate discourse in psychoanalysis proper from discourse in analytic psychotherapy (Labov and Fanshel 1977).

For example, our own investigations into analysts' conversational strategies have focused on the unilaterality of the analyst's verbal involvement. Our findings on analysts' verbal activity[2] demonstrate that in a productively evolving analytic process, there is no correlation between the patient's and the analyst's amount of verbal participation (Kächele 1983).

Operational measures for the analyst's vocabulary have to distinguish between form and content. The term 'vocabulary' refers to the number of different words (i.e. types) that are used by a speaker. Measures of types are interesting, since words stand for concepts (and therapy essentially consists of an exchange of concepts and beliefs, with assimilation of new material and accommodation of previous schemata). So the analyst's vocabulary at the beginning of the analysis will both shape and reflect the patient's experiential world. During the analysis, its evolution might run parallel to, or at least partly reflect, the conceptual and emotional learning processes taking place (French 1937).

RESEARCH ON VOCABULARY

Patients' variability in vocabulary has been a topic right from the beginning of formal psychotherapy research (Johnson 1944). Speech variability is calculated by dividing the number of different words (types, vocabulary size) by the total number of words (token, text size) in a given text. This ratio between types and tokens, or the type–token ratio, has usually been looked at as an indicator of the diversity of a text (Jaffe 1958). However, this measure is not independent of text size. Herdan (1960) therefore proposed the logarithmic type–token ratio, which was found constant for text samples of various lengths. According to Holsti (1969), 'the hypothesis that speech variability increases with successful therapy has generally been supported' (75). Although the type–token ratio has not been used very often in psychotherapy research in the past few decades, there was some activity in literary research at the end of the 1980s (Simonton 1990). In the context of psychotherapy research, a patient's increasing power of verbal versatility may be interpreted as a sign of working through and improvement, and thus as an objective measure for psychotherapeutic process in both macro- and microanalytic perspectives (Kächele and Mergenthaler 1984; Spence 1969).

With regard to research on the vocabulary of the analyst, relatively little work has been reported so far. We do not know, for example, what the expected vocabulary size for an analyst should be. Does it relate to professional training, to the number of books read, or to the fact that Freud had an unusually extensive vocabulary? Or is it simply that the analytic situation usually generates a different vocabulary because of the considerable situational constraints on language, as pointed out by Laffal (1967)? Of all these questions, we can answer very few at this time. What we can do, however, is report on some aspects of our research on two psychoanalysts with quite differing levels of clinical experience.[3]

Impact of the analytic setting

As a method of treatment, psychoanalysis takes considerable care to specify a setting that allows for uninhibited verbal interaction between the patient and

Table 15.1 Summary of patients and sessions

Patients of Analyst 011	Sessions
Initial interview (male patients)	32
Initial interview (female patients)	18
Short-term therapy (male patient)	27
Psychoanalysis (Franziska)	108
Psychoanalysis (Gustav)	106

the analyst. Whether the setting has a clear impact on the analyst's use of emotion-laden words is not clear. But since emotions in all psychotherapeutic work have been identified as the main domain of change-inducing interactions (Greenberg and Safran 1987), we felt that an investigation focusing on the emotional part of the vocabulary would prove promising.

The affective vocabulary as an empirical correlate of emotion processing was defined as 'all words that have an emotional connotation as a single word'. Our studies show that the emotional vocabulary of therapy comprises approximately 10 per cent of the total vocabulary, or about 4 per cent of all spoken words (tokens).

From one analyst (no. 011), we had collected a large sample of recordings of initial interviews, a sample from a short-term therapy, and large samples of recordings from two long-term psychoanalytic cases (see Table 15.1). We used an instrument called the Affective Dictionary Ulm (ADU) (Hölzer *et al.* 1992) to analyse the number of emotional words used by the analyst and the patients. The results are graphically represented in Figure 15.1.

The data demonstrate that there is a significant increase in the analyst's use of emotion words that parallels the increase in session frequency (i.e. the intensity of the therapeutic setting) (Hölzer *et al.* 1994). A closer look reveals that this effect is due, in part, to the influence of a distinct category of emotion words.

According to Dahl's (1991) theory of emotion, from which the Affective Dictionary Ulm is derived, two major classes of emotions can be distinguished: 'it-emotions', referring to wishes about objects (such as 'anger'), and 'me-emotions', that is, beliefs about the status of wish fulfilment (such as 'depression'). The strong correlation between speech-emotionality (in the analyst's vocabulary) and the intensity of the setting is almost exclusively due to an increase in it- (i.e. object-) emotions. It seems fair to speculate that the number of it-emotions serves well as an indicator of intensified therapeutic work on object relationships, including transference. This interpretation is based on our detailed session-to-session analysis of both the short-term psychotherapy case (Hölzer *et al.* 1990) and the four psychoanalytic cases (Hölzer and Kächele 1996).

The private vocabulary

Apart from a general strategy of lexical choice that is influenced by the psychoanalytic setting, we expect specific sets of vocabulary to affect the language of the analyst and patient. To identify these processes, it is useful to distinguish between two kinds of vocabularies:

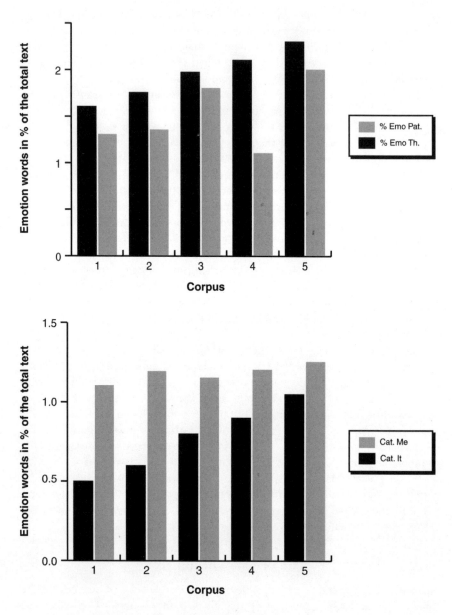

Figure 15.1 **(a)**: 'Affective density', i.e. number of emotion words in percentage of token. Corpus 1: Interview (male p.); 2: Interview (female p.); 3: Short-term therapy; 4: Psychoanalysis (male p.); 5: Psychoanalysis (female p.). **(b)**: It- and me-emotion words of therapist utterances in percentage of the total text. Corpus 1: Interview (male p.); 2: Interview (female p.); 3: Short-term therapy; 4: Psychoanalysis (male p.); 5: Psychoanalysis (female p.).

1   the Private Vocabulary (PV), that is, the set of types used by only one speaker, here denoted as patient's PV and analyst's PV;
2   the Intersectional Vocabulary (IV), that is, the set of types used both by analyst and by patient.

Since vocabulary measures have not yet been sufficiently validated, their interpretation up to now has been guided by clinical experience. Still, we believe that the following hypothesis has a certain face validity:

> The ability of a therapist to accommodate to the language of his or her patient, to bridge social differences, and to empathise with the patient should result in a low Private Vocabulary on the therapist's part.

In a recent study using verbatim material from the Penn Psychotherapy Project (Luborsky *et al.* 1988), we found a significant negative correlation (0.59; $p < 0.05$) for the size of therapists' PV with therapeutic gain for improved patients, as opposed to no significant correlation for non-improved patients. Between the therapist's level of clinical experience and the size of his or her PV, there was a negative correlation in both groups (Hölzer *et al.* 1996). Our conclusion is that experienced therapists tend not to distance themselves from the lexical choices of their patients.

The characteristic vocabulary

A slightly more sophisticated way to compute the private vocabulary results in what we call the 'characteristic vocabulary' (CV). Since many constraints operate in the use of language in actual discourse, we wanted to have a more specific – hence characteristic – sub-set of the analyst's vocabulary, that is, the part they are actively providing within the dialogue, not merely the part that indicates they are following the patient's lead. Here the decision as to whether a certain type belongs to the CV is based on frequency of occurrence. To be classified as characteristic, a word has to occur in the text of one speaker significantly more often than in the text of the other. Depending on the chosen level of significance, the magnitude of the CV may differ considerably. But it does not include words used by just one speaker; these would belong to the realm of the PV.

To illustrate this approach, we will compute the verbalizations of an analyst treating a woman with a severe case of hirsutism. The following description of the patient establishes the clinical context:

> Amalie X came to psychoanalysis because her low self-esteem had contributed to a neurotic depression in the previous few years. Her entire life history since puberty and her social role as a woman had

suffered from the severe strain resulting from her hirsutism. Although it had been possible for her to hide her stigma – the virile growth of hair all over her body – from others, the cosmetic aids she had used had not raised her self-esteem or eliminated her extreme social insecurity. Her feeling of being stigmatised and her neurotic symptoms, which had already been manifest before puberty, strengthened each other in a vicious circle; scruples from compulsion neurosis and different symptoms of anxiety neurosis impeded her personal relationships and, most importantly, kept the patient from forming closer heterosexual friendships. ... Clinical experience justified the following assumptions. A virile stigma strengthens penis envy and reactivates oedipal conflicts. If the patient's wish to be a man had materialised, her hermaphroditic body schema would have become free of conflict. The question, 'Am I a man or a woman?' would then have been answered; her insecurity regarding her identity, which was continuously reinforced by her stigma, would have been eliminated; and self-image and physical reality would then have been in agreement. It was impossible for her to maintain her unconscious phantasy, however, in view of physical reality. A virile stigma does not make a man of a woman. Regressive solutions such as reaching an inner security despite her masculine stigma by identifying herself with her mother revitalised the old mother–daughter conflicts and led to a variety of defensive processes. All of her affective and cognitive processes were marked by ambivalence, so that she had difficulty, for example, deciding between the different colours when shopping because she linked them with the qualities of masculine or feminine.

(Thomä and Kächele 1992: 79)

Using transcripts of eighteen tape-recorded sessions, we identified the analyst's characteristic vocabulary at the beginning of the analysis. From a total of 13,311 tokens, we found 1,480 types. About 10 per cent of the analyst's characteristic vocabulary comprised thirty-six nouns and eighty other words. In discussing the results of this study here, we first give the English translation, followed by the original German word and then the frequency of occurrence in parentheses. Our analysis used a 'lemmatized' version of the text, which reduces all inflected words to their basic form (e.g. replacing the plural form 'women/Frauen' with the singular form 'woman/Frau').

It is no surprise that the famous 'uhm/hm' (976) used by all analysts all over the world proved to be the most frequent and the most characteristic verbalization. There are any number of words that betray the analyst's so-called minor encoding habits, such as 'yes/ja' (678) – the dysfluency indicator once studied by George Mahl; other dysfluency indicators include: 'ah/äh' (395), 'also/auch' (238), 'that/dass' (200), 'something/etwas' (66), 'this/dieser, dieses' (60), 'than/als' (58) and 'uhuh/aha' (31).

Analysing a second set of eighteen sessions towards the end of the analytic process to check for these characteristics again, we did not find much change. These fragments of speech – out of conscious control – make up the linguistic fingerprints of any speaker. They are bad, but minor, speech habits that make for tedious reading in session transcripts. But they are in no way specific to the analyst's task, although they may be used as a screening device, especially when countertransference issues are being studied (Dahl *et al.* 1978).

As elements of style, nouns tell us what was being discussed, and how it was being shaped or framed. The characteristic noun vocabulary of the analyst is therefore very telling. In the eighteen initial sessions, the following nouns were highly characteristic ($p < 0.01$) for the analyst:

dream/Traum (88)
woman/Frau (31)
theme/Thema (18)
thought/Gedanke (17)
question/Frage (16)
anxiety/Angst (16)
hair/Haar (13)
cousin/Cousin (9)
demand/Anspruch (8)
madonna/Madonna (8)
notary/Notar (7)
insecurity/Unsicherheit (7)
seduction/Verführung (7)
comparison/Vergleich (7)

claim/Forderung (5)
mortification/Kränkung (5)
relief/Entlastung (5)
spinster/Jungfer (5)
tampon/Tampon (5)
breakout/Ausbruch (4)
conviction/Überzeugung (4)
dog/Hund (4)
intensity/Intensität (4)
lawyer/Jurist (4)
toilet/Klo (4)
uneasiness/Beunruhigung (3)
candidate/Prüfling (3)
shyness/Scheu (3)

Ordering the nouns into semantic fields, we found that they deal with four main areas. These are technical, emotional, sexual/bodily and topical concerns, as follows:

Technical items dream, theme, thought, question, demand, comparison, claim, conviction.

Emotional items anxiety, breakout, mortification, relief, insecurity, intensity, uneasiness, shyness.

Sexual/bodily items woman, seduction, spinster, tampon, toilet, madonna, hair.

Topical items cousin, notary, dog, lawyer.

From this tabulation of language used in the first eighteen sessions, we inferred that the analyst's interventions characteristically emphasized these four classes of nouns:

1 *Technical nouns* invite the patient's participation in the special analytic point of view.
2 *Emotional nouns* intensify emotions.
3 *Sexual/bodily-linked nouns* clearly refer to the patient's embarrassing sexual self-concept.
4 *Topical nouns* refer to the patient's life situation.

To deepen our understanding, we next subjected the use of the noun 'dream' to a more thorough examination. In the beginning of an analysis, it has to be conveyed to the patient that the analytic dialogue is an unusual dialogue insofar as the analyst may use highlighting as a style of intervention. Because the word 'dream' was a prominent characteristic part of the analyst's vocabulary (compared to that of the patient), we hypothesized that the analyst tried to intensify the patient's curiosity about dreams as a special class of reported material. Formally, the hypothesis was: In each of the sessions when the patient reports or speaks about a dream, the analyst focuses the patient's verbal activity by using the noun 'dream' relatively more frequently than does the patient. To avoid circularity – our hypothesis was built on findings from the eighteen sessions – we extended the database from the original eighteen sessions to include twenty-nine sessions that covered the period from the first hundred sessions. The results confirmed our hypothesis: In twenty-five out of twenty-nine sessions, the analyst used the noun 'dream' more often, based on the proportion of his speech activity.

The patient's usage of the word 'dream' had a mean of 0.13 per cent (s = + 0.02) of all words; whereas the analyst's usage of the word 'dream' had a mean of 0.57 per cent (s = + 0.35).[4] Certainly, these findings may be partially explained by the fact that the analyst uses shorter interventions, whereas the patient presents material in detail.

Based on these results, we assume that in the opening phase of the analysis, there was a systematic relationship between the patient's talking about dreams and the analyst's efforts to stay close and even sometimes to intensify the work on the reported dream. Whenever the patient used the noun 'dream', there was a variable response by the analyst in the majority of instances (even numerically greater than the patient's use). This may reflect the analyst's tendency to point to the phenomena more explicitly within a few sentences. Analysing a sample of sessions at the end of the treatment, we found that the noun 'dream' was no longer part of the characteristic vocabulary of the analyst.

SUMMARY

Techniques of lexical investigation allow us to identify the analyst's preferred conceptual tools. The analyst's vocabulary is part of a complex linguistic task taking place in a specially designed setting. Its study may help us to better understand what 'analysts at work' do. There is no standard vocabulary, but there may be components of verbalization that are an essential part of the analytic technology necessary to transform theory into practice.

NOTES

1 Partially based on verbatim material from the Ulm Textbank.
2 This is defined as the total number of words (tokens) occurring in a given text.
3 The empirical studies were performed with software tools provided by the Ulm Textbank (Mergenthaler and Kächele 1988).
4 The t-test for paired samples proves the significant difference (p < 0.001).

REFERENCES

Cassier, E. (1953) *The Philosophy of Symbolic Forms*, New Haven CT: Yale University Press.

Dahl, H. (1991) 'The key to understanding change: emotions as appetitive wishes and beliefs about their fulfilment', in J. Safran and L. Greenberg (eds) *Emotions, Psychotherapy and Change*, New York: Guilford, 130–65.

Dahl, H., Kächele, H. and Thomä, H. (eds) (1988) *Psychoanalytic Process Research Strategies*, Berlin: Springer-Verlag.

Dahl, H., Teller, V., Moss, D. and Trujillo, M. (1978) 'Countertransference examples of the syntactic expression of warded-off contents', *Psychoanalytic Quarterly*, 47, 339–63.

Flader, D., Grodzicki, W. D. and Schröter, K. (eds) (1982) *Psychoanalyse als Gespräch: Interaktionsanalytische Untersuchungen über Therapie und Supervision (Psychoanalysis as Discourse: An Interaction Analysis of Therapy and Supervision)*, Frankfurt am Main: Suhrkamp.

French, T. M. (1937) 'Klinische Untersuchung über das Lernen im Verlaufe einer psychoanalytischen Behandlung' ('Clinical investigations on learning in the course of a psychoanalytic treatment'), *International Journal of Psycho-Analysis*, 23, 96–132.

Freud, S. (1916) 'Introductory lectures on psycho-analysis', *Standard Edition*, 15–16, 1–482. London: Hogarth Press, 1953.

Greenberg, L. and Safran, J. (1987) *Emotion in Psychotherapy: Affect, Cognition, and the Process of Change*, New York: Guilford.

Grice, H. P. (1975) 'Logic and conversation', in P. Cole and J. L. Morgan (eds) *Speech Acts*, New York: Seminar Press, 41–58.

Herdan, G. (1960) *The Advanced Theory of Language as Choice and Chance*, Vienna: Springer-Verlag.

Holsti, O. R. (1969) 'A computer content-analysis program for analyzing attitudes', in G. Gerbner, O. R. Holsti, K. Krippendorf, W. Paisley and P. Stone (eds) *The Analysis of Communication Content*, New York: Wiley.

Hölzer, M. and Kächele, H. (1996) 'Analysts' work on emotion processing in four psychoanalyses', unpublished manuscript, Stuttgart: Stuttgart Kolleg.

Hölzer, M., Kächele, H., Mergenthaler, E. and Luborsky, L. (1996) 'Vocabulary measures for the evaluation of therapy outcome: re-studying transcripts from the Penn Psychotherapy Project', *Psychotherapy Research*, 6 (2), 95–108.

Hölzer, M., Scheytt, N. and Kächele, H. (1992) 'Das "Affektive Diktionär Ulm" als eine Methode der quantitativen Vokabularbestimmung' ('The "Affective Dictionary Ulm" as a method of quantifying a vocabulary'), in C. Züll and P. Mohler (eds) *Textanalyse: Anwendungen der Computerunterstützten Inhaltsanalyse (Text Analysis: Applications of Computer Assisted Content Analysis)*, Opladen: Westdeutscher Verlag, 131–54.

——(1994) 'Das emotionale Vokabular eines Therapeuten in Anhängigkeit vom Setting' ('The emotional vocabulary of a therapist depending on the setting'), *Psychotherapie, Psychosomatik und Medizinische Psychologie*, 44, 382–9.

Hölzer, M., Scheytt, N., Pokorny, D. and Kächele, H. (1990) 'Das "Affektive Diktionär Ulm": ein Vergleich des emotionalen Vokabulars von Student und Stürmer' ('The "Affective Dictionary Ulm": comparing the emotional vocabulary of the cases "student" and "forward" '), *Psychosomatik und Medizinische Psychologie – Diskjournal*, vol. 1, Thieme Verlag.

Jaffe, D. (1958) 'Language of the dyad: a method of interaction analysis in psychiatric interviews', *Psychiatry*, 21, 249–58.

Johnson, W. (1944) 'Studies in language behavior: I. A program of research', *Psychological Monographs*, 56, 1–15.

Kächele, H. (1983) 'Verbal activity level of therapists in initial interviews and long-term psychoanalysis', in W. Minsel and W. Herff (eds) *Methodology in Psychotherapy Research*, Frankfurt: Lang, 125–9.

Kächele, H. and Mergenthaler, E. (1984) 'Auf dem Wege zur computerunterstützen textanalyse in der psychotherapeutischen Prozessforschung' ('On the way towards computer assisted text analysis in psychotherapeutic process research'), in U. Baumann (ed.) *Psychotherapie: Makro/Microperspektive*, Göttingen: Hogrefe, 223–39.

Labov, W. and Fanshel, D. (1977) *Therapeutic Discourse: Psychotherapy as Conversation*, New York: Academic Press.

Laffal, J. (1967) 'Characteristics of the three-person conversation', *Journal of Verbal Learning and Verbal Behaviour*, 6, 555–9.

Langer, S. K. (1942) *Philosophy in a New Key*, Cambridge MA: Harvard University Press.

Luborsky, L., Crits-Christoph, P., Mintz, J. and Auerbach, A. (1988) *Who Will Benefit from Psychotherapy?*, New York: Basic Books.

Luborsky, L., Singer, B. and Luborsky, L. (1975) 'Comparative studies of psychotherapy: is it true that "Everybody has won and all must have prizes"?', *Archives of General Psychiatry*, 32, 995–1008.

Mergenthaler, E. and Kächele, H. (1988) 'The Ulm Textbank management system: a tool for psychotherapy research', in H. Dahl, H. Kächele and H. Thomä (eds) *Psychoanalytic Process Research Strategies*, Berlin: Springer-Verlag, 195–212.

Meyer, A. E. (1988) 'What makes psychoanalysts tick?', in H. Dahl, H. Kächele and H. Thomä (eds) *Psychoanalytic Process Research Strategies*, Berlin: Springer-Verlag, 273–90.

Ramzy, I. (1974) 'How the mind of the psychoanalyst works: an essay on psychoanalytic inference', *International Journal of Psycho-Analysis*, 55, 543–50.

Rosen, V. H. (1969) 'Sign phenomena and their relationship to unconscious meaning', *International Journal of Psycho-Analysis*, 50, 197–207.

Sandler, J. (1983) 'Reflections on some relations between psychoanalytic concepts and psychoanalytic practice', *International Journal of Psycho-Analysis*, 64, 35–45.

Sandler, J., Dreher, A. and Drews, S. (1991) 'An approach to conceptual research in psychoanalysis illustrated by a consideration of psychic trauma', *International Review of Psycho-Analysis*, 18, 133–42.

Simonton, D. (1990) 'Lexical choices and aesthetic success: a computer content analysis of 154 Shakespeare sonnets', *Computers and the Humanities*, 24, 251–64.

Spence, D. (1969) 'Computer measurement of process and content in psychoanalysis', *Transactions of the New York Academy of Science*, 31, 828–41.

Thomä, H. and Kächele, H. (1975) 'Problems of metascience and methodology in clinical psychoanalytic research', *The Annual of Psychoanalysis*, III, 49–119.

——(1992) *Psychoanalytic Practice, vol. 2: Clinical Studies*, Berlin: Springer-Verlag.

INDEX